THE SECRET SALES PITCH

An Overview of
Subliminal Advertising

by

August Bullock

Norwich

Visit our web site at **SubliminalSex.com** for information regarding live multimedia presentations, subliminal T-shirts, and wholesale and retail book orders.

Although the author has exhaustively researched all sources to ensure the accuracy and completeness of the information contained in this book, he assumes no responsibility for any errors, inaccuracies, omissions or any other inconsistency herein. The legal issues presented in Chapter 6 are in outline form only. Laws change rapidly, and readers should consult an attorney prior to incorporating subliminal techniques in their work.

Numerous trademarks appear throughout this book, including: Coca-Cola, Time, Benson & Hedges, Wallpaper, Health & Fitness, Chivas, Marlboro, People, Glamour, Smirnoff, Naturalizer, Sauza, Stay Pure, CosmoGIRL!, Cosmopolitan, Peter Heering, Jameson Irish, Spice Islands, Pomellato, Belair, Absolut, Newsweek, Virginia Slims, Three's Company, Montgomery Wards, San Francisco Chronicle, New York Times, Advertising Age, Just Do It, In-N-Out Burger, Gap, Burger King, Home of the Whopper, Have it Your Way, Microsoft, AutoZone, Plug it In, Taco Bell, Ford, Dodge, La-Z-Boy, Chevron, Star Wars, Spider-Man, Hulk, Imperial Savings, Dish Network, Playgirl, Playboy, Ruffo Research, Bally's Casino, Matilda Bay Wine Coolers, Seagram's, MortgageSave.com, America Online, Budweiser, Macy's, Haagen-Dazs, K Mart, ATT, Call ATT, 1-800 Call ATT, American Home, Circuit City, Chevron, Vectra, PhotoShop. None of the companies referred to herein have endorsed this book or are affiliated with it in any way.

This book hypothesizes how the illustrations herein are interpreted unconsciously, and how readers can create pictures that are unconsciously stimulating. The author's interpretations are based solely on the appearance of the pictures; he can only speculate as to what the artists who created the illustrations were thinking. Printed in Korea.

Bullock, August.
    The secret sales pitch : an overview of subliminal advertising / by
    August Bullock. — San Jose, CA : Norwich Publishers, 2004.
        p. ; cm.

    Includes bibliographical references and index.
    ISBN: 0-9742640-0-8

    1. Subliminal advertising. 2. Advertising. 3. Marketing—
Psychological aspects. 4. Marketing. 5. Subliminal perception.
I. Title.

HF5827.9 .B85 2004   2003109700
659.1/11—dc22   CIP

for s.a.b.

"If subliminal advertising did exist, there certainly would be textbooks available on how to practice it."

– from an article in *Advertising Age*

The illustrations in this book are meant to be viewed one at a time, in sequential order, as directed in the text. You will enjoy the illusions more if you resist the temptation of skipping ahead.

TABLE OF CONTENTS

The text is supplemented by Annotated Notes and References that begin on page 235.

Chapter One:
HUNGRY? EAT POPCORN!
THE HISTORY OF SUBLIMINAL PERSUASION

In the 1950s the United States had a problem. World War II had ended and the nation's factories were producing unprecedented quantities of consumer goods. Unfortunately, people weren't buying enough of them.

The hardships of the Depression and the conflagration that followed had left their mark on the public psyche. Most people were very frugal. They tried to make do with the things they had, and avoided buying things they did not need. Most products were well made and did not often have to be replaced.

Although this might seem like an ideal situation, the lack of consumption posed a serious threat to the postwar recovery. Manufacturers and advertisers responded by creating a new field of science, known as "motivational research." They hired psychologists and sociologists from universities, provided them with well-equipped laboratories, and asked them to develop innovative psychological techniques that would induce people to buy things. By the end of the 1950s, an estimated billion dollars a year was invested in motivational research, and another ten billion dollars a year was spent on advertising in general. These are enormous expenditures, considering that at the time a loaf of bread cost 17 cents.

The advertising researchers employed psychological methods that had previously been used to diagnose and treat neurosis. They discovered that people often bought things for *unconscious* reasons they were not aware of. In a process known as "depth probing," they ferreted out consumers' secret motivations about particular products by asking subjects to lie down and spontaneously disclose their innermost feelings. The researchers asked questions such as "What is your earliest memory involving a cookie?" or "How does eating a cookie make you feel?" They also employed *word association tests* ("cookies... mother... milk..."), *sentence completion tests* ("When my mother gave me a cookie I felt..."), and *projective tests*, in which the subject was shown a picture and asked to make up a story about it. They utilized *psychodramas*, in which subjects were asked to physically "act out" their feelings toward the product. *Focus groups* were used to "probe" several consumers at the same time. The sessions were often filmed and analyzed by teams of researchers.

The insights the motivational researchers acquired substantially improved the persuasive appeal of advertising. As an example, a cigar manufacturer ran an advertisement portraying a woman happily handing out cigars to her husband and her husband's friends. Although the ad seemed well designed, it had a negative effect on sales. Motivational researchers analyzed the problem and discovered that men unconsciously smoke cigars *because it irritates their wives*. Filling the house with smoke makes them feel dominant and important. The ad inadvertently deprived male viewers of their secret smoking pleasure, because it showed the woman encouraging tobacco consumption. When the picture was adjusted so that it no longer offended men's secret desires, sales increased dramatically.

In addition to psychological tests, advertisers developed electronic *equipment* that measured consumers' unconscious physical reactions to products, packages, and advertising. The devices they created detected minuscule amounts of sweat on the skin, tiny changes in heart and pulse rates, and minute muscular contractions that divulged the subjects' unconscious emotional states. In some supermarkets, sophisticated hidden cameras were used to monitor the eye movements of shoppers. The dilation of the shoppers' pupils revealed how interested they were in each of the products. The number of times they blinked per minute revealed their degree of tension. Many of the shoppers were found to be in mild hypnotic trances.

Most of these developments were first revealed by Vance Packard in *The Hidden Persuaders*, which was published in 1957. Written in an intelligent, nontechnical manner, the book quickly became a best seller and brought scientific advances such as depth probing into the public eye.

Hungry? Eat Popcorn

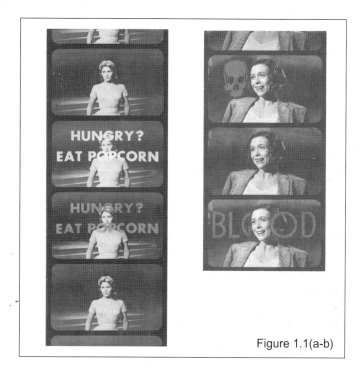

Figure 1.1(a-b)

About the time Packard's book was released, a prominent motivational researcher named James Vicary held a press conference in New York City. He revealed that he had conducted secret experiments in a New Jersey movie theatre using a device known as a "tachistoscope." A tachistoscope is a machine that can flash words or images on a screen for very brief periods of time – often as little as 1/300 of a second. Psychologists had discovered as early as 1917 that such fleeting images register *unconsciously*, and influence the viewer on a *subliminal* level, even though the images are not perceived consciously.

As illustrated in Figure 1.1(a), Vicary flashed the words "Hungry? Eat Popcorn" and "Drink Coca-Cola" every five seconds throughout the movie *Picnic,* starring Kim Novak. Over 45,000 movie-goers unknowingly participated. Vicary claimed that the flashed messages increased popcorn sales an astounding 57%. He offered the services of his company, the Subliminal Projection Corporation, to merchandisers and advertisers throughout the world. He assured his prospective customers that he could create subliminal advertisements for any number of products, in a variety of mediums. Vicary believed that subliminal advertising would benefit society enormously. The public would be able to watch television without enduring annoying commercial interruptions. Subliminal ads, secretly flashed every five seconds, would promote the sale of products without diminishing the entertainment value of the shows.

Although Vicary's sales figures were later shown to be exaggerated, his press conference generated an enormous amount of publicity for his ideas. For a while, many businesses attempted to cash in on the use of subliminal technologies. Several radio stations began marketing subliminal "whisper ads" in which messages such as "Buy Oklahoma Oil" or "Drink 7-Up" were secretly implanted beneath music played on the air. KTLA in Los Angeles signed a $60,000 contract in which it agreed to insert subliminal "public service" messages in television programming. As illustrated in Figure 1.1(b), *Life* magazine reported that frightening subliminal flash frames were inserted into at least two horror films in order to increase the audience's anxiety.

It soon became apparent, however, that the public was very disturbed by the idea of being subliminally manipulated. Instead of welcoming Vicary's proposals, most people were outraged by them. Angry editorials appeared in major periodicals of the day. Religious organizations declared that subliminal projection threatened personal liberty and would be used for brainwashing and political subjugation. *The New Yorker* proclaimed that minds were being "broken and entered." *Newsday* referred to the tachistoscope as the most "alarming invention since the atomic bomb." A letter from a prominent businessman published in the *Los Angeles Times* suggested that Vicary was as evil as Nazi war criminals and should be shot. A poll published in the *Public Opinion* Quarterly revealed that one third of the people interviewed claimed they would stop watching TV if the programming included subliminal messages.

Before long the outcry caused the advertising industry to reverse itself and condemn subliminal manipulation. Radio stations across the United States assured their listeners they would *not* use unconsciously perceived messages. The three major television networks insisted they would never use subliminal commercials. CBS publicly announced that the "legal, social, and ethical" implications of subliminal broadcasting precluded its use, at least for the time being.

During this period many bills were introduced on both the national and state level that would have made the use of subliminal devices illegal. Contrary to public opinion, however, *none were ever passed*. Strong lobbying efforts by advertisers blocked the legislation. Meanwhile, the media's zealous condemnation of unconscious manipulation calmed the public's anxiety. At the end of the 1950s, The Federal Communications Commission declared that no stations were using subliminal techniques, and it therefore was not necessary to ban them.

It is not suprising that advertisers secretly began studying subliminal technologies in earnest, at the same time they publicly denounced them as immoral. A 1958 article in the *Christian Science Monitor* entitled, "Ad Firms Ponder Success of Invisible Commercials," revealed that "a major firm" had circulated a confidential memorandum to its clients disclosing that "there was enough at stake" to continue its subliminal research. Undoubtedly many of the agency's competitors adopted a similar strategy.

For the next thirteen years or so the subject simply left the news. Very few stories dealing with subliminals appeared in popular media during the 1960s. Advertisers encouraged news outlets to avoid discussing the topic. The public was threatened by the idea of subliminal persuasion, and accepted the absurd notion that the advertisers had lost interest in it.

Subliminal Seduction

In 1969, while teaching a class at the University of Western Ontario, a media professor named Wilson Bryan Key noticed a strange optical illusion in an illustration accompanying an article in *Esquire* magazine. He and his students concluded it was just an interesting coincidence.

In the ensuing weeks, however, the professor and his students found similar illusions in other magazines. Key came to realize the hidden images were created deliberately in order to unconsciously influence viewers. In 1972 he published the results of his research in *Subliminal Seduction*.

I discovered a copy of his book in San Francisco around 1975 and immediately became engrossed in the subject. I began collecting my own subliminal examples, one of which appears in Figure 1.2. Please study it carefully before reading further.

Try Our Hard Pack

This Benson and Hedges advertisement appeared on the back cover of *Time* magazine in April, 1976. During this period, *Time* had a circulation of about four million and was read by about twenty million people. The cost of running a full page was approximately $75,000. The artwork could have cost $20,000. Since it was run many times in different periodicals, the total cost of the entire campaign probably exceeded half a million dollars.

Today, such an endeavor would be even more expensive. As I write this in 2003, running a full-page ad on the back cover of *Time* magazine costs $272,700. Thanks to computers, the cost of producing the artwork hasn't gone up as much, but could still amount to $25,000. In total, millions of dollars would be required to run the ad repeatedly in several magazines around the country.

With so much money at stake, the Benson and Hedges ad was certainly not created haphazardly. It was produced by a team of skilled technicians, utilizing research data accumulated over several decades. It was scrutinized and refined in the same manner that an artist works on a painting. Since most people barely glance at advertisements, and few read the copy, it was designed to influence a disinterested viewer in the space of a few seconds.

The picture portrays an attractive young couple sensually embracing each other. From the way they are dressed it appears they have been on a date, and have returned to one of their homes for a drink. A bottle of wine has been opened and two untouched glasses are on the table.

The caption proclaims "If you got crushed in the clinch with your soft pack, try our new hard pack." The play on the words "hard" and "soft" is difficult to overlook. Even on a conscious level, the ad seems to be promising male virility and potency.

The woman is extremely lovely. She is pressing herself against the man eagerly and seductively, as if she can't wait for him to return her caresses and make love to her.

The man is staring at the viewer with a strange look on his face. If you only glanced at the picture for a moment or two you would probably assume he is thinking, "If you smoked Benson and Hedges you'd have

Figure 1.2

beautiful women chasing after you too." If you study his expression, however, you will discover that it is somewhat ambiguous. He could be smug, but he also could be a bit nervous. His collar is too big, and a small amount of sweat appears on his nose. The aggressive advances of the beautiful young woman seem to be making him uncomfortable.

The man's expression suggests that he shares a secret with male readers that the woman doesn't know about.

Whatever could his secret be? I hung the ad on my wall for several weeks, and one morning it suddenly jumped out at me.

Look carefully at the man's left hand, the lower hand in the photo. It is resting gently against the lady's backbone.

The lady's backbone has been carefully airbrushed to resemble an erect, male phallus.

In the scale of the photograph it is approximately 6 1/2 inches long. The man's fingers are clearly wrapped around the base of the shaft. His left thumb is gently touching the ridge of the circumcised head.

Moreover, the tip of the penis is provocatively entering a large cylindrical curl formed by the lady's hair.

The phallus may take a few minutes to fully emerge in your consciousness, but when it does it will become dramatically obvious. A close-up is provided in Figure 1.3 on page 16.

The longer you look at the illusion the clearer it will become. If you put this book away and pick it up again tomorrow, the penis will seem even more apparent. The change in perception is usually permanent–you will never look at the picture again and only "see" a backbone.

You have just discovered a *subliminal embed*, an optical illusion implanted in the ad in order to influence you without your realizing it. Although it may at first seem unbelievable, subliminal messages of this kind have been commonly used in all forms of media for the last five decades. You probably have been exposed to millions of them in your lifetime.

The Not So Soft Sell

Once the subliminal content of the Benson and Hedges ad becomes conscious, the intent of it becomes fairly obvious. The caption "If you got crushed in the clinch with your soft pack, try our hard pack" unconsciously means "If you are nervous about sexual intimacy, smoke Benson and Hedges to compensate." The ad reinforces tobacco dependencies by upsetting the viewer (by triggering impotency anxieties), and then providing relief (smoking Benson and Hedges). Television mouthwash commercials that threaten the viewer with sexual rejection employ a similar (although less sophisticated) strategy.

Another way to understand how the ad "works" is to think about the fact that people smoke more when they are nervous. Accordingly, making them nervous increases their smoking. If the ad *consciously* upset the viewer (if the tag line said, "Hey, you're impotent, aren't you!") the consumer would feel resentful and avoid purchasing the product. Because the viewer is *subliminally* agitated, however, the anxiety/smoking "loop" is activated without awareness or resentment. Although it may at first seem counterintuitive, the "Secret Sales Pitch" is very logical.

Ernest Dichter, the self-proclaimed "father of motivational research," wrote in *The Handbook of Consumer Motivations:*

> We attempt to escape fear-producing stimuli. By producing fear we can alter people's behavior. When caught in fear, we regress step by step to ever more *infantile* and animalistic drives." (Emphasis added.)

The Benson ad unconsciously provokes *fears* of sexual failure. In response, the viewer engages in unconscious *infantile* fantasies of being breast fed and nurtured. On a subliminal level, the ad proposes that cigarettes are an alternative to Mommy's milk.

The Secret Sales Pitch

Wilson Bryan Key's books were exceedingly popular. *Subliminal Seduction* sold over a million copies, and the three books he wrote subsequently sold a million more copies collectively. From the late 1970s to the early 1990s, he appeared on countless radio and TV shows, and gave slide presentations all over the United States. He single-handedly made much of the world at least peripherally aware of subliminal advertising in media.

In some respects, however, his work was not taken as seriously as it should have been. Some researchers denigrated it as "pop psychology," and criticized it for lacking scientific credibility. Advertisers scoffed at it altogether. They claimed subliminal embeds are coincidences, and ridiculed

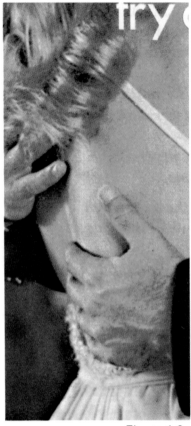

Figure 1.3

Key's less persuasive examples. As a result, the controversy fizzled to a draw, and has never been intelligently resolved. Although many people have heard of subliminal advertising, they don't understand the cognitive principles that underlie its effectiveness.

This book will explore how subliminal salesmanship has been routinely employed in every form of media, on many different levels, for many decades. It will:

1. Present many convincing examples, never before published in a book of this kind, that illustrate a variety of subliminal techniques;

2. Coherently explain how subliminal devices in media operate on a scientific, psychological level, and how they relate to published studies of perception;

3. Describe how anyone can use subliminal techniques to enhance art as well as advertising.

Readers might arguably be skeptical of any one of the individual advertisements or interpretations in this book. When all the evidence is considered, however, one cannot escape the conclusion that media plays with our minds in ways we are oblivious to.

Subliminal ads are particularly fascinating when they are viewed in conjunction with the psychological principles they illustrate. They reveal much about our psyches we would prefer to avoid. Analyzing how advertisers manipulate us unconsciously improves our understanding of both society and our secret selves.

Chapter Two:
MOMMY AND I ARE ONE
THE SCIENCE OF THE SECRET SALES PITCH

Hundreds of experiments conducted over the last 85 years have established that people are influenced by information they are not aware of. This phenomenon is known as "subliminal perception," and has been popularized in science fiction stories.

Most of the studies exploring subliminal perception have utilized a "tachistoscope," the device James Vicary experimented with in New Jersey. Typically, subjects are asked to look into the machine and are shown pictures and/or text for 1/300 of a second or less. Although the subjects consciously "see" only a flash of light, the unconsciously perceived fleeting images demonstrably influence their moods, fantasies, dreams and behavior. Subliminal presentations also produce measurable physical changes, such as involuntary muscular contractions and alterations in brain waves, heart rates, and the electrical conductivity of the skin.

The tachistoscope is most often used to "deliver" the stimulus because any combination of words and pictures can be inserted in the device, and the procedure can be easily duplicated by other researchers. However, subliminal stimuli can also be presented in ways that do not involve the use of flash frames.

The Holes Between Things

Please look at the tree in Figure 2.1 for one second, and then look away.

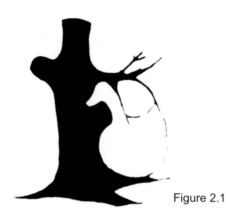

Figure 2.1

Now look at the tree in Figure 2.2 on page 20.

Did you notice the difference? A duck is hidden in the white spaces between the branches in the first picture, but not in the second.

The two trees were the stimuli used in an experiment conducted in 1967. College students were split into groups, and each group was shown either Figure 2.1 or 2.2 for one second.

None of the students were aware of the hidden duck. In the context of this book it's fairly obvious, but in the actual study more than half of the subjects could not find it, even after it was displayed for 30 seconds and after they were told, "there is a duck somewhere in the picture." You can experiment with this yourself by copying the illustration onto a blank piece of paper and briefly showing it to your friends.

Following exposure, the students were asked to imagine and draw a "nature scene" and label its parts. The drawings were rated by "blind" judges who did not know which group each viewer had been in. Incredibly, the students presented with the duck/tree stimulus drew more ducks and duck related imagery (such as water, birds, feathers, etc.) than the students who were shown Figure 2.2. The hidden image influenced them even though they were not aware of it.

The duck/tree illustration is a "figure-ground" illusion similar to the Subliminal Sex™ design on the cover of this book. The study reveals that people are unconsciously influenced by the *ground* even when they are consciously only aware of the *figure*. This was expressed in scientific language by N.F. Dixon, a respected researcher and the author of a comprehensive treatise entitled *Subliminal Perception*, who wrote:

> ...the distinction between figure and ground no longer seems to hold when the image is subliminal. In the latter case, even the 'holes between things'... may constitute information that is registered and stored for subsequent expression in dreams and imagery.

The experiment is particularly interesting because the subliminal duck exerted a significant influence, even though it is an emotionally neutral image. The subliminal stimuli used in advertisements are usually much more provocative.

The Unconscious Perception of Embeds

In addition to "figure-ground" illusions, "embedded" images, such as the penis/backbone in Figure 1.2, are also perceived unconsciously. This was demonstrated in a study published in the *Journal of Advertising* in 1984. Researchers Kilbourne, Painton, and Ridley had read Key's *Subliminal Seduction* and found two ads in national magazines that contained sexual subliminal embeds. One was a Marlboro Lights ad that depicted two cowboys riding on horseback through rocky terrain. A penis was concealed in the rocks. The other was a Chivas Regal whiskey ad, in which the back of a nude woman was embedded below the neck of the bottle.

The researchers hired a professional artist to remove the subliminals by airbrushing them out of the pictures. They then split the subjects in the experiment into two groups. For thirty seconds, the first group was shown the original ads (*with* the embeds), and the second group was shown the altered ads (*without* the embeds).

The unconscious arousal of the subjects was measured by monitoring their "galvanic skin response," minute changes in the electrical conductivity of their skin. The GSRs of the subjects who were shown the original, embedded ads were significantly *higher* (sometimes 20%) than the GSRs of the subjects who were shown the non-embedded ads.

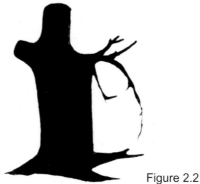

Figure 2.2

Interestingly, both sexes were more stimulated by the Marlboro ad (which contained a subliminal penis) than the Chivas ad (which contained a subliminal woman). This suggests that male genitalia is emotionally significant to both genders, and explains why subliminal erections appear in media so frequently.

The Unconscious Perception of Faint Images

"ESP" experiments, conducted by a psychiatrist named James G. Miller at Harvard in the 1930s demonstrate that very *faint* images are also perceived on a subliminal level.

Miller asked his subjects to sit in a chair facing what appeared to be a wall-sized mirror. He told them the purpose of the study was to investigate the ways in which people communicate *telepathically*, and then read them the following passage:

> It is common procedure in clairvoyance experiments for the subject to gaze into a crystal ball to help him find the answer he wants. This is usually done when the subject is asked to picture three dimensional objects. In this experiment, however, you are going to work with the flat surfaces of ESP cards. I am asking you therefore to stare into the flat surface of the mirror.

Miller then passed into an adjacent room carrying a large deck of cards. Periodically, he asked the subjects to guess which card he was mentally "sending" them. Secretly, he projected very faint images of the cards on the back of the mirror. The true purpose of the experiment was to see if the faint images would be perceived subliminally.

The results of the experiment indicated they were. When the projector was turned on, the subjects guessed the card correctly *more* often than they would have if their selection was based entirely on the laws of probability. When the projector was turned off, their performance dropped to chance levels. In all cases, they attributed their responses to ESP or intuitive flashes, and were not aware of the projections.

In a second phase of the experiment, Miller gradually increased the illumination of the images so that they would be readily apparent to any new person entering into the room. In spite of this, many of the subjects continued to believe the cards were products of their imagination. They were shocked when the existence of the projector was revealed to them.

The Corners Of Our Minds

R	X	H	G	B	R	D
T	E	Y	J	Q	L	R
Z	S	V	P	A	I	N
W	D	B	M	T	Q	Z
J	H	R	Y	G	V	S
Q	T	X	F	U	C	K
L	M	Z	D	J	B	M

Figure 2.3

Please look at the matrix of letters in Figure *2.3* for no more than *two seconds.* Somewhere in the matrix is a *red letter.* As soon as you identify the red letter, try and see as much of the rest of the matrix as you can.

P	X	H	G	B	P	F
Y	O	T	J	Q	L	H
Z	S	V	R	A	I	N
W	F	B	M	T	Q	Z
J	H	P	Y	G	V	S
Q	T	X	D	U	C	K
L	M	Z	F	J	B	M

Figure 2.4

When you are done, look at Figure 2.4 (above) in the same manner.

Did you perceive the difference this time? The matrix in Figure 2.3 contains the emotional words "F*CK," "PAIN," and "SEX." In the corresponding places in Figure 2.4 the more neutral words "DUCK," "RAIN" and "SOX" appear.

The two matrixes were used in a experiment published in the *British Journal of Psychology* in 1976. College students were shown either Figure 2.3 or Figure 2.4, on two occasions, for one second. They were given instructions very similar to those above.

Prior to the experiment, the researchers had determined that it was physically impossible to consciously perceive the hidden words in just a second or two. They also discovered, by using cameras that tracked eye movements, that the students would have time to scan the entire picture.

After being shown the matrixes, the subjects were given a standardized psychological test in which they were shown a picture and asked to write a story about it. They were instructed to describe what was happening, how it came to happen, and what would happen next. The stories were evaluated by judges who did not know which matrix the writers had been exposed to.

Incredibly, the students were influenced by the hidden words. Those exposed to the F*CK/PAIN matrix made up more stories involving violence, uncertainty, conflict, or loss. They also exhibited a marked tendency to use unpleasant words. The opposite was true of the subjects in the DUCK/ RAIN group.

Strange as it may seem, the students scanned the matrixes, read and understood the hidden words, and reacted to them emotionally, *without knowing they were there.* The experiment indicates that *incidental* information we see out of the *corners of our eyes* affects us, although we are unaware of it.

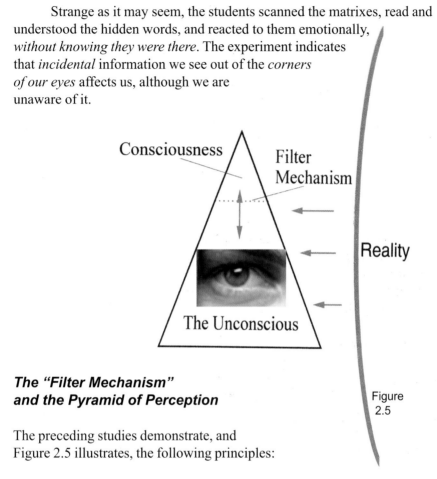

The "Filter Mechanism" and the Pyramid of Perception

Figure 2.5

The preceding studies demonstrate, and Figure 2.5 illustrates, the following principles:

1. The mind is separated into two independent divisions: the *conscious*, which we are aware of, and the *unconscious*, which we are not.

2. A phenomenal amount of data (far more than we realize) is collected unconsciously.

3. The data is read, understood, and cataloged in a remarkably short period of time.

4. A kind of *filter mechanism*, operating automatically without awareness, allows only a small part of the information to enter consciousness. The information blocked by the filter remains in the unconscious, and continues to affect the viewer.

The "filter mechanism" is necessary because it prevents the conscious mind from becoming overwhelmed. The conscious mind is a "sequential processor" that works relatively slowly and can only handle a few things at a time. The unconscious, on the other hand, is a "parallel processor" that operates quickly and can do many things simultaneously. The unconscious is faster, but the conscious is more logical and more adept at handling novel situations. The filter automatically analyzes all the information that is received by the senses, selects the really important things, and allows *only that data* into awareness.

We can observe the operation of the "filter mechanism" in our daily lives. When we are talking to a friend in a crowded cafeteria, for example, we are usually oblivious to the noisy chatter around us. If someone nearby happens to mention our name or starts talking about something important to us, however, we instantly become aware of the conversation. This is because our unconscious is constantly scanning the other discussions in the room. As soon as it detects something significant, the filter directs the information into awareness.

The filter mechanism is an integral part of our visual perception. The images that appear on a computer screen are merely the end result of processes that occur on the computer's hard drive. Similarly, what we are consciously aware of "seeing" is merely the end result of a perceptual "program" silently running on an unconscious level.

As I look around the room as I write this I am consciously aware of my desk, my computer, and a tree outside my window. The information initially falling on my retina, however, simply consists of light and color. My unconscious has to systematically interpret the data. It organizes the visual field into shapes, decides which are near and which are far, and cross-references my memory to see if any of them constitute known objects. It then assimilates all the information into a three-dimensional picture, which is the only thing I am aware of.

Human beings would not be able to function without the division between our conscious and unconscious selves. If we were aware of how the shapes and colors of the universe were being organized into familiar objects, our conscious "processors" would be so overloaded we wouldn't be able to function.

Hallucinogenic drugs may simulate such an overloaded condition. Some speculate that people under the influence of hallucinogens experience enhanced sensory perceptions, and become intellectually impaired, because the drugs allow too much data past the filter.

The Unconscious Perception of Visual Ambiguity

When the unconscious is presented with an *ambiguous* visual stimulus, such as the SEX design on the cover of this book or the penis/backbone in the Benson ad, it analyzes and digests both interpretations *but allows only one into awareness.*

Again, this is necessary for our survival. Ambiguous images sometimes occur in nature — the *space* between the trees in the forest for example might happen to look like a tiger. If you consciously perceived the tiger *instead* of the space, or the tiger *and* the space, you would become confused and your ability to function would be impaired. Accordingly, the filter selects what it considers to be the "best" interpretation, and allows only that into awareness.

Figure 2.6

My Wife and Mother In Law, the illustration in Figure 2.6, is a famous illusion often utilized in psychology texts. When first exposed to it, some people see a young woman, and some people see an old woman. The design, in fact, incorporates both images. The young woman is looking off in the distance, as portrayed in Figure 2.7(a), and the old woman is looking down to the left, as illustrated by Figure 2.7(b). What is a *chin* on the young woman is the *nose* of the old woman. If you get "stuck" and can't switch images, take a break and look at the picture again in a few minutes. At some point you will be able to see both images clearly.

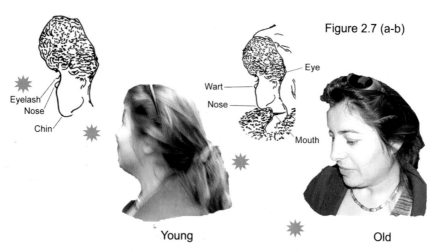

Figure 2.7 (a-b)

Young   Old

The illusion is fascinating, even if you are already familiar with it, because it graphically demonstrates the existence of the filter. When you first look at the drawing, the secondary interpretation (the one you don't "see") is automatically and completely blocked. Once it is revealed to you, however, you can manually flip the filter's "switch" and "see" either the old woman *or* the young woman. In other words, the filter at first operates completely without awareness, but then allows you to consciously control it. The filter is not capable, however, of allowing you to see *both* images at the same time.

Unlike the *My Wife and Mother In Law* illusion, the secondary (initially repressed) images in the SEX design and the penis/ backbone become *dominant* when they are pointed out. Once you become aware of them, you always "see" them when you look at the pictures. In a sense, the filter's "switch" becomes permanently stuck in the "on" position.

The main point to remember about "My Wife and Mother In Law" is that when you "see" the old woman you are *subliminally* perceiving the young woman, and vice versa. Like the duck in the duck/tree experiment, the *secondary interpretation influences you without you realizing it.*

Filtering Based on Context

Many external factors help the filter "decide" which of the two images is "best" and therefore should be allowed into consciousness. One of the most important factors is *context*.

For this reason, if you tell people who have never seen Figure 2.6 "I am going to show you a picture of an old woman," and then show them the picture, they are more likely to "see" the old woman than the young one. The opposite is true if you tell them you are going to show them a drawing of a young girl. This applies to all the illustrations in this book.

A related phenomenon occurs when you look at the sky on a rainy day. At first, you are usually only aware of clouds. If you study the clouds for a while, however, you will often discover hidden images embedded within them. The hidden figures are initially blocked because the filter concludes the "cloud" interpretation is more appropriate in the context of the scene.

Figure 2.8

These perceptual processes are illustrated by Figure 2.8 (above). When you read the word "Beautiful" you are inclined to interpret the first character as the *letter* "B." When we look at the bottom row, however, you are inclined to perceive exactly the same shape as the *number* "13." In each instance, your unconscious analyzes both possibilities, but then selects only the interpretation that is congruent with the overall context of the image.

Filtering Based on Gestalt Principles

The operation of the filter (and the effect of context) is closely related to the Gestalt school of psychology, a perceptual theory developed in Germany around the beginning of the twentieth century. The Gestalt school maintains that the unconscious organizes visual data so that we consciously perceive *whole* objects as opposed to separate *parts* of objects. This is illustrated by the examples shown in Figure 2.9 on the following page.

a. *Figure-ground:* As in the SEX design on the cover, the filter decides what the *figure* is, and suppresses the *ground*. In this case most people initially "see" the vase and then become aware of the faces.

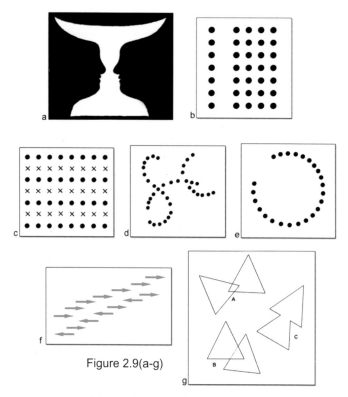

Figure 2.9(a-g)

b. *Proximity:* Objects that are close to each other are perceived as units. The dots appear to comprise vertical columns and not horizontal rows.

c. *Similarity:* Objects that are similar to each other also are perceived as units. We "see" horizontal rows of 0s and Xs, rather than vertical columns of alternating 0s and Xs.

d. *Continuation:* Similarly, objects that form lines or curves are perceived as units. The picture appears to consist of several wavy lines as opposed to random dots.

e. *Closure:* The filter prefers complete objects. We "see" a circle with a part missing, rather than a series of dots or an object resembling a sideways letter "C."

f. *Common direction:* Objects that appear to be moving in the same direction are also perceived as a unit. Note that it is much easier to interpret the top line than the bottom line.

g. *Symmetry:* The filter prefers symmetry. In example A, we "see" two triangles as opposed to an irregular shape. In example B, we are aware of a triangle covering part of another triangle, instead of a distorted, arrow-like shape. In figure C, we "see" an arrow, instead of two triangles.

The Filtering of Discordant Information

The unconscious is also inclined to suppress awareness of *discordant* information. The Benson penis/backbone clearly illustrates this principle. Since penises don't normally grow on backbones, the filter mechanism "cleans up" the picture by making it conform to our conscious expectations.

The repression of discordant information also made a lot of sense when we were in the jungle. Incongruous information (which was totally out of context) probably wasn't real, and consciously processing it impaired survival. When advertisers create embeds, they are capitalizing on an evolutionary weakness. We have no defense against "doctored" photographs because our perceptual processes developed long before the camera was invented.

Figure 2.10

Incongruency

The tendency of the filter to "clean up" images has been demonstrated experimentally. In a study conducted in 1949, subjects were *briefly* shown a series of "trick" playing cards, in which the colors of the suits were reversed as in Figure 2.10 (above). The viewers were not consciously aware of the adulterated nature of the cards, and perceived them to be normal cards. A red ten of clubs, for example, was either seen as black, or as a red ten of hearts. The filter altered the physical appearance of the stimuli in order to prevent the viewers from becoming confused.

When the cards were displayed long enough, the subjects' perceptual defenses no longer operated, and they became aware of the incongruity. However, it took a surprisingly long time for this to happen. Some viewers continued to see the distorted version of the cards after the exposure time was increased to a full second. As might be expected, others became disoriented and saw the cards as purple, or could no longer tell what they were looking at.

The Filtering of
Emotionally Disturbing Information

The filter also endeavors to block or alter the appearance of information that is *psychologically threatening*.

Dirty Word Experiments

In 1949, researcher Elliot McGinnies conducted a series of studies which later became known as the "Dirty Word Experiments." Using a tachistoscope, he presented both *neutral* words (such as "sleep" and "wood") and *taboo* words (such as "bitch" and "whore") to individual subjects for brief periods of time. He then asked each subject to identify the word. If the subject was unable to do so, he flashed it again for a slightly longer period, and then repeated the process. In this manner, he was able to determine the minimum amount of time each of the target words had to be shown in order for the subjects to identify them.

McGinnies discovered that highly emotional taboo words had to be displayed much longer than neutral words. For example, 1/25 of a second was required for the average person to recognize the word "sleep," but an exposure time four times longer was required to recognize the word "whore." The filter mechanism struggled to prevent the taboo words from entering consciousness, and succeeded in doing so until they were displayed for so long it could no longer block the stimulus.

Not surprisingly, McGinnies also discovered that the subjects' GSRs (galvanic skin responses) for the taboo words were higher than for the neutral words, when they both were perceived subliminally. Furthermore, as in the card experiment discussed above, he found that the filter *distorted the physical appearance* of the taboo words to make them more palatable. For example, when a disturbing word such as "penis" was displayed for a relatively long time, the subjects often "saw" a less disturbing word such as "pencil."

The "Dirty Word Experiments" were controversial, and generated a new area of research known as the "New Look" paradigm. The basic idea was that unconscious perceptual defenses, operating without awareness, *physically change the way things look.* Psychological defense mechanisms were studied by observing *perceptual distortions.*

Critics of McGinnies argued that the subjects in his experiments may have seen the taboo words, but were too embarrassed to admit it. Later studies eliminated this possibility. In 1958, for example, British psychologist N.F. Dixon utilized a device that split the field of vision in half, so that different stimuli could be presented to each eye. To one eye, he flashed a "dirty" or neutral word, and to the other eye, an innocuous beam of light. Dixon discovered the emotional content of "dirty" words presented to the one eye activated the defense mechanism and suppressed perception of the innocuous light beam in the other. Since the subjects were never asked which word they saw, and were only asked when the light beam became visible, the existence of the filter mechanism was confirmed.

More recent experiments devised by J.R. Stoop demonstrate the existence of the filter in a different way. Stroop presented threatening and neutral words, written in different colors, to subjects suffering from anxiety. He asked them to report the colors of the words, but to ignore their meanings. The subjects required more time to perform the task when the words were disturbing than when they were neutral. This was particularly true when the word related to a sensitivity of the viewer, as when the word "CANCER" was shown to a subject worried about health issues.

Distorted Room and Glasses Experiments

Distorted room experiments inspired by Adelbert Aames also illustrate how the unconscious physically alters the appearance of "reality" to protect us from anxiety. Mr. Aames was a multi-talented experimental psychologist who had also worked as a lawyer, painter, and physiologist. He invented the Aames room, which is depicted in Figure 2.11 on page 32. The man in the right rear window is actually quite normal looking. The room however, is distorted in such a way as to make him appear to have an enormous, unnaturally shaped head.

Figure
2.11

In the late 1940s, an experimenter was surprised to discover that a woman viewing the face of her *husband* through the window did *not* perceive it as unusually large. When the woman looked at the face of a man she *didn't know*, however, she reported it was misshapen. The researcher wondered if a strong emotional attachment between the viewer and person being viewed could "override" the normal perception-altering properties of the room. His hypothesis was confirmed when a series of newlyweds were asked to observe their spouses in the window. A significant percentage reported that the image of their spouse was not distorted, but rather the *room* was! When the viewers perceived people they were *not* emotionally attached to, the *faces* appeared altered, but the room did not.

Navy researchers encountered a similar phenomenon while experimenting with special vision-distorting eyeglasses. The researchers discovered that when enlisted men wore the glasses, they thought officers looked less misshapen than men of their own rank. Apparently, fear of the officers overcame the distorting properties of the glasses, in the same way the newlyweds' emotional feelings overwhelmed the influence of the Aames room.

Psychoanalytic Theory

The idea that the mind can repress or distort disturbing *visual* data overlaps with the idea that the mind represses awareness of disturbing *thoughts or emotions*. The latter is a fundamental proposition of modern psychology.

Sigmund Freud was the first person to convincingly propose that human behavior is guided to a large extent by unconscious influences we are not aware of. He was a doctor in the late 1800s who experimented with hypnosis as a means of treating mentally ill patients. He discovered that some patients, when hypnotized, became aware of powerful emotions and memories they had previously repressed. Sometimes when this occurred they experienced a cathartic outburst, after which their neurotic symptoms subsided. From these observations Freud developed *psychoanalytic theory*, which in its most simplistic form states the following:

The human mind is like an iceberg (quite like the pyramid discussed previously), and divided into two parts. The very top of it, the conscious, is the part we are aware of. It comprises our rational, logical selves, our sense of being, and our sense of morality.

The rest of the iceberg is the unconscious. It operates without our awareness, and it is egotistical, selfish, and self-centered. It is hedonistic and truly asocial, meaning it wants and desires gratification by any means. It is subject to drives and impulses that are often totally repugnant to the conscious mind. These drives and impulses might include seemingly unbelievable feelings such as the desire to murder the same sex parent, or to have sex with the parent of the opposite gender, or homosexual inclinations.

A barrier, or "filter mechanism" (as I call it) divides the two parts. Its purpose is to prevent the conscious from becoming overwhelmed with anxiety over what is going on in the unconscious. The barrier excludes or alters unconsciously threatening information through a process called "repression," so that the conscious does not become aware of it.

In a "normal" person, Freud believed, the filter is successful. The subject remains unaware of the repressed data and is able to develop more mature (and socially acceptable) means of seeking gratification. If the filter is not entirely successful, the subject may develop a neurosis. The threatening material can manifest itself in "maladaptive behaviors" such as stuttering, insomnia, or eating disorders, which appear to be unrelated to the original anxiety.

Freud's treatment involved helping the patient understand and deal with the unconscious conflict on a conscious level. At first, he used hypnosis to uncover the repressed material. Later, he developed other psychoanalytic techniques, such as the use of word associations, in which the patient was asked to spontaneously call out the first thing that came to mind in response to a stimulus. The goal was to get behind the "filter" and reveal the root of the problem.

The two systems of thought, the conscious and the unconscious, exist independently of each other, and are capable of having completely opposing points of view. It is possible, for example, for a person to love his or her mother on one level and despise her on the other. This, in fact, was the repressed conflict that led Sybil (the subject of the best-selling novel and popular movie) to defensively develop sixteen separate personalities.

Although it is still heatedly debated, psychoanalytic theory has evolved and become a cornerstone of modern psychology. Freud believed that repressed material is primarily sexual (often incestuous), or aggressive. However, as Robert F. Bornstein, a modern day subliminal researcher has pointed out, "more recent formulations suggest that a wide variety of anxiety-producing thoughts, beliefs, attitudes, and affective reactions may be subject to repression." In other words, the "filter mechanism" operates to "filter out" (and protect us from) *everything* that we find threatening.

The Social Façade

Many experiments confirm Freud's viewpoint that civilization is simply a thin veneer barely concealing our primitive selves. In *The Stanford Prison Experiment*, for example, conducted in the early 1970s at Stanford University, 24 students volunteered to create a simulated jail environment for a period of two weeks. They were arbitrarily divided into "prisoners" and "guards." The "guards" carried billy clubs and wore khaki uniforms, whistles, and intimidating mirrored sunglasses. The "prisoners" were strip searched, deloused with a spray, issued dress-like uniforms bearing identifying numbers, and forced to wear heavy ankle chains. They were incarcerated in small makeshift cells constructed in a university hallway.

The "guards" did not receive any specific training, and "were free, within limits, to do whatever they thought was necessary to maintain law and order... and to command the respect of the prisoners." Although they were given psychological tests prior to the experiment to ensure they were "normal," about *one third* of them became sadistic and abusive. The experiment had to be stopped in just six days, in part because some of the "guards" humiliated the prisoners in a "pornographic" manner at night, when they thought no one was watching.

The Evolutionary Perspective

From an evolutionary perspective, consciousness is a relatively recent development. It probably evolved about 200,000 to 500,000 years ago, around the time the first humans (protohumans) became capable of pre-planning activities. Consciousness developed as *an addition to* the existing (largely unconscious) protohuman mental structures.

The new addition of consciousness was very adept at dealing with novel situations, but it worked slowly and could only handle a few problems at the same time. The filter mechanism developed to restrict the amount of information the conscious had to deal with. This was true not only in regard to *seeing*, as was previously discussed, but also in regard to *thinking*. The filter developed as an *interface* that allowed the unconscious and conscious to efficiently operate in tandem.

The Evolutionary Basis of Attention: The filter promoted intelligence by allowing the conscious to focus on only a few thoughts at a time. To illustrate, when I was a law professor I had to perform many tasks simultaneously. I had to verbally address the class, and at the same time walk around the room. I had to construct paragraphs, and individual sentences within the paragraphs, and organize the material in a logical manner. I had to monitor the student's facial expressions to make sure they weren't bored. Because my conscious mind was incapable of processing so many thoughts simultaneously, my "filter" directed my *conscious* attention from subject to subject (Is the student in the back sleeping? What did I do with the chalk? Should I bring up "res ipsa loquitur" now?) while my *unconscious* did most of the work.

The Evolutionary Basis of Thought Repression: The filter also promoted intelligence by minimizing anxiety. The protohumans that preceded us had no sense of morality, and no sense of guilt. They would not hesitate to kill a sibling to eat its food, for example, if there was not enough food to go around. The new addition of consciousness gradually developed a sense of "right" and "wrong." As it became more moralistic, it became disturbed by the savage, amoral thought processes of the unconscious. The filter developed the ability to block (or repress) awareness of unpleasant unconscious thoughts, in order to protect the conscious from emotional turmoil that would have impaired its functioning.

Only the First Page: We human beings like to think of ourselves as the climax of evolution, the final result of a long tumultuous process of natural selection. In reality, we are a brand new, wholly undeveloped species. The pyramids, which mark the beginning of our civilization, were only constructed about 4,500 years ago. We think of 4,500 years as a long time, but in fact it is equal to merely *ninety* fifty-year lifetimes. One representative of every generation that has lived since King Tut could attend a fairly small party.

Human beings have only begun the evolutionary process. Our sun won't begin to exhaust itself for another ten *billion* years. A million years from now (when we have only used one *ten-thousandth* of the time we have left) *historians will consider our era as the beginning of the human species.* They will view us in much the same way that we view cave-people.

Accordingly, if the division between the conscious and the unconscious, and the savage impulses postulated by Freud seem primitive, that's because they are. Our mental structures were literally "born yesterday." We just emerged from the jungle, and have aeons left to develop. The idea that we are highly evolved and intelligent is a *gross perceptual distortion*— analogous to a one-day-old infant perceiving itself as a mature adult. It is easier to see ourselves as we really are, and to understand how advertisers manipulate us, if we view our species from this perspective.

How Advertisers Make Use of the Filter Mechanism

To briefly review, subliminal visual information can be "delivered" to the unconscious in many ways, including:

1. fleeting images (such as flash frames in movies)
2. figure-ground illusions
3. embedded illusions
4. faint double exposures, and
5. incidental (or seemingly insignificant) data (such as the taboo words in the matrix study).

The filter mechanism prevents much of the information from being perceived consciously. It does this by either *blocking* the stimulus all together, or *altering* its physical appearance. When determining what to allow into consciousness, the filter considers:

1. *Gestalt* principles, such as figure-ground, similarity, closure, etc.;

2. the degree to which the information is *discordant*; and

3. how *upsetting* the information would be if it were consciously perceived.

The following advertisements illustrate how these principles can be applied to advertising.

Figure 2.12

Fit at Any Size

The illustration in Figure 2.12 appeared on the cover of *Health and Fitness Journal* in 2000. Please study it for a moment before reading further.

The picture depicts a handsome young man and a beautiful woman riding a motorcycle. The woman is wearing a bikini, and sensually pressing against the driver as she smiles at the reader. The viewer is distracted by the fact that she looks somewhat vulnerable. The yellow text to the left, "Fit At Any Size," is a fairly obvious sexual innuendo.

Until it is pointed out, most people do not realize that the woman's right hand is *massaging the man's genitals*. A close up appears in Figure 2.13.

Figure 2.13

The sexual content of the picture is not debatable, and it is not really hidden in any way. Because it relates to a taboo topic and is contrary to our expectations, however, the filter mechanism automatically blocks awareness of it.

It is somewhat more obvious in the context of this book than it was in real life. Very few readers were aware of the cover's subliminal soft-porn content when they glanced at it in the supermarket.

Fancy A Dip?

Now take a look at the 2001 *Wallpaper Magazine* cover depicted in Figure 2.14. It portrays a striking photograph of two handsome young men and a captivating, bare-breasted young woman. Our attention is riveted by the fact that the woman's nipples are partially but not completely obscured by the "C" and the "A" in the suggestive phrase, "Fancy a Dip?" The subtitle "ripples, teak, brass, and ass" is also extremely provocative.

As in the previous example, however, most viewers probably don't realize that both of the woman's hands are massaging her companions' genitals. The fact that she is not wearing a top clearly suggests the three of them are naked. Again, the sexual content of the picture is not really hidden; it is suppressed by the filter mechanism.

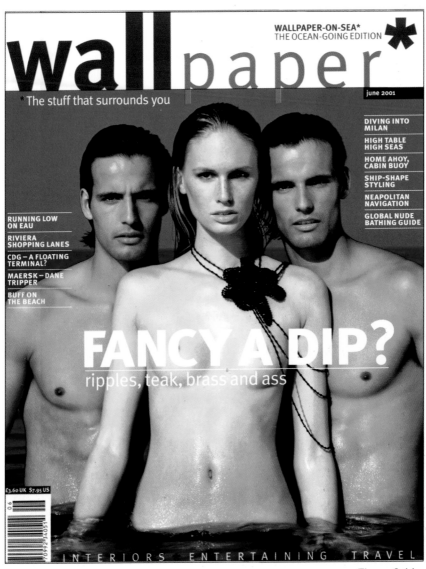

Figure 2.14

An embed on the inside of the magazine reinforces the sexual theme of the cover. The entire page is depicted on the upper left of Figure 2.15(a) (left). The woman and her two friends are shown walking naked on a beach. If you look carefully at the left hand of the man in front, you will find that a realistic, anatomically correct penis appears in the shadows on his palm. The phallus may actually have occurred naturally, and been photographically softened so that it only registers on an unconscious level.

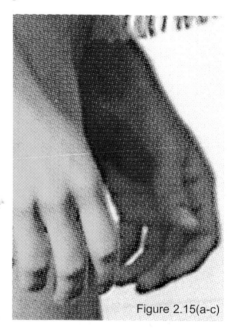

Figure 2.15(a-c)

Now go back to the complete *Wallpaper* cover. Do you notice anything unusual about the *faces*? They look remarkably similar. Although the woman's skin is much fairer than the men's, the nose, mouth, eyes, and hair of all three of them are very much alike. The models were chosen to look like *brothers and sisters*, as well as lovers. The cover not only subliminally portrays group sex; it depicts an incestuous *menage a trois*!

Three's A Crowd

The 1977 *People* magazine cover featured in Figure 2.16 was probably purchased by over a million people. Many more of them glanced at it while they were standing in checkout lines, or in doctors' waiting rooms. The scene features the cast of "Three's Company," a television situation comedy popular at the time. The show involved two women and one man who lived together platonically but flirtatiously.

Figure 2.16

   The cover portrays the man, John Ritter, playfully gnawing on co-star Suzanne Somer's shoulder. Mr. Ritter's tongue is curled up and pointing towards the top of his mouth. If you relax and focus on it for a while you will discover that a small, circumcised penis has been airbrushed underneath it. The penis is easy to see in the close-ups in Figure 2.17. It's purple, contains numerous veins, and seems to be emerging from some sort of compartment behind Mr. Ritter's teeth. It clearly could not be part of his mouth, or anything other than a miniature phallus.

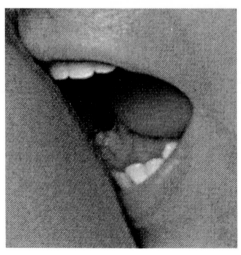

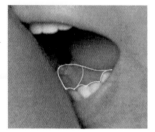

Figure 2.17(a-c)

Shave Your Man

How old is the woman in Figure 2.18? Please study the picture carefully before deciding.

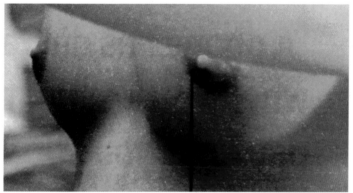

Figure 2.18

Now look at the entire page depicted in Figure 2.19, as it appeared in *Glamour* in 2001.

1 Don't sleep with make-up on

Regularly hitting the sack before any cleanser hits your face "will plug up pores and give you pimples," explains Marianne O'Donoghue, M.D., associate professor of dermatology at Rush Presbyterian–St. Luke Medical Center in Chicago.

Do use a 2-in-1 cleanser

Save time with a cleanser that removes makeup *and* tones skin. **Try** Lancôme Cleansing Water With Natural Extracts for Face and Eyes, $25, lancome.com.

2 Don't get beard-burned

Dancing cheek to cheek against a date's five o'clock shadow is like "washing your face with an SOS pad," explains Dr. O'Donoghue. If his kiss makes your skin red and raw, ask your dermatologist for a topical antibiotic like Cleocin T lotion to soothe it.

Do shave your man

Keep him clean and smooth by shaving him with an aloe-vera-based gel. (That way, the only thing that'll feel the burn is the bedsheets.) **Try** Nivea for Men Mild Shaving Gel, $3, at drugstores.

3 Don't pick your zits

"Squeezing pimples injects the dirt and bacteria from our fingers below the surface of the skin, which can cause infection," explains Dr. O'Donoghue. "Plus, breaking the skin will double the chances of scarring."

Do banish them with a zit zapper

Choose a clear, drying salicylic-acid gel that can be worn under makeup throughout the day. **Try** Bioré Blemish Double Agent, $7, at drugstores.

Figure 2.19

Amazing, isn't it? Although the torso unequivocally appears to have female breasts, in the actual ad it is attached to a man's head! (Sorry, but I only asked you how old the model was to throw you off.) The breasts are titillating (pardon the pun) and the nipples are erect and sexually stimulated. Even more astonishing, the torso appears to be pregnant!

When taken out of context, the image appears to be female. A viewer glancing at the complete page in *Glamour,* however, would "see" it as male. The principles of perceptual distortion cause its feminine character to be repressed, and perceived only on a subliminal level.

The woman in the picture is happily shaving her "boyfriend's" face. The "boyfriend" is subdued and passive. The picture (and its accompanying "advice article") are intended to stimulate the *Glamour* reader's latent homosexual impulses, as well as her fears of being rejected.

Many ambiguities in the text secretly support these objectives. "Do Shave Your Man," for example, on a subliminal level means "castrate your man," or "shave off his penis." It is a reference to the fable of Samson and Delilah, in which Delilah cut off Samson's hair in order to deprive him of his masculinity.

The large caption "Don't Get Beard Burned" unconsciously means "don't risk getting rejected (burned) by having a relationship with a male."

The small text in the lower middle of the page, "Keep him clean and smooth," again suggests that it is safer to relate to either emasculated males, or females. "That way the only thing that'll feel the burn is the bed-sheets" confirms that if you do so you won't get hurt, or "burned." "Try Nivea for Men Mild Shaving Gel" again stresses the desirability of mild, controllable men (or in the alternative, women).

Ambiguity in Text

As suggested by the "Shave Your Man" illustration, when a *word or phrase* has more than one meaning, the unconscious analyses all of them, although only one interpretation is generally permitted into awareness. The processing of ambiguous text is quite similar to the processing of ambiguous visual images. As one researcher put it, "What receives our attention and becomes conscious is only what is selected from alternative candidates." This is fairly obvious when you think about it. Reading the phrase, "to get the coconut, the monkey climbed the palm…" does *not* cause you to think about the palm of your *hand.* Your unconscious automatically suppresses that interpretation of the word "palm" because it is not congruent with the context of the sentence. Without you being aware of it, your filter mechanism:

1. scans the phrase and determines that it contains an ambiguous word;
2. analyzes all possible *meanings* of the ambiguous word;
3. determines the *context* of the phrase; and
4. *excludes* the inappropriate interpretations of the ambiguous word from consciousness.

This process promotes efficient language comprehension. It would be much more difficult to understand what the phrase meant if both the "hand" and "tree" interpretations were allowed to enter awareness.

From the perspective of advertisers, the important point is that the secondary, repressed interpretation is fully analyzed and understood *unconsciously*. You may only be aware of the palm "tree" meaning, but the palm "hand" meaning registers subliminally.

Advertisers routinely capitalize on this phenomena by utilizing text that has dual meanings. Sometimes they are very obvious, such as "Try Our Hard Pack," but often they are more hidden, as in the preceding "Shave Your Man" example. We frequently are unaware of the duality in advertising copy because we don't pay attention to the ads we are exposed to. If you flip through a magazine consciously looking for ambiguities, you will be astonished by the quantity you discover.

You will also be impressed by advertisers' creativity in this regard. Did you realize, for example, that "Taco Bells Hot New Hand-Held — Think Outside The Bun!" is a disguised referenced to masturbation, and therefore self-gratification by eating?

The Wine Sat There and the Smirnoff Flowed

The Smirnoff illustration in Figure 2.20 utilizes a subliminal technique that has not been discussed previously. Please study it carefully before reading further.

This ad appeared in *The New Yorker* and *Time* magazine in the late 1970s. At first glance, it appears to portray a mundane party scene. The copy, "The wine sat there and the Smirnoff flowed. Amusing," seems to suggest that serving Smirnoff will enhance the reader's social status.

Figure 2.20

If you study the photograph it soon becomes apparent that, oddly enough, it doesn't contain any faces. The only face you can see is the reflection of the woman looking in the mirror.

Figure 2.21

The woman looking into the mirror is slender and feminine. She has bare shoulders and is wearing a frilly purple dress. The reflection looking out of the mirror, on the other hand, is extremely masculine. The woman looking into the mirror has long hair tied in a bun, but the person looking back has a crew cut. The woman looking into the mirror is putting on lipstick, a feminine activity, but the person looking back could be smoking a cigarette and sneering. The arms of the two figures are raised above their heads and are pushing against each other, suggesting a male-female conflict is implied in the picture.

But where are the males? Discounting the reflection, there appears to be only one. He is sitting at the right side of the table.

We can't see his face, but we can tell that he is not the kind of super-masculine, sexually confident male typically portrayed in liquor and cigarette advertisements. Rather, he looks reserved, quiet, and repressed. His hair is balding and he is formally dressed, wearing a bow tie.

Although we can't tell what he is thinking, he appears to be somewhat nervous. Sweat is glistening on his forehead, and his jaw muscles are tense. His chair has been pulled away from the table, and he is leaning forward, clenching the napkin on his lap.

He looks as though he might be about to jump up from his seat. Why would he do such a thing?

Perhaps it is because the woman in the see-through blouse, standing in the center of the picture, is about to throw her drink in his face! Note how she is looking down at him, with her arm raised, and her glass aimed at his head.

The woman standing in the black dress, with her back to the reader, also seems ready to hurl her drink at the man. Notice the awkward position of her left hand as she reaches down to pick up her glass.

On a conscious level, the picture portrays an innocuous party. On a subliminal level, it portrays a heated argument reaching a crescendo as the women gang up on the man and finally let him have it. The ad satisfies the unconscious fantasies of women who drink heavily and are hostile towards men.

This hostility is symbolically represented by a small, menacing, skull-like face embedded in the space between the top of the liquid and the top of the glass on the table. A close up appears in Figure 2.22(b) (below). The face is glaring at the viewer with reddish, slanted eyes.

The copy, "The Wine Sat There And The Smirnoff Flowed," is cleverly ambiguous. The "wine" refers to the whiney, mousy man who is the object of the women's contempt. "The Smirnoff Flowed" literally, into his face!

As an additional enhancement, subliminal breasts have been airbrushed onto the *back* of the woman sitting in the chair. If you look at the close up, you will see that her back has been made to look like her front, complete with a sexy top and well-defined cleavage. This discordant, sexually provocative illusion demands our attention unconsciously.

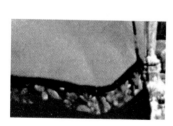

Figure 2.22(a-b)

Ambiguous Meanings

As the Smirnoff ad illustrates, the mind processes pictures with multiple *meanings* the same way it processes ambiguous *images* and *text*.

The picture is subject to two interpretations. One of the interpretations (the affluent party) is consciously acceptable. The other (the women assaulting the man) is threatening to the conscious, but appealing to the viewer's unconscious hostile fantasies. The filter represses the "hostile" interpretation, and allows only the "acceptable" interpretation into awareness.

Delivering subliminal content through the use of pictures with *multiple meanings* is extremely common in media. As will be discussed later, the ambiguity is often created by obscuring the facial expressions of the actors.

Distortion of Meaning

The Smirnoff ad also illustrates that in addition to distorting the *physical appearance* of a picture, the filter can alter and suppress its *meaning*.

In a study investigating this, bigoted individuals were shown a cartoon ridiculing bigotry. They were unable to consciously understand what the cartoon was driving it, even though it was obvious. The subjects' filters distorted the *meaning* of the cartoon, in order to protect them from its implied criticism.

Not surprisingly, when the filter blocks comprehension of the meaning of a picture in this manner, the blocked meaning continues to influence the viewer unconsciously. In the 1930s, researchers Malamud and Linder showed mentally ill patients pictures that related to their emotional disorders for a period of *thirty seconds*. Several minutes after the pictures were taken away, the patients were asked to describe what they had seen. The patients' responses indicated they were not consciously aware of the disturbing elements of the pictures. However, the disturbing elements they did not report "seeing" later emerged in their *dreams*.

For example, one subject was shown a copy of the painting *Immaculate Conception* by Bartolome Esteban Murillo (1617-1682), which portrays a maternal young woman surrounded by children (Figure 2.23). The subject was guilt-ridden because her younger brother had drowned while she was taking care of him. Her own child had later died from an infectious disease. Although she described the moonlight and the dress the lady in the

Figure 2.23

painting was wearing, *she did not mention the youths at all.* That night she dreamt she "saw herself soaring to heaven" surrounded by *winged children,* among whom she recognized her brother and infant child.

Another subject was a young man who felt sexually inadequate, and feared his wife was about to take away his children. He was shown a copy of the painting *Medea,* by Paul Cézanne (1829-1906). The painting portrays Medea, wielding a knife, about to murder the children she bore to Jason because he had been unfaithful to her. The subject described Medea as a man, and failed to mention the knife at all. That night, however, the subject dreamt that "all the meat" came off of his arm.

In the foregoing examples, the pictures that were presented to the subjects were not ambiguous. *When the picture is ambiguous, as in the Smirnoff ad, it is easier for the filter to block the threatening meaning because a more palatable interpretation is available.*

The Law of Exclusion

The Viennese psychologist Otto Poetzl explored how subliminal information affects the *dreams* of viewers as early as 1917. He exposed subjects to
pictures for 1/100 of a second and asked them to draw and describe what
they had seen. Because the images were displayed so briefly, the subjects
usually could only recall a few elements of them. As in the examples discussed above, however, the subjects often dreamt about the parts of the
pictures they did not report "seeing." Poetzl concluded that threatening information in the images was repressed, stored in the unconscious, and subsequently processed during sleep. He labeled this phenomenon the "Law of
Exclusion," referring to the fact that the disturbing material was "excluded"
from awareness. His research constituted the first hard evidence supporting
Freud's psychoanalytic theories.

More recent studies have validated and expanded upon Poetzl's research. In the 1950s researcher Charles Fisher successfully replicated his
experiments. Fisher also recovered subliminally presented material immediately following exposure through the use of word association and psychological tests. He found that subjects who ordinarily did not dream while
sleeping were more inclined to process subliminal data while they were
awake. Researcher Howard Shevrin has noted that the early Poetzl studies
"have stood the test of time" because "much more registers of a stimulus
during a brief flash than can be consciously reported: moreover, what is *not*
reported can be recovered in dreams and other forms." (Emphasis added.)

In an article written in 1986, Dr. Shevrin also remarked that an amazing amount of information is recorded unconsciously, even when the stimulus is presented for only one *thousandth* of a second. He noted that the
more threatening a stimulus is the more likely it is to be repressed, and the
greater impact it has on a subliminal level.

Evidence of the Unconscious Through Hypnosis

Hypnosis played an important role in the early exploration of the
unconscious. Freud discovered that when he hypnotized mentally ill patients,
he found they often suffered from repressed traumas they could not remember
consciously. When he helped them to recall the traumas, their neurotic
symptoms (such as psychosomatic blindness) sometimes subsided. These
observations led him to develop his psychoanalytic theories. Other

psychologists, prior to World War II, used hypnosis to investigate Freud's hypotheses.

Dream Theory

Freud theorized that the barrier between the unconscious and conscious relaxes during sleep. Information that is subliminally perceived during the day is processed when we are dreaming. Since our unconscious thoughts are often consciously disturbing, when we wake up we don't remember what we actually dreamed. Rather, we recall a *sanitized* version in which the original information is distorted and represented symbolically. Freud believed that analyzing and interpreting the *symbols* in dreams reveals unconscious conflicts.

In 1924 researcher G..Roffenstein tested this hypothesis by hypnotizing a female subject and suggesting she dream of having intercourse with her *father.* He further instructed her to distort the dream and hide its contents so as to make it entirely innocuous, so that she could tell any stranger about it "without embarrassment."

The woman fell into a hypnotic sleep. Although she could not remember the instructions, when she awoke she reported:

> I dreamt about my father, as if he presented me with a great bag, a great traveling bag, and he gave me a large key. It was a very large key. It looked like a key to a house. I had a sad feeling, and I wondered about it being so big; it couldn't possibly fit. Then I opened the bag. A snake jumped out right against my mouth. I shrieked and then I awoke.

Roffenstein's study corroborated Freud's dream theory. The instructions he gave the patient mirrored what Freud hypothesized occurs naturally. The snake, the key, and the other symbols that appeared in the subject's dream were remarkably similar to the symbols that Freud's patients reported dreaming about. Roffenstein's results supported Freud's view that his patients actually dreamt about incestuous activities, but only remembered them in a disguised form when they woke up.

Farber and Fisher achieved similar results in 1943. A male patient was hypnotized and told a dream "would come" to him about a young woman nursing an infant. When he awoke, he reported that he took the "Mount

Pleasant" streetcar to the top of a tall hill. He made a drawing of the incline that looked very much like the profile of a large breast. Apparently, he had dreamed about being breast-fed and nurtured, but only remembered a sanitized, socially acceptable version of his dream when he awoke.

Inducting Neurosis

Freud theorized that neurosis is the result of unconscious conflicts. In 1932, A.R Luria artificially instilled neurosis in subjects by hypnotizing them and telling them they had stolen money from a friend. When the subjects awoke, they did not remember what Luria had told them, and they were not aware of feeling distressed. Nonetheless, psychological tests and physiological monitors revealed that they were experiencing anxiety on an unconscious level. In a similar manner, hypnotic suggestions have also been used to artificially generate psychosomatic illnesses.

Rationalizing Behavior

Freud theorized that humans "rationalize" their behavior — meaning they falsely ascribe rational, consciously acceptable motives to conduct that in truth is motivated by unconscious impulses. Interestingly, when people are hypnotized and instructed to perform a bizarre act after they wake up, they often do. When asked why they performed the bizarre act, they usually *confabulate* a "logical" reason for it. No matter how far-fetched the rationalization is, they generally believe it, and are not aware that their actions were induced by the hypnotic instruction. This behavior mirrors Freud's theories about rationalizations, and again illustrates the existence of unconscious thought processes.

As an example, a doctor entered a hospital ward, put his umbrella in the corner, and hypnotized one of the patients. He told the patient he was going to leave temporarily, and instructed him to open the umbrella and hold it over his head when he returned. The patient was awakened, and the Doctor left and returned to the ward as planned. The patient held the umbrella over the doctor's head. When asked what he was doing, the patient replied, "Its raining outside and I thought you would open the umbrella in the room before going out." Although he seemed embarrassed, the patient was totally unaware of why he had acted in such a manner.

Brain Waves and Psychoanalysis

Current research has uncovered additional support for psychoanalytic theory in a more scientific manner.

In 1996, for example, the distinguished psychologist Howard K. Shevrin published a lengthy experiment in which neurotic subjects were psychoanalyzed by a team of psychotherapists. The doctors compiled a list of words that related to a.) The subject's *symptoms*, and b.) *Unconscious conflicts* that were causing the subject's symptoms. The subjects were then exposed to the words both *sub*liminally, so they were not aware of them, and *supra*liminally, so they were aware of them. Their brain waves were recorded to measure their reactions.

One of the subjects was a thirty-year-old man who was terrified of social situations. As a young child he was closer to his father, who was a compulsive gambler, than to his mother. When the subject was five, his mother threw his father out of the house. The mother then took a night job, and left the subject alone or in the care of an emotionally distant adult. Dr. Shevrin and his colleagues concluded that although the man was outwardly soft-spoken, he inwardly was extremely angry. He avoided social settings because he secretly was afraid he would be unable to control his unconscious rage.

Dr. Shevrin further concluded that "power," "take control," and "violence" were "conflict" words that related to the man's emotional disorders. When the subject was exposed to these words at subliminal speeds, the brain wave patterns he generated indicated he processed the words extensively on an unconscious level. Conversely, he processed neutral words superficially. The man was unaware of the psychological significance of the conflict words, and of his inner hostility. The results of the experiment supported the psychotherapists' analysis of the man, as well as psychoanalytic theory in general.

Stranger Than We Think

A broad insight that can be derived from the foregoing studies is that we are all a lot stranger than we think. We consciously appear and pretend to be "normal," but when you scratch the veneer of our psyches it becomes obvious we are anything but.

Advertising is a reflection of our selves because it has to appeal to both what we *really* are, and what we would like to *think* we are. It is not surprising, therefore, that it too becomes more and more bizarre as we peer beneath its surface superficialities.

Natural Disorientation

The Naturalizer ad in Figure 2.24 dramatically portrays a series of very attractive women, all clad in slinky black dresses and sexy black boots. Each of them is wearing a string of white pearls, symbolically suggesting bondage, and has her neck exposed, suggesting submission. (Animals display their necks in a similar manner when they submit to their adversaries.) The outline of the pearls (particularly on the woman in front) is phallically shaped.

After you have finished studying the picture, please turn the page and look at Figure 2.25.

Figure 2.24

Did you realize that the person at the rear of the procession is a *man*? He looks like a rock star wearing a dress. He is sporting sideburns and the slight stubble of a beard. His thick biceps and short-nailed, large, masculine hand reveal his true gender.

This ad takes advantage of the Gestalt principle of similarity. When you look at the entire picture, your unconscious determines that since all the figures have long hair and are wearing dresses, boots, and pearls, they must all be women. The filter concludes that the masculine appearance of the person on the far left is an error, and corrects it. When you look at the man outside the context of the ad, however, his sex seems obvious.

The Naturalizer ad fulfills female viewers' unconscious fantasies of being manly. Like the "Shave Your Man" ad, it also appeals to their repressed homosexual feelings. Freud believed that even "normal" people have latent homosexual impulses they are not aware of. Common sense tells us this must be true. Most people do not appear to be exclusively either masculine or feminine; rather their sexuality falls on a continuum between the two extremes. Media constantly stimulates and plays with our conflicting unconscious sexual inclinations.

Figure 2.25

Staying Pure

The advertisement in Figure 2.26 appeared in 2001 in *Maxim*, a men's magazine that competes with *Playboy* and features erotic photographs of nude women. The ad ostensibly portrays a beautiful woman playfully biting into a lime.

Or is it a woman? The model has an incredibly large nose, and a very masculine-looking, prominent chin. "Her" neck is large and manly looking, as is her hand. Her fingers are fairly large, and the nails are very short. Her breasts are not visible, and there is no indication of a cleavage. Odd as it may seem, "she" appears to be a man in drag.

The model's right eye is very masculine, and the hair falling over her left eye infers that she is hiding something. Perhaps she is thinking about the subliminal penis behind her hand. The tip of it is hidden beneath the lime, between her first and second finger. The base of it appears just below the pinky, and the tip is obscured by the lemon. It is outlined in red in the close up in Figure 2.27 on page 56.

On a conscious level, the ad appears to stimulate heterosexual fantasies associated with Sauza *Horni*tos Tequila. On an unconscious level, however, it portrays a man in drag coyly licking a phallus. The caption, "Way Purer Than Most Of Your Thoughts" reinforces the male readers' subliminal perception of the picture.

The ad contains another interesting illusion. If you look at the *left* side of Figure 2.27 you will find the green top of a Sauza bottle cap. To make the illustration, I photographed an actual Sauza bottle, cut out the green cap on my computer, and laid it into the picture. If you look at the complete ad in Figure 2.26 you will find that a remarkably clear *subliminal* bottle cap appears in exactly the same location.

Figure 2.26

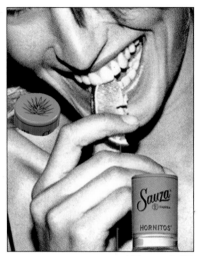

Figure 2.27

The Sauza companion ad depicted in Figure 2.28 is equally bizarre. It appeared in *Stuff,* another men's magazine, in the same year. Many people think the model wearing the leather jacket looks like a homosexual. The "woman" appears to be a man in drag. Her chin is more prominent than Jay Leno's. She has an enormous Adam's apple, and her hair grows very far down the back of her neck. Her eyebrow seems to be painted, and the make-up on her eyelid is extremely thick. It is hard to understand why the creative director would select such an unattractive model, unless "she" was intended to be subliminally perceived as a gay man. The copy "The Tequila Is Pure. Your Intentions Don't Have To Be" again appeals to the reader's unconscious understanding of the picture.

Both of these ads stimulate male homosexual *fantasies*. Because the fantasies are taboo, however, the ads also generate unconscious *anxiety*. The tag line, "Sauza. Stay Pure," reinforces this dichotomy by warning "Look out! You are becoming sexually stimulated by a man! Repress those feelings!"

This duality ironically sells the product in two ways. The pleasure of the forbidden sex is associated with the tequila, and, at the same time, the anxiety the ad engenders stimulates the desire to drink.

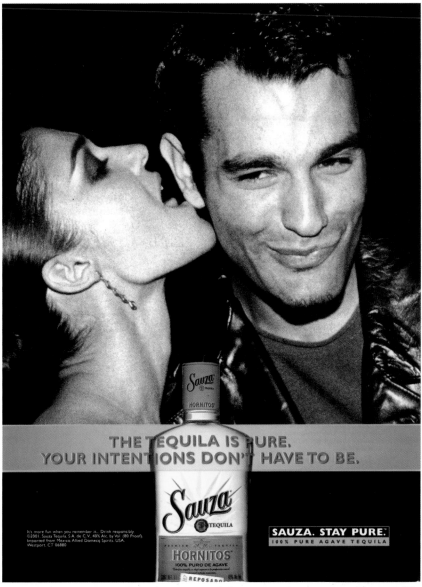

Figure 2.28

The Cosmo Scene

The illustration in Figure 2.29 appeared in 2001 in *CosmoGIRL!*, a version of *Cosmopolitan* marketed towards teenagers.

At first glance it portrays three groups of young men and women holding each other. The primary group consists of one man and two women at the lower left of the picture. The two women seem to be fondling the man. The dark-haired woman, who is kneeling, has her left hand on the man's chest and appears to be staring lovingly into his eyes.

If you study the picture, however, you will soon realize that she isn't really looking at the *man*; she is looking at the light-haired *woman* standing *behind* him.

The light-haired woman is returning her affectionate gaze. The two women are sensuously touching the tips of their fingers together on the man's chest. The dark-haired woman's left elbow is gently caressing the light haired woman's knee. On a subliminal level, the two women are secret lovers.

The homosexual fantasies inspired by the photo are reinforced by an embedded sexual graphic. If you look in the dark space between the dark-haired woman's chin and the thumb on the man's right hand, you will discover a perfectly formed female breast. The nipple is touching the dark-haired woman's Adam's apple.

The man appears to be caressing the back of the dark-haired woman's head in an affectionate manner with his left hand. From another perspective, however, he is attempting to induce her to pay more attention to him.

An extra pair of hands inexplicably appears in the space between the inside of the man's right elbow, and the dark-haired woman's left hand. Two feminine fingers with long nails appear to be sensuously caressing a female thumb.

The extra fingers don't really "fit" in the photograph. They can't belong to the light-haired woman because her right hand is on the man's biceps, and her left hand is on the man's chest. They can't belong to the dark-haired woman because her left hand is on the man's chest, and her right arm couldn't be long enough to comfortably snake around in front of her and reach the man's side. Even if it was, two of the "extra" fingers have *long* nails, and the dark-haired woman's left hand seems to have *short* nails. The extra hands subliminally represent the women's erotic relationship.

Figure 2.29

By now you may have noticed that all the men in the photograph are expressionless, dull, and robot-like. The two women towards the rear look like twins. The one on the left is oblivious to her partner and could be thinking about her girlfriend.

The woman on the right rear has a subliminal penis. It is short, circumcised, and erect. It appears in the genital area of her pants, with the head pointing towards her companion's navel. Just below it, a mouth-like organ can be seen kissing her partner's genitals.

The woman to the rear left also has a penis, although it is more symbolic. It appears as a long dark shadow extending from her genital area, as if she had a huge erection pressing against her companion's crotch.

On a conscious level, the *Cosmo* scene portrays heterosexual couples eagerly embracing each other. On an unconscious level, however, it depicts the women ignoring the men and bonding sexually and emotionally with each other. The woman to the right rear is gazing wistfully at the audience, inviting the female teenage *CosmoGIRL!* reader to join them.

Subliminals in Our Daily Lives

In our daily lives, subliminally perceived information plays an important role in the formation of our attitudes, beliefs, and world view. Our behavior is strongly influenced by information we are not aware of. When we sense someone is lying, for example, our skepticism of their credibility is often derived from subtle mannerisms and body language we are not cognizant of consciously. When we meet a new person, our first impression is the result of subtle cues we do not consciously think about. Many studies have explored how unconsciously perceived information is assimilated and influences us.

Subliminal Influences on Attitudes

In a 1993 experiment, for example, subjects were shown either a subliminal "happy" face or a subliminal "angry" face. Following the subliminal presentation, they were shown a *supra*liminal (consciously perceived) series of Chinese symbols. They were asked to indicate whether they thought each of the symbols represented a "good" or "bad" concept. The subjects' impressions of the symbols were affected by the subliminal faces. The subjects were more likely to rate the symbols as "good" after they had been

Figure 2.30(a-d)

shown the subliminal "happy" face, and "bad" after they had been shown the subliminal "angry" face.

In a related study, subjects were subliminally shown words that connoted either "honesty" or words that connoted "nastiness." They were then read a biography of a fictional person who was sometimes honest and sometimes mean-spirited, and asked to evaluate the fictional person's behavior. The subjects were more likely to rate the character as "honest" when they were subliminally exposed to the "honesty" words, and more likely to rate the person as "mean" when they were exposed to the subliminal "nasty" words.

Unconscious Learning

A great deal of hard *knowledge* is assimilated unconsciously. Psychologists have long been aware of the distinction between *explicit* and *implicit* learning. "Explicit" learning refers to the process of *consciously* assimilating and cataloging information, such as studying the events that led up to World War II, or the symbols of the elements of the periodic table. It is the kind of learning we engage in when we go to school, or study textbooks. "Implicit" learning, on the other hand, takes place automatically and *unconsciously*, without us realizing it. This is the manner in which we learn how far away to stand from someone when we talk to them, or how to make people like us, or how to be persuasive. A child learning a language does so *implicitly*, with little effort and enormous success. An adult learning a language generally does so *explicitly*, with considerably more effort and much less success.

Numerous studies have explored how we learn without being aware that we are learning. In one experiment, *amnesiacs* were repeatedly asked to play a game that involved moving rings around three poles in order to achieve a specified order. Each time they played, their performance improved, even though they could not remember having played the game on prior occasions. Implicitly, they learned to perform the task more efficiently, although they were not consciously aware of how they acquired the skill.

Other studies have investigated how *normal* people unconsciously assimilate new ideas and information. Musically untrained subjects, for example, were asked to listen to a series of ballads and then compose a song themselves. They were able to apply musical principles they had no conscious knowledge of, and could not describe.

Incredibly complicated materials can be learned unconsciously. This was illustrated by a study in which college students were asked to quickly locate visual targets on a computer screen. The location of the targets was determined by a complex mathematical formula. The students unconsciously applied the formula and mastered the task, but could not consciously deduce what the formula was. They were unable to identify it even when they were offered a one-hundred-dollar reward.

Unconscious Conditioning

The assimilation of *knowledge* without awareness is related to the phenomenon of *unconscious conditioning*. Most people are familiar with Pavlov's experiments, in which dogs were fed shortly after a bell was rung. The dogs acquired a "conditioned response" and thereafter salivated whenever they heard the bell. Recent research has determined that such conditioning occurs even when the subject is unaware of both the stimulus and the resulting reflex. Rats have been conditioned even when they are under the influence of *anesthesia.*

Humans have been conditioned by subliminal stimuli under experimental conditions. In one study, subjects were given a mild electric shock when they were shown a subliminal "angry" face, but not shocked when they were shown a subliminal "happy" face. The subjects acquired a conditioned reflex, and exhibited higher skin conductance levels when they were subsequently shown the "angry" stimulus. Similar results were achieved by other researchers, using subliminal snakes and spiders as the "anxiety" stimuli, and subliminal mushrooms and flowers as the neutral images.

We are all conditioned by subliminal stimuli in our daily lives. Whenever we act a certain way, and those around us respond favorably, we are conditioned to act that way in the future. When our actions have adverse consequences, we are conditioned to conduct ourselves differently in the future. Although we are cognizant of the major events that comprise this process, we are oblivious to most of the subtle influences that shape our personalities and guide our behavior.

This was illustrated by a study performed at Indiana University. Students were asked to state, one at a time, all the words they could think of. Every time they uttered a *plural* word, the researchers subliminally *approved* by softly murmuring "mmm-mmh." After twenty minutes, many of the subjects generated twice as many plural words as members of the control group (in which subliminal approval was not given.) None of the subjects realized the "mmm-mmhs" had anything to do with the words they selected.

Naturally, advertisers long to secretly condition us to purchase their products. In an article in the *Wall Street Journal*, a "communications research manager" working for Coca-Cola was quoted as saying:

> We nominate Pavlov as the father of modern advertising. Pavlov took a neutral subject and, by associating it with a meaningful object, made it a symbol of something else...that is what we try to do...

Conditioning in a Marketing Context

Although most of the studies investigating unconscious conditioning in a marketing context have been performed in secret, researcher Gerald Gorn published a revealing paper on the subject in 1982. As a preliminary matter, he established that:

1. The subjects in his experiment considered *blue* pens and *beige* pens to be equally visually appealing, and
2. The subjects in his experiment *liked* the music from the movie "Grease," but *disliked* classical East Indian Music.

Gorn then split the subjects into four groups. Each group was shown either the blue pen or the beige pen, paired with either the liked or disliked music. At the conclusion of the study, the subjects were told they could choose either one of the pens as a gift. By a ratio of 3.5 to 1, they chose the pen color that was shown in conjunction with the music they *liked.* They exhibited a similar tendency to *not* choose the pen color that was shown in conjunction with the music they *disliked.*

Although they were not aware of it, the subjects were *subliminally conditioned by the music* to prefer one pen color over the other. When they were asked why they had chosen the pen they selected, more than 50% said they simply "liked" the color. This could not be the *real* reason for their choice, however, because the preliminary part of the experiment had established that the subjects considered the blue and beige pens to be equally appealing. The real reason for their choice had to be the *music*, because the music was the only variable. Nonetheless, only two percent of the subjects realized that the sound track had anything to do with their choice.

The Gorn study is particularly interesting because the subjects were conditioned after hearing the music only once. Commercials on TV, as we all know, are played over and over again.

Not "Random" Choices

Other studies have explored the Gorn conditioning phenomenon in other contexts. At the University of Warsaw, for example, students were interviewed by a researcher and asked to state their name and "birth order." When they predictably inquired what "birth order" meant, the interviewer either *scolded* them for their ignorance or reacted *neutrally* by merely answering the question. The students were then asked to go into an adjacent room and give a slip of paper to "whichever of two researchers was not busy." Both of the researchers in the other room were equally "not busy;" however, one *physically* resembled the interviewer and one did not. Remarkably, 80% of the subjects who had been *scolded* chose the researcher who did *not look like* the "birth order" interviewer, whereas only 45% of the subjects who had received the *neutral* treatment did so. The subjects did not realize that the "birth order" interview had influenced them. As in the Gorn study, almost all of them believed their selection (of researchers) was completely random.

In another experiment, subjects were exposed to either *achievement* words such as "strive," or *affiliation* words such as "friend," while conducting a seemingly unrelated task. They were then paired with an *incompetent* partner (who was secretly a confederate experimenter), and asked to solve a puzzle. The situation presented a dilemma. In order to succeed the subject had to *humiliate* the partner; in order to be *nice* to the partner the subject had to perform the task poorly. Amazingly, the subjects who were exposed to the achievement words were more likely to choose the success/ hostility option, whereas subjects who were exposed to the affiliation words were more likely to choose the cooperation/friendship alternative. None of the subjects were aware of the influence of the priming words, and simply attributed their behavior to their desire to either solve the puzzle or get along with their co-worker.

These studies illustrate that there is really no such thing as random behavior. When we believe we are acting spontaneously, we secretly are reacting unconsciously to subliminal cues we are unaware of.

The Cumulative Effect

Even if the subliminal effect of the *individual* ads we are exposed to is small, the *cumulative* effect of being exposed to millions of them, from childhood though adulthood, must be significant. If attitudes and behavior can be molded by just *one* subliminal presentation, the influence of *decades* of presentations must be pervasive.

In addition, the studies discussed so far measured the affect of *benign* subliminals, such as happy faces, achievement words, or murmured "mmm-mmhs." Advertisers employ *emotionally provocative* stimuli, targeted towards particular psychological weaknesses. The overall impact of these psychological "arrows" is much greater than society is willing to acknowledge.

Subliminal Staying Power

The *longevity* of emotionally relevant subliminals was dramatically demonstrated by B.W. Levinson in 1965. Dr. Levinson was a surgeon who staged a mock crisis in the presence of ten patients undergoing anesthesia just before they were operated on. After they became unconscious, he exclaimed: "Just a moment! I don't like the patient's color. Too much blue. Her lips are much too blue! I'm going to give her a little more oxygen." In each case, the operation proceeded, and the patients recovered normally. One month later, they were hypnotized and asked if they could remember anything that occurred during the surgery. Remarkably, four out of ten were able to give almost verbatim accounts of the seemingly life threatening incident! Even though they were under anesthesia when they heard it, they unconsciously remembered the statement long after they recovered, and long after it had ceased being important.

Drive Activation

The idea that emotionally upsetting images have powerful subliminal effects is supported by an area of research known as "psychodynamic drive activation." Extremely *disturbing* subliminals, aimed at *particular* unconscious *conflicts,* can increase neurotic disorders.

"Drive activation" research was initiated in the 1970s by Dr. Lloyd Silverman, a psychologist working at the Veteran's Administration Hospital in New York City. Dr. Silverman wanted to experimentally test Freud's theory that neurosis arises from repressed unconscious conflicts. Freud believed the speech difficulties of stutterers are related to their toilet training. He theorized that stutterers unconsciously associate *talking* with *defecation*, and have "conflicting wishes and inhibitions relating to expelling and retaining feces."

In a fascinating experiment, Dr. Silverman subliminally exposed a group of stutterers to a picture of a *dog defecating*. He then counted the number of times they stuttered when they paraphrased a story printed on a card. He utilized a similar procedure with another group of stutterers, who were subliminally shown a neutral picture of a bird.

Interestingly, the subjects who were shown the defecating dog stuttered more than the subjects who were shown the neutral image. The results of the experiment did not prove that improper toilet training causes stuttering. However, the study did suggest that:

- When people suffering from a behavior disorder (in this case stuttering)
- are subliminally exposed to a disturbing image that relates to an unconscious anxiety associated with the disorder (in this case the defecation image)
- the behavior disorder can be increased without the viewer understanding why (in this case the subjects stuttered more).

Dr. Silverman concluded:

> ...when a drive related stimulus registers subliminally, it makes contact with whatever congruent drive derivatives are active in the individual at the time; *for a person predisposed to pathology, the result is often an intensification of the particular kind of disturbance to which he is generally vulnerable.* (Emphasis added.)

Disturbing subliminals have been shown to impact many different kinds of people, with many different kinds of disorders. For example:

Schizophrenics in a mental hospital exhibited increased "pathological thinking" after they were subliminally shown a picture of a charging lion with bared teeth. The patients' pathological thinking was measured by psychological tests, and by observing their outward behavior. Many of the subjects became confused and disorganized, and laughed inappropriately after the subliminal presentation. They also exhibited tic manifestations. One patient became extremely disoriented when he was subliminally shown the torso of a nude woman.

Suicidal patients at Bronx State Hospital became more depressed after they were subliminally exposed to the phrase, "DESTROY MOTHER," accompanied by a picture of a young woman attacking an older woman with a knife. Freud believed that depression is caused by repressed hostility. The researchers theorized that the subliminal image "activated" the patients' animosity towards their mothers, and therefore increased their melancholy. In a related study, depressed young women became more downcast after they were exposed to the subliminal stimulus "CANNIBAL EATS PERSON."

Homosexuals recruited from ads in the Village Voice in New York City were subliminally exposed to the phrase "F*CK MOMMY," accompanied by a picture of a nude man and woman in a sexual pose. The incest related stimulus increased the subjects' homosexual drives. This was measured by asking them to rate "how sexually attracted" they felt towards pictures of men and women in a college yearbook, and to indicate how strongly they would like to have sex with a man and woman of their choosing.

Freud believed that male children are sexually attracted to their mothers. He further theorized that men become homosexuals when they are unable to successfully repress such feelings. Modern evidence suggests that Freud was incorrect, in that homosexuality appears to be a genetic *characteristic* and not a psychological *disorder*. Nonetheless, Dr. Silverman's study suggests that homosexuals are psychologically sensitive to, and sexually aroused by, subliminal incest stimuli.

Relevant Subliminals Are More Effective

When the subliminal images discussed above were *switched*, so that" F*CK MOMMY" was shown to stutterers and schizophrenics, "CANNIBAL EATS PERSON" was shown to homosexuals, and a DEFECATION stimulus was shown to depressed patients, *they ceased having an influence*. Dr. Silverman discovered that the subliminal effect occurred only when the message was *relevant* to the viewers' psychological issues.

Furthermore, the messages only had an effect when they were perceived *unconsciously*. They ceased to have an effect when they were shown long enough for the viewers to become aware of them.

Drive Activation In Advertising

The foregoing studies suggest that some products can be sold by stirring up, or "activating" unconscious anxieties. Advertisers can make use of "subliminal drive activation" when:

1. the consumer suffers from unconscious anxiety, *and*
2. the anxiety causes the consumer to engage in a neurotic indulgence (such as smoking, drinking, over-eating, self-medicating, etc.)

Subliminally increasing the *anxiety* exacerbates the *neurosis*, which in turn triggers an increase in *consumption*. Repeated exposure to the ad conditions the viewer to associate the desire to indulge with the product in question. The Benson penis/backbone ad utilizes this approach; it stimulates the desire to smoke by triggering fears of sexual inadequacy.

The 20/80 Rule

20% of consumers account for 80% of the consumption of many items. This is known in the industry as the 20/80 rule. For this reason, advertising is generally directed towards the heavy users of a given product. Heavy users of alcohol, of course, are alcoholics. Heavy consumers of cigarettes are habitual smokers. At least some of the people who buy lots of food are chronic over-eaters. Members of these groups often have emotional problems that inspire their over-indulgence, and make them particularly susceptible to subliminal influences. Advertisements directed towards them often seem to *utilize intensely disturbing embedded imagery* that seems quite bizarre when perceived consciously. Advertisers make the embeds as emotionally provocative as possible, in order to "activate" unconscious anxieties related to the consumption of the product they are selling.

Nostalgia Sweepstakes

The Peter Heering Liqueur ad in Figure 2.31 appeared in *People* Magazine in 1981. It was targeted at middle-aged readers who were teenagers in the 1950s. The predominately black and white color of the ad is reminiscent of 1950s television shows.

The copy inspires nostalgic fantasies by imploring the viewer to "Return to the Fabulous Fifties, when a dime set the rock 'n roll music blasting, and a cherry cola was the soda drinker's dreamboat." On a conscious level, the ad suggests that Peter Heering mixed with cherry cola is a love substitute for the reader's lost "dreamboat."

The ad contains many secrets, however. If you turn it upside down, you will become aware of a skull in the center of the glass. It is white, with black eyes and a black nose and mouth. It is adjacent to the row of medals at the bottom of the bottle. You will find it easily in the close-up in Figure 2.32 on page 73.

Figure 2.31

If you turn the ad sideways, just above the lime you will see a dead looking head, cut off at the forehead. This is shown at the upper right of Figure 31(a).

If you turn the ad right side up again you will discover a drowning, Frankenstein-like head to the right of the lime. The fluid level is just above his nose. The close- ups in Figures 2.32(b) and (c) (in the middle of the right column) only show the head, but if you study the ad you will discover the creature's entire body can be found in the glass. Two feet appear at the far right at the bottom of the liquid, and are connected to a surrealistic torso. It seems to be wrapped up in a kind of straightjacket, unable to move as its nose sinks below the top of the fluid. This image is harder to "see" than the skull, but it's extremely unsettling once you find it. It "activates" unconscious feelings of helplessness and suffocation.

Layer upon layer of other disturbing images also appear in the glass. In addition to cartoon images that seem to represent the "fabulous fifties," a middle-aged woman wearing glasses can be found behind the "RR" on the bottle, just above the label.

The subliminal meaning of the "Return To The Fabulous Fifties" theme in the copy reinforces the unconscious anxieties triggered by the embeds. When middle-aged people reminisce about how wonderful things were when they were young, on an unconscious level they necessarily contemplate the fact that they have left their teenage years behind. The ad ostensibly opines, "Weren't the fifties great!" but secretly suggests, "God you're old! What happened to your youth? Where did you go wrong? Why didn't you accomplish what you wanted to?"

Just as stimulating anxieties relating to defecation causes stutterers to stutter more, stimulating feelings of loss, failure, aging, decay, helplessness, hopelessness, suicide, and death encourages sensitive habitual drinkers to drink excessively. Incredulous as it may seem, pictures of skulls, dead bodies, drowning corpses, and other highly emotional graphic images are often subliminally embedded in liquor and other advertisements because they encourage "maladaptive behaviors" that advertisers consider desirable.

Figure 2.32(a-c)

On the Rocks

The ad in Figure 2.33 appeared in *Newsweek, Penthouse,* and *Scientific American*. Please take a long look at it before reading further.

A man's head appears in the bottom of the glass. It is lying on its side and is apparently severed at the neck. It is easier to see if you turn the ad ninety degrees sideways, so that the glass is at the bottom of the page.

The head is fairly large and occupies about one half the scotch in the glass. The hair, and particularly the part, are quite visible. The eyes are melancholic, and a perfectly formed ear appears on the right. Although the image is impressionistic and not literally drawn, viewers consistently describe the head as belonging to "a young man who is either drunk, dead, or very sad." It is outlined in Figure 2.34(b) on page 77. The glass has been turned on its side so the head is upright. Figure 2.34(a) is a true copy of the original.

The "mouth" resembles the blade of a knife. If you follow it down you will find a handle, appearing as a dark, rectangular, vertical shape at the bottom of the glass.

Once you "see" the "mouth" knife, you will discover more cutlery in the picture. Both of the "eyes" fall within the contour of a "blade" that has a gray handle at the bottom of the glass. More knives appear to the right and left. A total of seven appear in the picture. The knives are outlined in white in Figure 2.34(c).

If you focus your attention above and to the left of the man's head, you will find the profile of part of a woman's head. (Figure 2.34(c)). It appears to have been cut off below the eyes. Her "chin" begins at the extreme left of the glass, adjacent to where it says "John Jameson" in *light* letters in the middle of the bottle. If her eyes were not cut off she would be looking at the word "Jameson" in heavy *black* letters on the top of the bottle. Her slightly reddish lips are clearly drawn, and a single white tooth is visible at the top of her mouth. The glass of scotch appears to be a collage of severed body parts creatively woven together and circumvented by a ring of sharp blades. Many other images can be found embedded within the picture.

The Jameson Irish ad sells scotch by stimulating unconscious anxieties about impotency and castration. The castration theme is reinforced by the fact that the top of the letters "I" and "J" in the script word "Irish" are cut off, as is the top of the bottle.

If you like Scotch, you'll love light Jameson Irish.
Try a glass of Jameson Irish the way you would your favorite Scotch.
You'll notice how much it tastes like fine Scotch — only lighter and more delicate. Not smoky tasting like Scotch.
The dedicated Scotch drinker will instantly appreciate this flavor difference.
Though it may take a little time getting used to saying, "Jameson Irish on the rocks, please."

Jameson. World's largest-selling Irish Whiskey.

80 & 86 PROOF • CALVERT DIST. CO. N.Y.C.

Figure 2.33

The ad also encourages the viewer to wallow in and succumb to feelings of despair and self-destruction. It subliminally suggests that consuming "Scotch On The Rocks" will enable the reader to avoid sex ("I'm too tired"), and give up on life ("Get drunk and you wont have to deal with your problems"). Provocatively, it infers that the reader's life is "on the rocks," and that Jameson Irish provides the solution.

Regressing to Infancy

As I noted in Chapter One, the "father of motivational researcher," Ernest Dichter, wrote in *The Handbook of Consumer Motivations:*

> We attempt to escape fear-producing stimuli. By producing fear we can alter people's behavior. When caught in fear, we regress step by step to ever more infantile and animalistic drives.

A experiment in the 1970s validated Dichter's observations. It revealed that people engage in unconscious, oral fantasies when they feel rejected and insecure.

The college students who participated in the study were told that the researchers were investigating how people form friendships at first sight. They were asked to stand, one at a time, and state their names, while the rest of the students rated how likeable they were.

The subjects were then divided into two groups. One group was told they had received high ratings, and the other was told they had received low ratings. In actual fact, the groups were divided arbitrarily, and the ratings were discarded. The secret purpose of the procedure was to create a pool of people that felt "accepted" as well as a pool of people that felt "rejected."

The researchers hypothesized that the "rejected" students would engage in repressed oral fantasies — that the loss of esteem they suffered would cause them to unconsciously imagine themselves being *nurtured and breast-fed as infants*. To test this, both groups were subliminally exposed to the word "milk." They were then briefly shown a list of *supra*-liminal (consciously perceived) words. After the list was withdrawn, they were asked to recall as many of the words as possible. As the researchers anticipated, the "rejected" students recalled more words related to breast feeding, such as

Figure 2.34(a-d)

"milk," "bottle," "nipple," "smell," and "taste" than did the "accepted" students. The effect was considerably stronger in subjects who had indicated prior to the experiment that they used food as a substitute for affection.

The study suggests that stimulating unconscious anxiety is particularly useful to advertisers when the product they are promoting is associated with infantile, oral fantasies. The following cigarette ad illustrates this point.

The "Spirit" of Marlboro

The Marlboro Lights ad in Figure 2.35 appeared in *Penthouse* magazine and portrays a smoking cowboy about to lasso a fleeing, wild horse. The facial characteristics of the lead horse he is chasing are distinctly feminine, and the picture unconsciously appeals to male fantasies of domination and subjugation. The dark horse in the middle has masculine characteristics, but the Marlboro man is going to race ahead of it and make the lead female his own.

A much more bizarre message, however, is conveyed on a deeper subliminal level. The illustration contains numerous embeds intended to "activate" powerful emotions related to death, suicide, and smoking.

The most obvious of these is a skull/ghost creature floating in the clouds between the cowboy and the front horse. It is outlined in black in the key in Figure 2.36(b) on page 87. Its mouth is open, emphasizing the oral theme of the picture.

Another skull can be found to its immediate left. It is outlined in white in the key in Figure 2.36(a).

Between the two skulls and the lead horse's mane is a perfectly formed, realistic-looking wolf's head. The "lone wolf" is unconsciously associated with feelings of alienation and estrangement, as well as a wild, unfettered, but difficult existence. This particular wolf looks a bit depressed.

A large, oval, impressionistic face can be found in the clouds to the right of the central horse. Its mouth is open and it seems to be exhaling white clouds (as though it were smoking cigarettes). It is outlined in black in Figure 2.36(b).

A profile of a man's face can be found between the dark, middle horse, and the leading horse. It is facing to the left and has a clearly defined pointed nose and chin. It is outlined in white in Figure 2.36(c).

Incredibly, as the cowboy pursues the lead female, he himself is being pursued by death. A ghoulish, white creature can be found directly behind him, underneath his left arm (the right arm as you look at the picture). The image is also outlined in white in Figure 2.36(c). The ghoul's head is attached to a body, superimposed over the dark, middle horse. No matter how furiously the cowboy rides he will never be able to escape his ultimate demise, the evil "spirit" of Marlboro!

The ad is intended to stimulate unconscious suicidal fantasies. Although ostensibly it stresses that Marlboro Lights are healthier because they

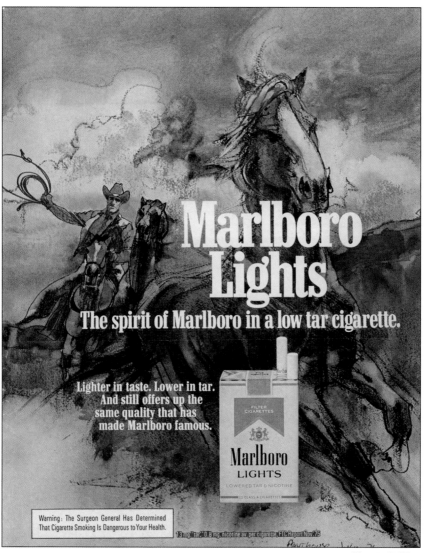

Figure 2.35

contain less tar, on a subliminal level it "activates" the parallel thought that all cigarettes are a form of poison. If the ad declared, "Marlboro Lights Are Better Because They Take Ten Years Longer To Give You Lung Cancer!" the viewer would be horrified and imagine helplessly dying in a hospital. The copy (and embeds) in the actual ad conjure up similar mental images, but they are repressed and experienced unconsciously.

Smokers may be in denial about it, but cigarette consumption is a form of self-destruction. The Marlboro Lights ad is aimed at heavy smokers who secretly feel that "life is just too hard," and unconsciously wish to hasten their departure from this world. Paradoxically, the ad also stimulates *fears* of dying, and therefore engages the desire to *suck and be nurtured.*

It is interesting to note that the ad was drawn and not photographed. The artist must have worked very hard to create the hidden illusions.

Anxiety, Depression, and Addiction

The relationship between drinking, smoking and anxiety has been established both experimentally and by statistical surveys. *One half* of the heavy drinkers in North America suffer from psychiatric disorders. People who drink and smoke excessively are likely to be anxious, and people who suffer from depression and anxiety disorders in adolescence are more likely to become addicted as adults. Among schizophrenics, the number of cigarettes smoked per day is correlated with psychological distress as well as neuroticism. Interestingly, people who are easily *conditioned* (in the Pavlovian sense) are more likely to suffer from clinical anxiety. This could be due to the fact that they are more easily influenced by subliminal advertising.

Moderate drinkers often consume alcohol in social settings when they feel happy, but heavy drinkers often indulge when they are depressed. Since heavy drinkers gradually come to associate feeling unhappy with imbibing, studies have shown that "negative mood inducers can increase the desire to drink even when alcohol cues are absent."

Similarly, college students experienced increased tobacco cravings when they were asked to imagine negative "scripts" designed to put them in a bad mood. Viet Nam veterans suffering from post-traumatic-stress disorders experienced increased smoking withdrawal symptoms when they were exposed to trauma-related words such as "gook," "chopper," and "bodybags." Smokers who were made to feel nervous by being asked to speak in public smoked more cigarettes.

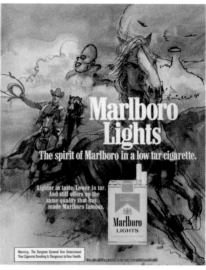

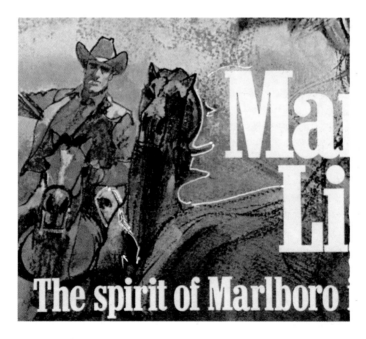

Figure 2.36(a-c)

In these studies, the subjects were consciously aware of *the negative mood inducers* that stimulated their addictions. Advertisers use *subliminal* triggers to avoid offending the viewers. Subliminal advertisements generate feelings of anxiety and depression, and "activate" addictive behaviors associated with these emotional states.

Drive Activation in Everyday Life

"Subliminal drive activation" is something we all experience in our daily lives. We only need to think about it to become aware of it.

Once when I was driving my car down the freeway, for example, I started having a very pleasant reverie about living in New York during my twenties. I suddenly realized that a song was playing on the radio that I had often listened to during that period of my life. The song had "activated" all the memories I associated with it. It was not hard for me to become aware of the connection, because the memories were very pleasant.

On another occasion, I was having a glass of wine in a nightclub when I suddenly became depressed for no apparent reason. After several minutes of self-analysis, I realized that a woman on the dance floor looked a lot like an ex-girlfriend who had rejected me. I further realized that her companion physically resembled me. The woman and her dance partner had apparently subliminally "activated" self-esteem issues associated with my break-up. Identifying the connection between my mood change and the subliminal (unnoticed) stimulus was more difficult than in the previous example, because the emotions involved were slightly more upsetting. If the subliminal had been delivered in the form of an embedded illusion or a flash frame, or if the psychological issues involved were *extremely* disturbing, I would probably not have been able to determine what had caused me to feel anxious.

Lloyd Silverman, who initiated the "psychodynamic drive activation" experiments discussed previously, commented on this phenomenon. He described a young woman undergoing analysis who wanted very much to have a child. One day the woman received a birth announcement from a close friend whom she had always viewed as a rival. The birth announcement intensified the woman's competitive feelings towards her friend, and her desire to bear a child of her own.

Shortly after she received the announcement, the woman became very anxious while reading a magazine article. When she discussed the incident with her therapist, she suddenly realized that the author of the article was named "Rothchild." Her friend's last name was "Roth." Reading the article had made her feel depressed, because she had unconsciously interpreted "Rothchild" to mean "child of Roth."

Dr. Silverman also described a 25-year-old man whose wife had become pregnant. The man and his spouse were ambivalent about having a child, and were contemplating an abortion. Through analysis, the man came to realize that he unconsciously associated his unborn child with his younger *brother*. He had always been jealous of his brother, particularly when his brother was born. The man realized he unconsciously was contemplating the abortion because he secretly longed to eliminate his sibling rival.

While the man was wrestling with these insights, he experienced a severe mood swing while walking down the street. He looked up and saw a sign that said "floor scraping." Because he was in therapy, he realized that he had unconsciously associated "floor scraping" with *abortions*, and had become depressed as a result.

The "floor scraping" example is more disturbing than the "Rothchild" example because the unconscious drives involved are more upsetting. While it's not that hard to confess that we secretly feel jealous of our friends, it's much more difficult to admit we fantasize about assassinating our brothers and sisters.

Therapeutic Uses of Subliminals

Psychodynamic drive activation can be used to *diminish* anxiety as well as increase it. Dr. Silverman exposed male college students to subliminal messages that read either "BEATING DAD IS BAD," "BEATING DAD IS OK," or the control stimulus "PEOPLE ARE STANDING." He wanted to test the theory that attitudes towards competition and aggression in boys are molded by their competitive feelings towards their father. He theorized that "BEATING DAD IS BAD" would stimulate unconscious anxieties and *diminish* performance in a dart-throwing contest, while "BEATING DAD IS OK" would have the opposite effect. As he anticipated, the students who were shown the subliminal "BEATING DAD IS OK" stimulus received the highest dart-throwing scores.

Similarly, the phrase "MOMMY AND I ARE ONE" subliminally shown beneath a silhouette of two people joined at the hips has been shown to have therapeutic effects. Researchers theorize that during infancy most of us experience our mother as comforting, nurturing, and an unconditional source of food and love. Although conflicts often develop later in life, our initial relationship with our female parent is usually extremely gratifying. As a result, most of us harbor unconscious wishes of "oneness" or "merger" with the "good mother of early childhood."

Schizophrenics evidence diminished pathologies when they are exposed to the "MOMMY AND I ARE ONE" stimulus. Patients undergoing treatment for insect phobias and other disorders get better more quickly. "Normal" people have more pleasant thoughts and memories when they subliminally view the phrase. In contrast, the subliminal presentation of "NO ONE LOVES ME" causes unconscious distress with measurable physiological consequences.

Love Food

Therapeutic subliminal messages that reduce unconscious conflicts probably are not as useful to advertisers as subliminals that stir up anxiety. Making people feel good encourages them to feel satisfied, and does not motivate them to purchase or consume products.

Nevertheless, advertisements and packaging for food products sometimes do seem to have happy or friendly images embedded in them. In the "Spice Islands" ad in Figure 2.37, the white clump of salad dressing forms the head of a satisfied hippo-like creature with sleepy eyes. It is facing towards the left of the page. The creature's left eye (the right eye as you look at it) is a dark horizontal line in the middle of the white clump. The mouth is formed by a dark, triangular shadow appearing between the two vertical avocado slices at the bottom of the page.

A large "Ronald McDonald" like set of smiling lips also appear on the right side of the clump, just next to the word "Love" in "Love Foods From California." Both the hippo and the smiling lips are outlined in Figure 2.38 on page 86.

Another cute, comical happy face can be found to the left of the clump. The two adjacent olive slices form eyes, the horizontal avocado slice (second from the bottom) forms a kind of face, and the dash of red tomato between the two is a tongue. Although the image is figurative and not literal, its positive emotional state is clearly conveyed.

The ad radiates good vibes on many levels. "Love Food From California" means both "Give your love to food," and "Food is a substitute for

Figure 2.37

Figure 2.38(a-b)

the love you are lacking." The happy creatures in the salad promise contented companionship. If you look carefully at the cookie packages the next time you are in the supermarket, you will probably be able to find similarly playful playmates hidden within them.

Perceptual Vigilance

The unconscious is *vigilant* or constantly "on the lookout" for information that is psychologically threatening. When subjects are shown pictures at subliminal speeds, so that they are only aware of flashes of light, the images that are psychologically disturbing appear to "stand out" more than images that are emotionally neutral.

Moreover, when agoraphobics (people afraid of open spaces), social phobics (people afraid of people), and obsessive (compulsive) patients are asked to listen to something in one ear, they detect fear relevant words played in the other ear more easily than "normal" subjects under the same circumstances. Anxious mothers whose children are about to undergo surgery show an enhanced ability to detect threat words embedded in white noise.

In the jungle, the tendency to unconsciously pay attention to things associated with danger was a beneficial characteristic. In modern society, it is a psychological weakness exploited by advertisers. Without being aware of it, we all scan the media searching for ads that relate to our personal peculiarities. Paradoxically, the ads that are most meaningful to us on a subliminal level are the ones we are least likely to understand consciously, because they are the most threatening.

Accordingly, men who smoke cigarettes and are sensitive to impotency issues are unconsciously on the lookout for ads like the Benson penis/

backbone. At the same time it is more difficult for them to "see" the phallus because their filter mechanisms work harder to keep them from becoming aware of the hidden image. The same is true of women who drink heavily and are hostile towards men, in relation to the Smirnoff drink-in-the-face ad.

No matter how unusual your personal Achilles heel may be, at least some of the ads in the world are targeted towards you. These are the ads your unconscious pays the most attention to, and ironically, the ones you are least aware of being influenced by.

Banishing the "White Bear"

The more people try to consciously *not* think about something, the more they dwell on it unconsciously. This was revealed in a study in which subjects were asked to *not* think about a "white bear." The researchers discovered that a) the subjects tried to distract themselves by thinking about something other than "white bears," and b) the subjects unconsciously remained vigilant for "white bear" related stimuli. In other words, the unconscious associations they had for "white bears" remained "activated," even though they were consciously thinking about other things.

The "White Bear" paradox provides interesting insights. People who believe they are adept at "not thinking about their problems" are secretly thinking about them a great deal (although not in a healthy, constructive way). They also become more vigilant to subliminal cues that relate to the subject they are trying to avoid.

Moreover, suppressing thoughts makes them more intense. When subjects were asked to remain emotionally detached while watching a grisly movie about (faked) sawmill accidents, they reported feeling *less* upset than viewers who were asked to become emotionally involved in the film. The "detached" observers, however, exhibited *higher* skin conductance levels than the "involved" viewers, indicating they were more upset unconsciously.

Similarly, when male college students were asked to conjure up memories of their mother and father, and then shown pictures of nude women, they reported being *less* sexually aroused than students who were *not* asked to conjure up such memories. The students who thought about their parents, however, exhibited *higher* skin conductance levels than the students who did not think about their parents, revealing that they were more aroused unconsciously.

These studies suggest that repression and denial are not altogether effective defense mechanisms. Although they minimize conscious distress, they exacerbate unconscious anxiety. This view is corroborated by the fact that subjects who are inclined to *forget* briefly-flashed tachistoscopic images are more likely to *dream* about them, and more likely to have *bad dreams*.

As I alluded to previously, the Sauza "STAY PURE" ads illustrate how advertisers capitalize on the fact that the things we avoid thinking about become unconsciously more exciting. By subliminally admonishing susceptible viewers to "STAY PURE" and *refrain* from having homosexual fantasies, the Sauza ads galvanize exactly the opposite behavior.

The Nature of the Unconscious

When you think of the unconscious as "a seething cauldron of sexual and aggressive drives," it is easy to imagine it as a dim-witted ape. Actually, despite its moral turpitude, the unconscious is extremely intelligent and creative. It thinks and solves problems, it can write poetry, and it makes long term plans. It reads and understands at an incredibly rapid rate. It's not as adept at dealing with novel situations as the conscious mind, but in many respects it is remarkably clever.

In computer terms, the unconscious utilizes an altogether different "operating system" than the conscious mind. This is evidenced by the following:

The unconscious is a parallel processor. As discussed previously, the unconscious is capable of performing a multitude of "sub-programs" while our conscious focuses on individual tasks.

Space-time associates do not exist unconsciously. Events in the unconscious are not catalogued according to when and where they occurred, as they are in the conscious. Rather they are connected in a seamless, free-flowing web of emotions and subject matter organized somewhat like the Internet. Free associating, or letting your mind wander from topic to topic, is quite like jumping from site to site while surfing the Net.

Unconscious associations "fan out." Unconscious associations are loose and free flowing, and "fan out" in a wildly uninhibited manner. This was demonstrated in studies in which subjects were subliminally shown the picture of a pen and a knee depicted in Figure 2.39.

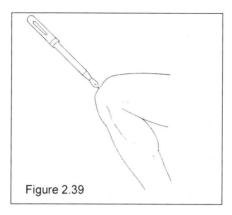

Figure 2.39

Following exposure, they were given a variety of psychological tests, and their dreams were recorded. The subliminal "pen-knee" stimulus provoked three *levels* of responses:

1. Thoughts associated with the *meaning* of the word "pen" (such as "pencil") and the *meaning* of the word "knee" (such as "calf"), and
2. Thoughts associated with the *sound* of the words "pen" and "knee," such as "pennant" and "banner," and
3. Thoughts associated with the *rebus* of the "pen" and "knee," which is "penny." These included words such as "coin," "bank," or "money."

The unconscious is Freudian. Unconscious associations are often Freudian in nature. Subjects who are subliminally exposed to the words "room" or "water" and then asked to free associate often elicit "mother"-related words. Similarly, when subjects are subliminally presented with the word "cow" and asked to free associate, they often respond with oral, passive terms like "suck" or "warm" rather than barnyard words like "bull" or "grass."

The unconscious is creative. Great artists, such as Bob Dylan, seem to have an uncanny ability to get behind the "filter" and allow universal unconscious emotions to manifest themselves in their art. *All Along the Watchtower,* as an example, is a fabulous, song/poem that doesn't make much literal sense but is nonetheless intensely meaningful unconsciously. The opening line "There must be some way out of here, said the joker to the thief," "activates" unconscious associations relating to helplessness, imprisonment, feelings of guilt associated with stealing from others, feelings of being violated and stolen from, feelings that life is a cruel joke, life is a competitive game, and so on. On a more conscious level, the associations are brilliantly woven into a tapestry of medieval images involving castles and barefoot women. The total effect is incredibly powerful, although as you listen to the song you don't really know why.

In numerous interviews Dylan has stated that he doesn't "write" his songs, he "discovers" them. They seem to emerge from his unconscious with little conscious intervention. Other artists have made similar self-observations. Paul McCartney reported that he wrote the melody to "Yesterday" in his sleep. Samuel Taylor Coleridge made a similar claim regarding his composition of his poem "Kubla Khan." Gertrude Stein and other writers are said to have successfully used "automatic writing," a hypnoidal trance state in which the hand is dissociated from consciousness and allowed to create on its own. Visual artists have successfully used a similar technique known as "automatic drawing."

Art makes more of an impact on us when it "activates" universal feelings. Carl Jung, a psychologist who was initially a follower of Freud but then broke away and developed his own theories, believed that all humans share an inherited mental state he called the "collective unconscious." Jung noted that people from very different parts of the world create similar symbols, which are often given similar meanings. Stories of floods, for example, play a prominent role in many cultures and religions, and are often associated with cleansing and rebirth. Works of art that relate to these "archetypal" images (such as "All Along the Watchtower") are inspiring because they resonate with unconsciously shared emotions.

The unconscious never sleeps. The unconscious is an idea generator that never rests. It is constantly problem-solving without our being aware of it. On occasion we all experience sudden insights, in which inspirational thoughts or solutions to complex problems unexpectedly leap into our minds. This occurs when ideas that are generated unconsciously are allowed past the filter. We experience an abrupt" Aha!" as we become aware of them.

Thinking in Reverse

It's fair to say that most of the time our actions are motivated by psychological considerations, and we confabulate consciously acceptable *excuses* for our behavior. Our analytical thought processes are flawed in a similar manner.

Our greatest intellectual deficit is that we automatically think in reverse. When presented with a problem, we pick the *conclusion* that is most emotionally appealing, and then work backwards to construct an argument to defend our choice. Obviously, in the long run we would be better off if we analyzed the facts and accepted the conclusions that logic led us to, regardless of emotional considerations. In other words, our thinking would be improved if we employed the algorithm: "Facts - Analysis - Conclusion," rather than "Conclusion - Utilize Facts to Construct Argument to Support Conclusion."

The great thinkers of our species have clearly utilized the former methodology. The insights they formulated seem like amazing breakthroughs largely because *psychological considerations* prevented society from becoming aware of them at an earlier date. Copernicus's revelation that the earth was not the center of the universe, Darwin's theory of evolution, and Freud's discovery of the unconscious are all examples of this. Conversely, the NASDAQ bubble of the late 1990s is an example of "normal" *reverse* thinking. Multitudes of people accepted the emotionally gratifying conclusion that Internet stocks would always go up, and worked backwards to construct an argument justifying that belief.

Consciously thinking about *how* we are thinking causes us to think more logically. When we are not thinking about *how* we are thinking, the unconscious takes over, and we are more likely to think in reverse. This was illustrated by a study in which subjects were told a story about a person who didn't win a lottery because she took the advice of a friend, instead of following her intuition to buy a ticket with her "lucky" number on it. After hearing the story, the subjects were asked to state the first thing that came to their minds. Most of them declared the friend was to blame, and that the person should never listen to the friend again. When asked to reflect on the matter, however, most of the subjects realized the result was due to chance, and that listening or not listening to the friend could not possibly affect the likelihood of future winnings.

The Dual Fit

Like the pieces of a puzzle, effective advertising "fits" the duality of the mind. It presents two appeals: one that is congruent with our underlying, emotional reason for consuming a product, and another that reinforces our confabulated, consciously acceptable excuse for doing so. When the two appeals are *similar*, and the underlying "pitch" is *not* threatening, we can easily become aware of both of them. When the two appeals are *divergent*, and the unconscious appeal involves some kind of *taboo*, becoming aware of the "secret" message jolts our senses.

The Nightmare in the Magazine

The jewelry ad in Figure 2.40 is incredibly creative and seems to incorporates many different subliminal techniques in an imaginative manner. Please study it carefully before reading further.

The ad appeared in a 2002 edition of *Wallpaper*, a magazine geared towards affluent consumers. At first glance it appears to portray a beautiful woman wearing a semitransparent nightgown, erotically and sensually interacting with two men. The willingness of her participation is implied by the salacious manner in which she appears to be undressing herself. The filter mechanism initially blocks it, but her left hand (out of view on the right side of the picture) is caressing her companion's genitals.

If you study the expression on her face, however, you will discover that it contains an element of fear and anxiety.

A bizarre subliminal illusion secretly reinforces this interpretation. If you switch your figure-ground, and focus on the *dark* space, not the light space, in the area between the woman and her long-haired companion, you will discover a demonic humanoid-shaped spirit. It is easier to "see" if you flip back and forth between Figure 2.41 on page 100 and the complete ad. The spirit's head is looking towards the left. It is formed by the dark space between the woman's neck and the neck of the long-haired man. The spirit's chin is formed by the nape of the woman's neck and her shoulder. The creature's nose is highlighted by light shining on the woman's hair.

When you locate the spirit's head in the complete ad, you will see the demon creature has a *body*. It is black, and formed by the woman's negligee and arm. It seems to be helping to undress her. The line marking the edge of the woman's negligee may have been redrawn, in order to properly form the shape of the spirit's neck and torso.

MICHEL COMTE

Milano Rome Florence Venice Capri Paris Monte Carlo Cannes Madrid

Barcelona Marbella Lisbon Antwerp Moscow Tokyo Osaka Singapore Taipei

Pomellato
www.pomellato.it

Figure 2.40

Figure 2.41

The interior of the head contains a green, ghoulish death mask, representing the evil mind of the spirit. A close up is provided below in Figure 2.42. Its eyes are formed by dark triangles, and its nose is a slightly lighter shade of green.

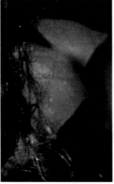

Figure 2.42

The person on the right side of the photograph is handsome, angelic, and extremely feminine. Although it is difficult to interpret his expression because the top of his head has been cut off, he does not seem to be evil. The profile of a light-colored, subliminal dove is superimposed on the left side of his chest (on the right side of the picture). The head of the dove is looking at the woman, and appears just below the circular part of the chain encircling the man's neck. The vertical edge of the picture cuts through the dove's back.

The angel man himself is swan-like, and (like the woman) has an incredibly elongated neck. A series of light-colored marks appear on his torso, adjacent to the vertical part of his necklace. The marks emphasize his vulnerability and represent wounds from previous battles.

The man on the left side of the picture is considerably more wicked. His sullen, dark eyes are transfixed on his hand as he prepares to violently rip the necklace from the woman's neck.

Remarkably, a subliminal *witch* is embedded in the evil man's head. The illusion is similar to the Old Lady/Young Lady discussed in the beginning of this chapter. The man's *nose* forms the witch's *chin*. The dark indentation just above it forms the witch's *mouth.* The witch's nose is partially obscured by the name of the artist, which is written vertically in white letters. The witch's *eye* is formed by a *dark triangle* to the left of the letter "o" in "Comte." If you study the witch's outline in Figure 2.43(a) you will be able to locate the unaltered image in Figure 2.43(b).

Figure 2.43(a-b)

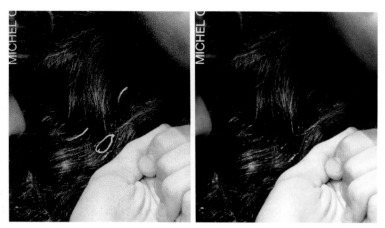

Figure 2.44(a-b)

Another creature is embedded in the woman's hair, just above the evil man's hand. If you look at Figures 2.44 (a) and (b), you will discover a hairy little animal, somewhat like Chewbacca in *Starwars*, sucking on the side of the man's thumb.

The woman's hand at the bottom of the complete ad is suprisingly large, and its nails are quite short. It seems unlikely that such a lovely model would have such a masculine looking appendage. Furthermore, her left arm is enclosed in the sleeve of her negligee, but her right arm is bare. Although it is possible that her negligee has simply been pulled up to her elbow, it is more likely that the hand at the bottom of the picture doesn't belong to her, but to a man standing *behind* her.

Part of that person's other arm constitutes the flesh-colored object at the lower right of the picture, behind the "P" in "Pomellato." The hidden person appears to be undressing the woman with his right hand, and reaching for the genitals of the "angel" with his left.

The Nightmare ad is as intensely emotional and powerful as any briefly observed graphic image could possibly be. If there was a "Oscar" for subliminal advertisements (and perhaps some day there will be), it would definitely win 1st prize.

Like a good poem, or a well-written novel, it is subject to more than one interpretation. It could portray the woman's rape fantasy, in which she is savagely, although erotically, attacked by both demons and her angel lover. The conflicted expression on her face reveals both her horror as well as her delight at being the object of such attention.

The ad also suggests a moving and dramatic story. The woman is being raped and pulled into the netherworld by dark, evil spirits, as her angel lover struggles to save her. She and her protector are emotionally bound by the necklaces they both wear, which are symbols of their impermeable attachment. The evil man/witch is about to rip her necklace from her throat, but her angel savior will intervene and rescue her in the nick of time.

Dreaming of Demons

As noted previously, people who unknowingly look at *figure-ground* illusions when they are awake often dream about them when they are sleeping. The hidden figures they are *not* aware of emerge in their dreams.

Otto Poetzl, the first scientist to investigate this phenomenon, believed that visual perception is analogous to photographic processes. A person exposed to a picture records the entire image instantly, but does not "print" and "develop" hidden images within the picture until he or she is sleeping.

Modern day experiments have confirmed that the Poetzl effect occurs even when the figure-ground image is presented for only a *fraction* of a second. Accordingly, many *Wallpaper* readers who viewed the Pomellato ad (and the spirits it secretly contains) must have had *nightmares* as a result.

Vicary Misapplied

When James Vicary held his historic press conference in 1957, he claimed that subliminally flashing "Hungry? Eat Popcorn" during the movie *Picnic* had increased popcorn sales 57%. When his alleged "experiment" was replicated, it was discovered that he may have exaggerated the results in order to promote his business, the "Subliminal Projection Corporation."

Some defenders of the advertising community have seized upon the discrediting of Vicary's allegations as evidence that subliminal messages do not influence behavior. This is patently illogical. "Hungry? Eat Popcorn" is an innocuous command that is unconsciously irrelevant. To be effective, subliminal messages must resonate with powerful unconscious emotions. All the ads in this book clearly illustrate this point.

The Viewpoint of Psychologists

Experimental psychologists working out of universities and hospitals are under a great deal of economic and social pressure to distance themselves from the apparent use of subliminals in advertising. It is harder for them to obtain grants and their teaching positions are jeopardized if they express viewpoints that are perceived as excessively radical. Publicly proclaiming they think "subliminal penises" or "monsters" are embedded in mainstream periodicals probably doesn't further their careers. There is no penalty, however, for downplaying the subliminal controversy, and it is therefore not surprising that many of them choose to do so.

An article published in the psychological text *Scientific Approaches to Consciousness* illustrates this point. Oblivious to the obvious, the author concludes, "Subliminal techniques of the sort now used in laboratory research *could possibly be develop*ed for use in mass media to produce significant influences on behavior." (Emphasis added.)

Despite the pressure, some researchers feel the evidence of subliminals is so persuasive they are compelled to comment on the controversy. Some years ago, I wrote to N.F. Dixon, who was then the world's leading authority on subliminal perception and a professor at University College London. Dr. Dixon is the author of *Subliminal Perception*, a comprehensive and widely respected treatise on the subject. I sent him three ads: the Benson penis/backbone in Figure 1.2, the Smirnoff "drink-in-the-face-ad" in Figure 2.20, and the Jameson Irish "decapitated head" ad in Figure 2.33, as well as the interpretations and general theories presented in this book. I asked him to comment on them. The following are excerpts from his kind reply:

Dear Mr. Bullock,

Many thanks for your most interesting letter of 16 October and the fascinating examples of advertising which appear to be using embedded figures.

I must say I found your interpretations, particularly of the Smirnoff ad, very convincing and ingenious.

My own views, (and I have read Key's book), are as follows:

1. I am quite ready to believe that some ads contain deliberately embedded emotive stimuli...
2. Theoretically, in the light of the many researches referred to in my book ... it is highly likely that unconsciously received material that touches on a particular drive or conflict area (e.g. castration anxiety) has an effect on the psychopathology and behavior of people who are sensitive to the issues being represented.

Researchers Kilbourne, Painton, and Ridley have also taken an unequivocal stand on the issue. In their paper regarding the Marlboro Lights penis/rock experiment, which was published in the *Journal of Advertising* (and discussed in the beginning of this chapter), they wrote

> The use of sexual embedding in magazine advertisements has been documented by Key and substantiated by the authors of the present study. ...finding ads with clear, unambiguous embeds did *not* present a formidable task. (Emphasis added.)

It is likely that in the future more reputable researchers will be willing to address the widespread use of subliminal devices in media.

The Private vs. the Public Sector

It's important to realize that the studies discussed in this chapter represent only the visible "tip" of the research "iceberg." They were performed by psychologists and educators working in the public sector, and are available in most libraries. The bulk of subliminal research, in contrast, has been conducted in secret by advertising and marketing firms. It constitutes "intellectual property" that is rarely, if ever, revealed to outsiders.

Private motivational research is vastly superior to its public counterpart, for the following reasons:

More money: Private industry has invested a staggering amount in mapping the consumer psyche. In 1957 alone, one billion dollars was reportedly spent on marketing research. By 1999, the total amount spent on all advertising expenditures amounted to 215 billion dollars. To place these sums in perspective, the entire Apollo moon landing program only cost NASA a *total* of 31 billion dollars between 1960 and 1969.

More freedom: Researchers in the public sector are restrained by political and ethical considerations. To receive funds, they have to apply for grants from public agencies. Research that is controversial is discouraged, and experiments that adversely affect the participants are prohibited. Researchers in the public sector, for example, probably would not be allowed to significantly reinforce the alcohol addictions of alcoholics, even if the subjects consented.

Researchers in the private sector are not subject to such limitations. Finding ways to increase alcohol, cigarette, food, and other addictions is their job. Uninhibited creative thinking is not only encouraged, it is demanded.

More motivation: Private researchers are highly motivated because the insights they acquire result in increased company profits and personal promotions. Public researchers, on the other hand, are concerned with theoretical discussions that only incrementally advance their careers.

Clearer results: In the public arena, researchers accumulate data by administering laborious psychological tests to small numbers of subjects. Each experiment can take years to set up, fund, and execute. In the "real world" fast lane, researchers can simply run a test ad in one location, and a control ad in another, and note the difference in sales. The sales figures provide precise, mathematical evidence indicating which techniques are effective and which are not. In addition, focus groups, individual depth interviews, and consumer surveys can investigate the subliminal influence on particular psychodynamic populations. In a literal sense, to advertisers the world is a laboratory, and all the people in it are guinea pigs.

Accordingly, there is little doubt that research conducted in the public sector, including the studies reviewed in this chapter, provide only a tiny glimpse of the volumes of research secretly compiled by the communications industry. If Lloyd Silverman showed that maladaptive behaviors can be stimulated by the subliminal presentation of disturbing, psychologically relevant images, there is little doubt that advertisers have spent billions of dollars exploring every nuance of that phenomena.

Chapter Three:
BOPPED DOING THE BUMP
REBUTTING THE DENIAL

Too Many Coincidences

Advertisers deny they use subliminal techniques. They claim that the embeds and other devices that appear in media are coincidental. There are far too many "coincidences," however, for their denials to be taken seriously.

For example, consider just how many "coincidences" appear in the Benson and Hedges penis/backbone ad. The lady's backbone "happens" to be shaped like a penis, the tip of which "happens" to be entering a cylindrical curl, which "happens" to be formed in just the right place in the woman's hair.

The subliminal meaning of the *text* "happens" to be consistent with the subliminal meaning of the picture. On a conscious level, "If You Got Crushed In The Clinch With Your Soft Pack, Try Our Hard Pack" innocently suggests Benson and Hedges are desirable because they come in boxes. On an unconscious level the phrase menacingly queries, "Do *you* suffer from impotency?"

If you ignore its subliminal content, the ad seems idiotic. The caption is convoluted, confusing, and unpersuasive. Since many cigarettes are sold in boxes, it emphasizes a characteristic of the product that is not unique. It is hard to understand how a team of highly paid, talented, creative people working on a multi-million-dollar campaign could conceive of such an uninspiring concept. On the other hand, if you accept the idea that the ad is "subliminal" it seems ingenious, and every aspect of it makes sense.

So many coincidences appearing in *one* ad strongly suggest that subliminals do not appear in media by accident. Advertisers' denials seem even more implausible, however, when you consider that *series* of ads often incorporate similar subliminal techniques.

Bopped Doing the Bump

The Benson and Hedges ad in Figure 3.1 also appeared in *Time* magazine, just a few months before the penis/backbone ad. It depicts a man and a woman dancing together in a sexual manner. As in the penis/backbone ad, the woman looks confident and available but the man looks distressed. The caption, "If you got *bopped doing the bump* with your soft pack..." predictably suggests "If you failed to perform successfully..."

Like the penis/backbone ad, the picture also contains a subliminal phallus. It is small and erect, and has been airbrushed onto the genital area of the man's pants in an anatomically correct location. It is a lighter shade of purple than the man's slacks, and points to the right, complete with testicles. You will find it easily in the close-up in Figure 3.2 on page 110.

Figure 3.1

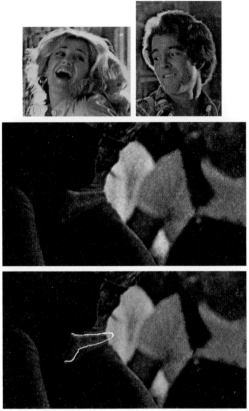

Figure 3.2

The Unhappy Honeymoon

The Benson and Hedges ad in Figure 3.3 appeared in both *Time* and *McCalls*. It portrays a middle-aged couple, just married, apparently on their honeymoon. The woman is holding up a sexy nightie and looking wistfully at her new husband. She is hoping he will make love to her but she is fearful he will decline. The groom is indifferent to her advances. He is taking a sweater out of the suitcase, implying he is going to change into street clothes instead of undressing for bed.

The caption, "America's Favorite Cigarette Break," suggests that smoking Benson and Hedges is a way of avoiding sex. "Cigarette break" is another oblique reference to impotency, which is reinforced by the fact that the cigarette is broken. The man's attention is focused on the male reader. The ad capitalizes on the fact that men in the groom's age bracket often experience diminished sexual abilities.

Figure 3.3

The Monster Bash

The Benson and Hedges ad in Figure 3.4 depicts three clusters of people at a party. The smokers seem to be benefiting enormously from their cigarette addictions. The woman in the sequined jacket at the far right is a smoker, and she is enjoying the attentions of a younger man wearing a bow tie. The fingers of her right hand are massaging his glass, and her left hand, holding her cigarette, is wrapped around the outside of the word "party."

The handsome man in the blue suit smoking on the far left side of the photo is even more popular. He is surrounded by beautiful, adoring females, one of whom is holding up her glass as if she were begging to "receive" his cigarette.

The couple in the middle is the most interesting. At first glance, it appears that the woman's left hand is resting on the shoulder of the man with the bow tie. That hand, however, belongs to the blonde-haired man standing behind her. Although you can't see his mouth, and the left side of his face is in shadows, the blonde-haired man seems to be distraught.

The woman's left hand is actually hidden behind the "p" in the words "hard pack." She is deftly rubbing her thumb and index finger together. She appears to be dissatisfied with the blonde-haired man, and is making puckering gestures towards the viewer with her mouth.

On a subliminal level, the woman is propositioning the reader. She is rejecting the blonde-haired man because of his disappointing sexual performance. The blonde-haired man is understandably upset. He is trying to push the bow-tied man aside, to come between the woman and the reader. Meanwhile, the handsome man in the blue suit on the left is pointing over his shoulder and laughing as he tells his female companions, "Ha ha! Did you hear that that blonde-haired guy has a *softie?*" The caption "If you got crunched at the party with your soft pack, try our new hard pack," suggests "If you got *rejected* at the party because of your sexual inadequacies, smoke Benson and Hedges."

The picture also contains several interesting embeds. The most dramatic is a "subliminal gorilla monster" that appears *in the space* between the handsome man's tie and his hand. It consists of a leathery, brown head, looking towards the reader's right shoulder. The monster is reaching up and about to suck a brown, penis like appendage coming out of the man's tie, just below the knot. The image is outlined in Figure 3.5 on page 108. Figure 3.5(c) is a true close-up of the original.

Figure 3.4

Since the "subliminal gorilla monster" is a good-looking guy, its not surprising that he brought a girlfriend to the party. If you study the close-ups of the handsome man's hand in Figure 3.5(b) and 3.5(c), you will see

Figure 3.5(a-c)

that a face is has been embedded on the underside of it, beneath the pinky. The face is looking down the front of the red dress worn by the woman holding the glass. The creature's Medusa-like hair is formed by the man's fingers.

The hand creature has a body and is wearing a dress. Its shoulder and arm are formed by the feminine "tie" on the blouse of the blonde woman in the background. The right side of the blonde woman's "tie" forms a "V" neck on the hand monster's outfit.

One more interesting illusion can be found in the original ad. Look again at Figure 3.4 and focus on the *space* between the bow-tie man's head (on the right side of the picture) and the woman he is talking to. The cheek and ear of the woman in the background form the profile of a female breast. It is pointing towards the right of the picture, and the bow-tie man appears to be giving it a kiss.

The Woman's Perspective

The ad in Figure 3.6 deals with the flip side of impotency anxiety. It portrays a woman, not a man, sitting on a suitcase with a disturbed expression. She is holding a passport and appears to be detained at customs in an airport.

On a conscious level, the ad doesn't make a lot of sense. How could such a dreary and unpleasant scene possibly sell cigarettes?

Figure 3.6

It does so by presenting a subliminal *rape*. The two men have over-powered and violated the woman. They have penetrated her suitcase, rav-aged her intimate, personal belongings, (including her wallet and under-wear), and left them callously strewn about the counter when they were done. They are holding her captive as they debate their next move. The woman's legs are spread because she feels humiliated and defeated.

Figure 3.7

The close-up of the woman's face in Figure 3.7 tells the story clearly. Her cheeks are flushed and her lipstick is smeared because *the men forced her to kiss them*.

Whereas male sexual anxiety often involves fears of impotency, fe-male sexual anxiety often involves fears of being violated. The ad stimu-lates women's infantile desire to suck (and therefore smoke) by making them feel threatened and upset. It also appeals to men, by satisfying uncon-scious male fantasies of subjugating females.

Here Comes an Offer

Continuity in subliminal content is not limited to Benson and Hedges ads. Each of the three Belair ads portrayed in Figure 3.8, 3.10, and 3.12 "coincidentally" contain very similar embeds.

Figure 3.8

The woman in the blue T-shirt in Figure 3.8 has an erect penis thrusting out of her genital area. Both she and her boyfriend seem very excited about it. It is hard to imagine what it is supposed to be (other than a penis) because the tip of it extends beyond her thigh. You will find it easily in the close-ups in Figure 3.9 on the next page.

Figure 3.9(a-b)

Figure 3.10

In Figure 3.10 a very large circumcised phallus appears on the man's stomach between the lady's elbow and the top of his shorts. It is pointing down and slightly to the left. The tip of it ends around his navel area. It is outlined in the close-ups in Figure 3.11 on page 120. It is interesting to note that the woman appears older than the man and the genital area of her bikini is bulging.

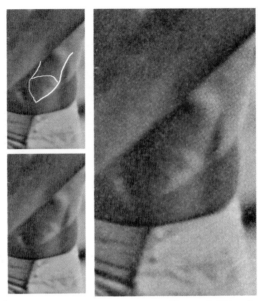

Figure 3.11(a-c)

The lady in Figure 3.12 is also sporting a penis. Her phallus is a flaccid, faint, double exposure falling out of the right side of the bottom of her bathing suit. A close-up appears in Figure 3.13 on page 122. Its size and location are, more or less, anatomically correct. The penis appears as a dark shadow on her left leg (the right leg as you look at the photo). Like the other Belair women, she seems confident and impressed with herself. The caption reads "Here comes an offer..."

Advertisers Are Freudians

In addition to denying they use subliminals, many advertisers also insist they have no interest in psychology. An account executive for the cigarette "Virginia Slims" expressed this viewpoint when he declared:

> Subliminal stimulation is not purposely used by the Leo Burnett Co. in the development of Virginia Slims advertising. The reason is we are advertisers, not psychologists. Our expertise is in the communication of ideas and images, not in the probing and stimulation of the subconscious.

Figure 3.12

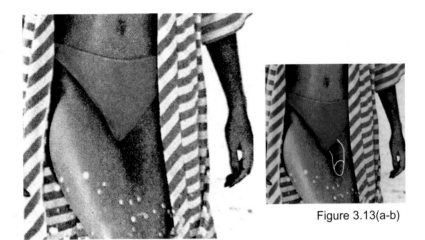

Figure 3.13(a-b)

Such assertions are contradicted by the fact that ordinary college text-books and marketing journals emphasize the importance of appealing to unconscious motivations. For example, the 1994 college marketing text-book *Consumer Behavior* states:

> Researchers have found that much of a person's actions are determined by influences of which he or she is, at the time, completely unaware…. The motives that exist at the *unconscious level*…[are an]…area reserved for some specially trained psychologists and psychiatrists. To understand this point better, you may wish to review …the theories of Sigmund Freud. (Italics in original.)

Consumer Behavior goes on to disclose that "a major ad agency" representing the roach killer "Combat" conducted a study to determine why a plastic bug-killing device wasn't selling as well as expected. The study revealed that many women view the roach "as symbolizing men who had mistreated them in the past." The research director concluded that "killing roaches with a bug spray and watching them squirm…" allows women "…to express their hostility towards men." The insights provided by the study enabled the ad agency to improve the "Combat" campaign.

Older materials are even more revealing. A 1958 article entitled "Motivation Research and Subliminal Advertising" stated:

...The advertising psychologists are fairly well agreed that there are three levels at which people are motivated to purchase goods.... The third is the subconscious level, comprising that complex, hidden maze of all market motives of which the consumer himself is not aware. At this level...analysts contend that the pleasure of women who bake cakes is the symbolic acting out of the birth of a child; or that people who eat prunes are tightwads, and that tightwads are the product of fastidious toilet training in childhood.... (Emphasis added.)

Consumer Behavior and Behavioral Sciences, another college textbook published in the mid 1960s, stated that "...basic behavioral patterns may be determined by desires located in the unconscious personality." The text noted that *pathological gamblers* unconsciously desire to lose in order to punish themselves for being unconsciously aggressive. *Bargain hunters* yearn to outsmart others and express aggression towards their mothers, whom they secretly view as cold and refusing. *Constipated individuals* psychosomatically give themselves digestive disorders in order to "'withhold' from the world." The article also noted that some consumers are secretly motivated by *homosexual* and *oedipal* tendencies.

Damned If They Do

Advertisers are not evil conspirators. They are intelligent, creative people faced with a difficult dilemma. The competitive pressures of the marketplace force them to use subliminal techniques, and at the same time require them to deny they do so.

Agencies must use all cost-effective means of persuasion in order to remain competitive. Producing a subliminal ad doesn't cost much more than producing a non-subliminal ad, because in both cases an ad has to be conceived and created. Furthermore, *running* the ad costs much more than *producing* it, so that even a nominal increase in sales improves the bottom line. Consider the math: if subliminals are incorporated into a campaign that grosses a hundred million dollars a year, and the subliminals cause sales to increase only one percent, the additional million dollars in revenue more than covers the cost of incorporating the subliminals. In other words, unconscious persuasion is *cost-effective* even when it only *modestly* increases purchasing behavior.

Subliminals in advertising are probably *more* than modestly effective. The subliminals used in the studies discussed in Chapter Two exerted a significant influence even though they were usually benign and presented on only one or two occasions. The subliminals used in media, in contrast, are emotionally provocative and presented repetitively.

No matter how much advertisers would like to, most of them cannot admit they use subliminals. A tumultuous outcry followed Vicary's "Hungry? Eat popcorn!" press conference in New Jersey. Vicary merely flashed innocuous commands like "Drink Coke" during a movie. A much greater outcry would result if advertisers admitted that, for decades, they had secretly embedded pornography in materials viewed by children.

The advertiser's dilemma is analogous to the predicament of politicians. Most people realize politicians have to accept contributions from special interest groups in order to raise the funds to get elected. They also realize elected officials must vote in accordance with the wishes of the special interest groups that support them. Politicians have to deny being influenced by such contributions, because they couldn't get reelected if they didn't.

Most voters don't take politicians seriously when they insist campaign contributions do not affect them. In the same way, the public should not take advertisers seriously when they deny they use subliminals. They couldn't tell us if they wanted to.

Market forces also motivate media professionals to pretend they are unsophisticated and not psychologically oriented, as the representative of Virginia Slims asserted. The public would feel threatened and defensive if advertisers admitted they were clever and manipulative. Advertising works best when we believe it is unpersuasive. Paradoxically, advertisers must convince the public their work is ineffectual, and at the same time they must convince their clients they can deliver sales.

The Media Filter

Thus far, at least, market forces have also restrained the mainstream media from exposing the use of subliminal techniques. Although a few courageous individuals have addressed the controversy, for the most part the communications industry has either ignored or trivialized the subject. Most newspapers, magazines, and television stations rely on advertising revenues for survival. They are naturally reluctant to criticize advertising because advertisers provide their income. In a sense, the media sanitizes and represses the truth about subliminal persuasion, to prevent the public from becoming upset about it.

The Role of Images

Figure 3.14

Most modern marketing textbooks accept the media's trivialization of the subliminal controversy. *Visual Persuasion: The Role of Images in Advertising*, published in 1997, provides an interesting example. The author remarks that "scholarly opinion" on the topic of subliminal advertising "tends to be skeptical…." He further states "…there may be *some* reason for supposing that subliminal advertising can work *occasionally,* although the evidence is by no means unequivocal." (Emphasis added.)

The text analyzes the visual techniques used in a number of ads, one of which is reproduced in Figure 3.14 on page 125. The author's *entire* commentary about the illustration states:

> An Absolut Vodka ad, labeled "ABSOLUT ATTRACTION," shows a martini glass next to a bottle of Absolut; the glass is bent in the direction of the bottle, as if being drawn toward it by some invisible force...

If you study the ad, you will see that it is quite provocative. The bending stem resembles a developing erection. The light colored shape in the interior of the container looks like a hot flame, or perhaps a woman's vulva.

The most intriguing aspect of the picture, however, is a figure-ground illusion that the author did *not* comment upon. If you focus on the light colored space *behind* the glass for a few moments, the shape of a woman's buttocks will emerge. The bottom rump is especially clear. It is formed by the lower edge of the bent glass; the dark shadow along the bottom of the container erotically forms the dark space between the woman's cheeks. The woman's skin has been extended slightly over the edge of the glass to accentuate the illusion. The upper cheek is enhanced by an almost vertical curved shadow inside the glass, to the left of the flame.

A Confidential Admission

There are many advertisers in the world, and it is therefore not surprising that despite the pressure not to, some of them privately admit using subliminals. The following are excerpts from a letter sent to me by one such individual, who contacted me in response to an ad I ran in the trade journal, *Advertising Age*:

Dear August,

...I'll get right into your questions. I am familiar with Key's book.... I know lots of advertisers and filmmakers who use subliminal techniques. The advertising business is such that a person who *does not* use them doesn't understand his craft very well. Obviously, it follows that I have used subliminal techniques myself.

The very nature of subliminal imagery rests on the dual meaning.... Its power lies in the fact that you are *not* conscious of the message....

A little bit about myself and my work. I am the art director for a retail advertising agency. We are full service, which means that we do TV, radio, and all forms of print advertising. My job is mainly involved with concept formation for advertising, and then supervising the production of said concept through the finished product.

...I don't want to get too technical and end up in hot water.... Subliminal imagery is not openly discussed with people outside the ad industry very often, most advertisers taking the position that it doesn't exist. Frankly, I had second thoughts about answering your letter when I found out you were writing a book.... The types of subliminal manipulation you mentioned, i.e. dual sound tracks, double exposures, airbrushing, etc., are all in use today...

An Inadvertent Admission

The ad I ran in *Advertising Age* said "SUBLIMINAL ADVERTISING. Writer seeks correspondence with knowledgeable persons. Strictly confidential." To my amazement, I received the following reply from the executive director of a "media communications" company that inadvertently admitted using subliminal techniques. Apparently, he misunderstood my ad and thought I was seeking employment! His letter stated:

Your advertisement in ADVERTISING AGE aroused a bit of interest inasmuch as *we are working in the area of subliminal advertising.* (Emphasis added.)

However, since the ad was so brief, we have no way of qualifying it to know if what we have in mind is somewhere within the realm of what you have in mind.

Please write and explain exactly what you wish to get into in the area of subliminal advertising; whether you are seeking employment, freelance assignments, offer consulting services or ????

Cordially,

XX
Executive Director

I wrote back to the "Executive Director" and explained that I was writing a book and would like to interview him. Unfortunately, I never heard from him again. Whenever I called he was "not available," and the many messages I left were never returned. I wish now that I had told him I was interested in providing "consulting services," but I didn't think of it at the time.

Like Terrorist Cells

The advertising industry has always been extremely secretive. Employees are required to sign nondisclosure agreements in which they promise not to discuss their work with anyone, not even their spouses. In meetings with supervisors, they are frequently reminded of the importance of maintaining absolute confidentiality. If they are caught discussing company business at a cocktail party, or anywhere else, they are immediately fired.

Advertisers are generally not very friendly with each other. Although it's easy to imagine them sitting around, joking about the genitalia they have embedded in cigarette ads, such a scenario is not very realistic. They are extremely competitive. They keep their distance, even at social gatherings within the companies they work for. In a way, the advertising industry is organized like terrorist cells; everyone is isolated from one other and no one knows what anyone else is up to.

In society in general, some people consider the existence of the unconscious to be self-evident, and are fully cognizant of the pivotal role it plays in human affairs. Other people are extremely threatened by the concept. They rarely think about unconscious motivations, and are rarely aware of their own unconscious thoughts.

Within the advertising industry, a similar continuum exists regarding subliminal manipulation. Many advertisers deliberately use subliminals, and assume that in order for an ad to be effective it must have a subliminal slant. Other advertisers are repulsed by the idea, and never think about using subliminal techniques. Still others use subliminal devices but *deny*, in the psychological sense, that they do so. They rationalize their behavior in order to deal with their conflicting emotions. A copywriter, for example, told me she never used subliminal techniques, but then admitted she routinely crafted slogans *with dual meanings*. She told me she incorporated ambiguity into her work so that if she "got caught" she would "have an excuse" for the sexual phrases she had created. Many marketing professionals are interested in this book because it presents ideas they already know about *in ways they never thought of.*

The study of subliminal techniques is currently not included in most educational curriculums. Therefore, advertisers who have the drive and the aptitude must implicitly learn about subliminals on their own, or find mentors who are willing to reveal their professional secrets to them. Advertisers who lack the psychological orientation remain oblivious to the entire concept.

As a result of the subliminal scandals of the 1950s, and the nondisclosure agreements they have signed, most advertisers are extremely reluctant to discuss their work. Those that are willing to be interviewed exhibit a complete spectrum of responses. Some become extremely uptight, cross their arms, insist they don't know anything about subliminal techniques, would never use them, and are sure they wouldn't work anyway. A few are surprisingly candid. Still other advertisers wink and nod, and let you know they use subliminals without verbally admitting it. One executive I spoke to was not the least bit surprised by the examples I showed him. He readily agreed that many of the ads in this book contain convincing embeds. When I asked him if he had ever personally used subliminal techniques, he just smiled. "You can't interview me, " he said.

Protesting Too Much

Many advertisers go overboard when they try to distance themselves from the subliminal controversy. Consider the following quote, which was written by a partner in a firm that created an ad that was analyzed by Bill Key in *Subliminal Seduction*. When questioned about the ad in the 1980s the partner stated:

> …I don't know the advertisement you are referring to, but it really doesn't matter. If it was an ad done in this agency, the charges Dr. Key makes are ridiculous. We never have and never will do advertising that stoops to that level of taste or stupidity.
>
> The purpose of this agency is to create intelligent and tasteful advertising that reaches or surpasses our client's goals and, at the same time, nurtures and rewards everyone in this organization.

The partner's suggestion that he did not know *Subliminal Seduction* featured an ad his firm created is about as believable as J. Edgar Hoover's assertion that "there is no Mafia." He implies that Key's allegations were never brought to the Board's attention by an employee, business competitor, or client. Wouldn't the company whose product was featured in the ad want to discuss Key's observations? Wouldn't the firm and the client have had meetings to consider what, if anything, should be done? Wouldn't the legal department have been consulted? Wouldn't potential new clients have wondered if their ads were also going to be dissected in a book on subliminal advertising? The partner's denials would be more credible if they were *less* emphatic.

No Gallup to This Poll

A number of published studies have purported to confirm the ad industry's view that subliminal advertising is a myth. These materials are not convincing when they are objectively analyzed.

A 1994 article entitled "The Answer is No: A National Survey Of Advertising Industry Practitioners And Their Clients About Whether They Use Subliminal Advertising" is a good example. Two marketing researchers conducted a poll in which they mailed a questionnaire to 750 randomly chosen advertising practitioners. 36.1% of the advertisers they wrote to filled out the questionnaire and mailed it back. Of these, 66% indicated they believed advertisers "place subliminal messages or imagery in advertisements." About 50% thought subliminal techniques were "effective." 7.1% thought the firm they *currently worked for* "used subliminal messages or imagery..."

These figures seem remarkably high when you consider that the respondents were not compelled to answer. They were free to avoid the questions by *not* writing back to the researchers. The voluntary nature of the poll skewed the results *in favor of advertisers.*

This bias is easily illustrated. Imagine writing to all the *Ford* salesmen in America and asking them if they thought *Toyotas* were better cars than Fords. Very few, if any, would write back and say, "yes." If they thought Toyotas were better, they simply wouldn't reply at all. On the other hand, if they thought Fords were better, they would be inclined to write back, because they would want to confirm they were selling the "better" car and support the company they worked for. Moreover, some salesmen who secretly preferred Toyotas would *lie* and pretend they preferred Fords, because they would think this was expected of them. From this perspective, its amazing that such a high percentage of the advertisers in the survey admitted they knew about subliminals and/or made use of them.

Despite this, the authors of the study characterized the poll as providing proof that subliminals are *not* deliberately used in media. They suggested the recipients did not always understand the questions, and proposed other convoluted arguments, to rationalize the data they were uncomfortable with. The title they used, "The Answer Is No...," is conclusory and misleading. Anyone superficially scanning the article would acquire an erroneous impression of its content.

Scientific Disinformation

A few supposedly scientific studies have purported to "prove" subliminal embeds and other techniques don't affect consumer behavior. One article that is often cited in support of this proposition is "Subliminal Advertising: What You See Is What You Get," by Timothy Moore. The author concludes:

> Subliminal stimuli are usually so weak that the recipient is not
> just unaware of the stimulus, but is also oblivious to the fact

that he/she is being stimulated. As a result, the potential effects
of subliminal stimuli are easily nullified by other ongoing
stimulation…

It is likely that psychologically *irrelevant* information is disregarded
and/or overwhelmed in the manner that Mr. Moore suggests. Every day, we
subliminally perceive enormous amounts of irrelevant *incidental* information, such as objects we see out of the corners of our eyes, and conversa-
tions we overhear but don't pay attention to. We generally do not respond to
this data because it is not important emotionally. Psychologically *significant* information, however, is stored, processed, and reacted to in many
ways.

Other studies cited by the ad industry are misleading and use flawed
methodologies. In an experiment published in the *Journal of Advertising*,
for example, subjects were asked to leaf through a "dummy" magazine containing a variety of advertisements. Some of the ads were taken from Key's
books and were presumed to *contain embeds*. Other "control" ads were
taken from popular magazines published in the same time period, and were
presumed to *not contain embeds* because the author of the study did not
find any in them. After the magazine was taken away, the subjects were
asked to recall as many of the ads as possible. Because the subjects' memories of the two groups of ads were similar, the author concluded that subliminal advertising is ineffective.

The experiment is invalid because the "control" ads probably contained subliminal devices the author had not detected. As demonstrated by
the Benson and Hedges and Belair series, similar ads often incorporate similar
subliminal techniques. It may be easy to "see" the subliminals when they
are pointed out, but it is not easy to discover them. You can test this yourself
by showing the penis/backbone ad to people not familiar with this book.
Most of them will not be able to find the hidden phallus, even if you tell
them the picture contains "an optical illusion" and let them look at it for as
long as they like. Moreover, the author of the "dummy magazine" study
was a consultant for ad agencies, and probably wasn't terribly motivated to
find embeds in ads that did not appear in Key's book. Since he did not
publish the particular ads used, it is not possible to examine them.

It is interesting to note that the Kilbourne (Marlboro Lights penis/
rock) experiment discussed in Chapter Two *found* a subliminal effect using

a more objective procedure. Kilbourne and his colleagues created the control ads by *removing* embeds they discovered in a liquor and cigarette ad. The control ads were therefore *identical* to the experimental ads, *except* that they did not contain the embeds that had been removed. The subliminal ads (*with* the embeds) elevated the skin conductance of the subjects significantly more than the non-subliminal ads (*without* the embeds).

Subliminal advertising is a psychologically threatening subject involving billions of dollars. It is not surprising that it is controversial, or that a great deal of disinformation has been generated about it. Other pro-industry studies utilizing questionable methodologies are discussed in the footnotes. For serious researchers, suggested experiments are included in Appendix B.

With Their Hands in the Cookie Jar

People in media get caught using subliminals all the time. When they do they invariably try to wiggle out of it by claiming it was an "accident," or the work of "disgruntled employees."

Slipped in the Shorts: The March 26, 2001 edition of *Newsweek* reported that during an episode of the television show *Three's Company* (remember Figure 2.16?) John Ritter's penis fell out of his jockey shorts and was clearly exposed for half a second. The "accident" was finally discovered by an "eagle-eyed *Nick at Nite*" viewer, and had never been complained about in previous airings. The studio quickly snipped out the offending frames.

Obviously, such an event could not occur by mistake. Imagine how many people – the director, actors, camera-persons, make up artists – are involved in shooting a television program. How could every one of them fail to notice Mr. Ritter's genitalia flying out of his underwear? And even if it did slip by everyone during the shooting, how could it not be discovered when the show was edited?

A Dramatic Bedroom Setting: A similar phenomenon appeared in the *Montgomery Wards* catalogue depicted in Figure 3.16. If you look carefully at the shadows below the plant on the right hand side of the bed, you will discover the word F*CK written in thick, light-colored letters. According to the *San Francisco Chronicle*, Wards "blamed a disgruntled employee of an outside photo studio for the graffiti." The article went on to report that, "the word, scrawled on the negative after the photo had been taken," was "so light and badly written that one would have to look closely to notice it. It went undetected throughout the catalogue's preparation." The text in the ad appropriately suggested "Create a dramatic bedroom setting."

Rats: During the presidential campaign in September, 2000, George W. Bush ran an attack ad in which he criticized Gore's prescription drug plan as being overly bureaucratic. At the end of the commercial, the phrase "bureaucrats decide" appeared, then fragmented and danced around the screen. An "eagle-eyed" Democrat discovered that on one and only one frame the word "RATS" appeared subliminally in large letters, for 1/30 of a second. The fleeting image is reproduced in Figure 3.15. The ad cost 2.5 million dollars and was run on 217 stations a total of 4,000 times.

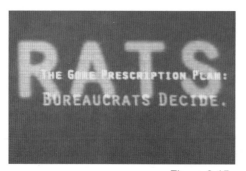

Figure 3.15

The New York Times reported that the commercial was produced for the Republican National Committee by Alex Castellanos, a respected "veteran advertising strategist." Predictably, Mr. Castellanos insisted that the use of the "RATS" was "purely accidental." "We don't play ball that way," he declared. "I'm not that clever."

Figure 3.16

The Lion King: In 1995, a number of religious groups complained that the word "SEX" was subliminally embedded in the Walt Disney movie *The Lion King*. The word appeared momentarily in dust that arose after Simba flopped down a hill. For the most part, the mainstream press ridiculed the allegations. This is not suprising, considering the enormous amount Disney spends every year advertising in newspapers.

Russian Imitators: An article appearing in the *San Francisco Chronicle* in August, 2002 reported that *one fifth* of all Russian TV programs contain subliminal flash frames. Administrators in Moscow announced a plan to electronically monitor all Russian TV channels and crack down on the perpetrators.

Serving Themselves

When they feel it's in their interest do so, advertisers readily admit using subliminal devices.

I'm Your Penis: An article in *Marketing and Media Decisions* in 1988, for example, reported that Shelly Palmer, a well known advertising agency owner and jingle creator, "is not even shy about the word 'subliminal.' He confesses outright to having altered the sound waves of voice and music in current broadcast ads for Seagram's Mixers, Bally's Casino, and Matilda Bay Wine Coolers." The article explained that Mr. Palmer "modifies the frequencies of sound waves" to mimic sounds like ice-crackling noises that help build thirst at parties. Mr. Palmer was quoted as saying, "In a spot for Seagram's mixers...we've interspersed all kinds of interesting noises. They're always present, but you wouldn't be able to hear them," at least not in the traditional sense. Mr. Palmer reportedly hoped that the subliminal sounds would "woo unsuspecting customers."

If advertisers admit using innocuous subliminal sounds like "ice-crackling" noises, it's hard to believe they don't secretly use more provocative sexual stimuli. For example, a popular television commercial features a lively song that declares, "I'm your Venus, I'm your fire of joy...!" It's easy to imagine how a master sound technician could embed the word "penis" over the word "Venus," so that the sexual word was only heard on a subliminal level.*

*See page 257.

Such a technique may have been utilized in "Staying Alive," the Bee Gee's theme song to the film *Saturday Night Fever*, starring John Travolta. The chorus can either be heard as, "UH UH UH UH, staying alive, or F*CK, F*UCK, F*CK, F*CK, staying alive."

The Saintly President: In a 1988 article in *Advertising Age*, a video-editing artist bragged that he had "touched up" the tape for a Presidential primaries television commercial, so that a thin "halo" of saintly light appeared around George Bush's head. In contrast, photos of Bush's opponent, Bob Dole, were "flipped" so that Dole's hair was parted on the wrong side and his face looked awkward. The flipping was apparently intended to be perceived subliminally. "It's nothing anyone would notice," the artist explained.

Cinematic Subliminals

The movie industry has admitted experimenting with subliminal techniques since the 1950s, as illustrated by the film clips featured in Figure 1.1 on page 9. When I mentioned to a retired senior executive for a major studio that subliminals often appear in movies, he replied, "we never denied it."

Wilson Bryan Key reported that Warner Brothers admitted using several fleeting images of frightening death masks in the horror film, *The Exorcist*. Directed by William Friedkin and first released in 1973, *The Exorcist* is a creative masterpiece. It has won multiple awards and is considered to be one of the most disturbing pictures of all time. The death masks appear at least twice. The first mask is displayed during Father Karras' dream sequence (about a third of the way into the film) as his mother emerges from the subway. The second appears during the final exorcism, momentarily replacing Regan's face as she writhes on the bed.

The mask from the dream sequence is reproduced in Figure 3.17 on page 139. As you can see, it is extremely distressing. It looks like an enraged, demonic, cave-creature about to viciously attack the viewer. Its thin face and bared teeth arouse primordial fears of being hunted and eaten. The blood-red eyes point in slightly different directions, suggesting that the beast is deranged and unpredictable.

Most people feel a jolt of apprehension when the masks appear. They are displayed just around the *threshold* of consciousness. Viewers who know the masks are incorporated in the film usually perceive them consciously.

Some viewers who do not know they are incorporated in the film also perceive them consciously, even though they are not expecting them. Other viewers never become aware of the fleeting masks. They do not realize there is anything unusual about the sequences, except that watching them makes them feel anxious.

Viewers who consciously perceive the death masks often do not realize how disturbing they are. When they are shown the still frame in figure 3.17 after watching the movie, they frequently remark that the demon is more horrifying than they thought. The filter endeavors to block awareness of the masks because they are threatening and discordant. If it cannot block them completely, the filter sanitizes and distorts the images to minimize the viewer's anxiety.

Also, when viewers consciously perceive the death masks in the movie, they tend to "forget" seeing them when the movie is over. The filter makes the conscious memory of the masks fade away the way dreams fade in the morning, or the way traumatic memories are repressed. The masks can have a subliminal effect, even when they are initially perceived consciously.

The Exorcist also contains frightening fleeting images that are displayed much more briefly. During the final exorcism Regan's arm restraints break off, and the blanket covering her body violently flies off the bed. For a brief instant, the ghoulish skull depicted in Figure 3.18 appears at the upper center of the screen. The blanket forms a shroud around the creature's head. Orange material flows out of its mouth, reminiscent of the green vomit ejected by Regan in the preceding scenes. Although Director William Friedkin obliquely refers to the death masks in the DVD commentary, he does not refer to the blanket ghoul. The ghoul is invisible when watching the movie, but easy to "see" if you stop the action on a DVD player.

Another fleeting image occurs after Father Karras invites the demon to leave Regan and enter his body instead. Karras falls backwards, and when his face reappears at the bottom of the screen it looks white and similar to the death mask in Figure 52.1. The transition only lasts for a few frames, and his appearance returns to normal as he regains his standing position.

Over the past few decades, cinematic and video artists have employed faster and faster scene changes in their work. This information is often presented too quickly for the conscious mind to follow. In this sense, the use of subliminal cuts has become common and accepted. This is illustrated by the fact that the 2000 digital version of *The Exorcist* contains many fleeting

Figure 3.17

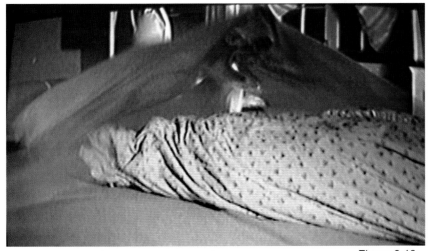

Figure 3.18

images, presented around the threshold of consciousness, that did not appear in the original video.

A Different Sense

The Exorcist also uses techniques that are *subliminal* in a more artistic sense. At a dramatic moment in the film Regan's mother hears horrible noises emanating from Regan's bedroom. She races upstairs and discovers Regan stabbing her genitals with a crucifix. The mother tries to protect Regan, but is viciously slapped to the ground. Furniture flies about, and Regan's head spins around 180 degrees until it is facing *backwards* in relation to her body. In an evil, *masculine* voice, she says, "Do you know what your daughter did?" The action is so fast-paced and disturbing that most viewers do not *consciously* realize that the voice belongs to Burke Dennings, a character in the movie that Regan had previously *murdered.* The dramatic impact of the scene is enhanced because the viewer *unconsciously* identifies the voice, and *unconsciously* realizes Regan is bragging about her crime.

Freidkin used the same technique in another part of the movie, when Father Karras meets Regan for the first time. Regan rhetorically asks in a male voice, "Can you help an old alter boy, father…?" The viewer doesn't consciously realize it, but the voice belongs to a homeless person Karras had previously encountered on the subway.

Subliminal Sounds in Movies

Director Friedkin reportedly also utilized disturbing subliminal *audio* techniques in *The Exorcist*. According to Wilson Brian Key, he inserted the sound of enraged swarming bees and a pig being slaughtered in the soundtrack. The recordings were electronically altered to prevent the listener from consciously identifying them.

Other filmmakers have applied similar audio techniques. In *The Silence of the Lambs,* sound engineer Ron Bochar created the "ambiance" of Hannibal Lecter's cell by slowing down the sound of a lunatic screaming, processing it, and playing it in reverse. Gunshots were embedded into the sound of pounding typewriter keys in the beginning of *All the Presidents Men,* foreshadowing the conflict between the power of the press and the power of the presidency. Alfred Hitchcock experimented with subliminal sounds in 1936 in the movie *Secret Agent.* As early as 1933, the "voice" of

King Kong was created by recording the roar of lions at the San Diego Zoo and playing them in reverse.

Embeds In Moving Pictures

Embeds (like the penis/backbone) and *figure-ground* illusions can be incorporated into films and television commercials. As a movie executive explained, "one technique works for all mediums."

An interesting movie embed appears in Figure 3.19 (below). Please study it for a moment before reading further.

The image is taken from the 2002 movie *Tomb Raider,* which features the fictional character Lara Croft. Ms. Croft is a beautiful, ingenious woman with the athletic ability of Batman and the charming self-confidence of James Bond. Although she is distinctly feminine, she also has a great deal of masculine sexual power. All the men she associates with are clearly her subordinates.

In the movie, during her tenacious pursuit of the bad guys, Ms. Croft drives a dog sled across Siberia into the mouth of a mountainous cavern. As shown in Figure 3.20, as the camera pans down the face of the cliffs a majestic snowy white horse momentarily appears embedded in the rocks. The camera movement makes the complete horse appear slightly blurry, but

Figure 3.19

as Lara approaches the opening of the cave the left hoof and lower face of the horse come into focus.

Most people can consciously identify the horse after looking at it for a few seconds. They are not able to do so when watching the film, however, because the image passes by too quickly.

White horses are inspiring symbols. They represent power, freedom, speed, pride, sexuality, and spiritual transcendence. Knights in shining armor ride on white horses, as do "good guys" in cowboy pictures. ("Bad guys" ride black horses.) Carl Jung believed white horses symbolize life as well as "the uncontrollable instinctive drives that can erupt from the unconscious...." Adolescent girls are often infatuated with white horses and unicorns, which are winged white horses with phallic shaped horns.

In *Tomb Raider*, the white horse subliminally embedded in the mountain enhances the viewers impression of Ms. Croft as a dynamic, free spirited, morally pure individual with both masculine and feminine sexual power. The forceful, obedient sled dogs phallically extending in front of her as she enters the cave further symbolize her manly energy.

The Totality of Circumstances

The circumstantial evidence of subliminal advertising can be summarized as follows:

- Subliminal devices influence human behavior.

- Many ads seem to contain subliminal devices.

- The subliminal content within *particular* ads is consistent.

- The subliminal content within *series* of ads is consistent.

- The communications industry started investigating subliminals in the 1950s. Since then more money has probably been spent on motivational research than the space program.

- Mass media is a "laboratory" in which advertisers can freely experiment on the public.

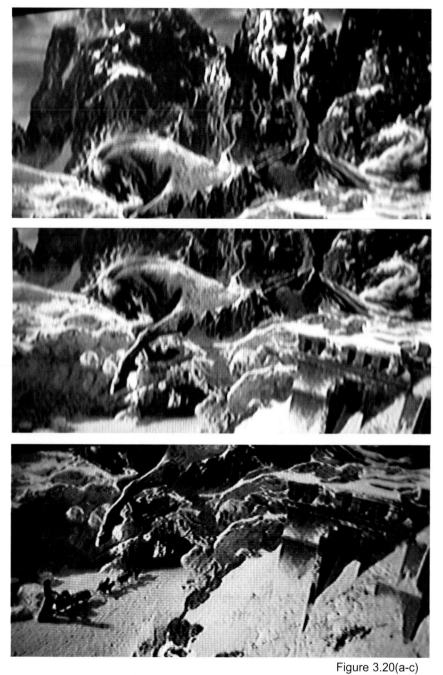

Figure 3.20(a-c)

- Using subliminals is profitable even if the subliminals only negligibly increase sales.

- Most advertisers couldn't admit using subliminals if they wanted to. Their assertions that they have no interest in psychology are implausible.

- The movie industry openly uses subliminals.

- Some advertisers admit using subliminals.

- Advertisers admit using less controversial forms of subliminals when they feel it is in their interest to do so.

- Media professionals frequently get caught using subliminal techniques.

Hard Evidence

The existence of subliminal advertising will never be proven beyond the circumstantial evidence outlined above. Even if a prominent advertiser admitted using subliminal techniques, the controversy would continue because others in the industry would deny doing so. The whistleblower would be chastised, personally attacked, and accused of suffering from emotional problems. The debate will probably never come to a dramatic close, but will be resolved gradually as people become more aware of, and willing to accept, the unconscious emotions that secretly motivate us.

The Subliminal Continuum

Subliminal advertising is a continuum, not a light switch that is either "on" or "off." The subliminal content of some ads is intended to be perceived only on a deeply unconscious level. The subliminal content of other ads is presented just below our threshold of consciousness, so that we become aware of it as soon as we think about it. Ads can fall anywhere between these two extremes, as the chart in Figure 3.21 illustrates.

---

*Many of the terms refer to federally registered tradmarks.

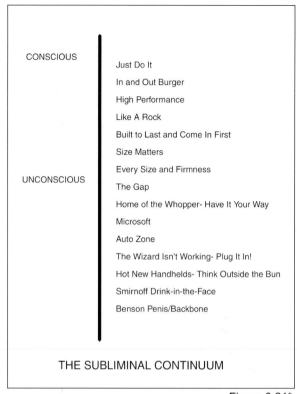

Figure 3.21*

We all realize that advertisers routinely try to add a libidinal "charge" to the text of media by using ambiguous sexual terms. If we are aware of their effort, we perceive the result as an *innuendo*. If we are not aware of their effort, the affect is *subliminal*. Whether something falls in the innuendo or subliminal category is determined by the structure of the phrase and the extent to which our attention is directed towards it.

"Just do it" is a rudimentary example of a phrase whose hidden meaning falls on the edge of consciousness. Ostensibly it means "don't be inhibited, don't be afraid of failure, go for the gusto in sports and in life." On a slightly deeper level it refers to sexual intercourse. To most people, the sexual connotation becomes obvious as soon as they think about it. Other people probably always make the association. Some people might find the idea threatening and avoid seeing the ambiguity at all. In any event, when our attention is exclusively directed at the sports meaning, the sexual meaning is "activated" unconsciously.

Media is saturated with such sexual ambiguities, all of which fall at different points on the continuum. Other popular, almost conscious examples include "High Performance" (in a car ad), "Like A Rock," and "In-N-Out Burger."

Somewhat more subliminal examples include: "Fords Are Built to Last and Come In First," "Size Matters" (in a poster for a Godzilla movie), and "Every Size and Firmness" (in a mattress ad on the radio). "The Gap" refers to female genitalia and an emotional void that can be filled by pampering oneself by buying clothes. The slogan, "Burger *King* — Home of the Whopper - Have It Your Way" makes an allusion to large penises and the desire to dominate and control. These are somewhat obvious when you think about them, but not so obvious when you are thinking about other things.

Further down the continuum scale, considerably more secretive examples include: "Microsoft" (which refers to an undersized, flaccid nerd-like penis), "Auto-Zone" (which refers to the clitoris, a "zone" utilized for masturbation), and the slogan "The Wizard Isn't Working — Plug It In, Plug It In! (which employs a strategy similar to the Benson penis/backbone ad). As I noted previously, "Taco Bells Hot New Handhelds — Think Outside The Bun," subliminally refers to *masturbation* and *food* as a substitute for sex.

The Smirnoff drink-in-the-face ad and the Benson penis/backbone ad are at the furthest end of the continuum, because they are understood only on the deepest unconscious level.

The fact that Bill Gates may have picked the name "Microsoft" for other reasons is irrelevant. The emotional "secret" meaning at least partially accounts for the way it "sticks in our minds."

Television commercials can deliver subliminal content by moving too fast for us to consciously process the data. A popular truck commercial, for example, uses the following script:

> California is about **bigness**
> **Big** waves (picture of beach)
> **Big highways** (picture of freeway from helicopter)
> **Big whatever** (picture of homosexual male weight lifter)

> Now Dodge Quad Cab **nails that bigness thing**
> With **four big wide opening doors**
> A big **full-sized bed**
> This truck **hangs out** at your Dodge Dealer

The ad contains a homosexual theme that becomes fairly obvious when you slow down the action and analyze the commercial's ambiguities. An image of a homosexual-looking male weightlifter is presented as the announcer proclaims "Big whatever." On a conscious level the viewer associates "big whatever" with the model's well developed pectorals. On a subliminal level, however, the phrase refers to the weight lifter's genitalia and "activates" repressed homosexual fantasies. "Highways" refers to free and uninhibited lifestyles. "Four big wide opening doors" refers to the two mouths and two anuses involved in homosexual sex. "Full sized bed" requires no explanation, and "hangs out" refers to exposed genitalia.

Like "innuendoes," advertisements also often contain subliminal *inferences* that range along the "continuum" in a similar manner. Classic mouthwash commercials, for example, infer that users of that product will have more success with members of the opposite sex than consumers who do not use mouthwash.

On a slightly deeper level, many modern commercials and television shows portray women who are bossy and condescending to their male partners. Men are often depicted as childish and inept. To some extent, the stereotypical roles of the 1950s have been reversed. Mass media frequently flatters women because women consume more than men. Although the subliminal inferences of such scripts often do not register consciously, they resonate with the viewer's unconscious feelings.

Advertisers often use *humor* to disguise hostile subliminal inferences. The humor makes it easy for viewers to avoid recognizing the true meaning of the script. A popular television commercial, for example, portrays a married couple driving in their truck with their son in the back seat. The son has just arrived on a visit from college. The parents are very glad to see him, until the son mentions that he intends to eat all the family's cereal as soon as they get home. The father slams on the brakes and leaves the son stranded on the side of the road. The commercial jokes that the cereal is so delicious it is more important than familial relationships. On a subliminal level, it capitalizes on unconscious feelings of enmity between parents and their college-aged offspring.

When you look at the complete continuum, it becomes clear that many ads are "subliminal," and subliminal ads are everywhere. Ambiguous slogans and hidden inferences may not be as shocking as the penis/backbone or other examples in this book, but they are based *on the same psychological principles*. The argument that subliminal advertising does not exist at all is contradicted by the fact that less dramatic, indisputable variations of it can be found in every form of media.

Chapter Four:
DISTURBING TABOOS
THE COURAGE TO LOOK

The unconscious has no moral inhibitions, and neither does the advertising that appeals to it. This chapter explores subliminal content that violates powerful social taboos.

How Mom and Lazy Boy Celebrated Father's Day

Most people are familiar with the psychological theory that young boys are unconsciously sexually attracted to their mother, and jealous of and hostile towards their father. Freud referred to this as the Oedipus complex, after Sophocles' play, *Oedipus Rex.*

The ad in Figure 4.1, which appeared in *Parents* magazine, stimulates this drive. It is appropriately captioned "How Mom and La-Z-Boy celebrated Father's Day."

It portrays a young boy approaching his mother with flowers, while his father looks on in the background. As soon as you think about it, it is difficult to overlook the mother's sensual appearance. She is leaning back in her chair in a suggestive manner, with her hair tousled and unkempt. The third finger of her right hand is deftly massaging the crease of the book on her lap. Her middle fingers are awkwardly extended, as though they were legs spread in a sexually provocative position.

Most shocking, however, is the unbelievably sexual way her left hand is gliding up and caressing her son's arm.

The son, meanwhile, is standing with his genitals pushed against the arm of the chair. A black, vertical shadow on his shorts (just above the center of the wood) forms the shape of an erection. As he stares at his mother's lap and offers her flowers, he looks very much like a nervous young man on a first date.

In the background, Dad is extremely anxious. Although his face is obscured by his hand, his eyes reveal his agitation. He is staring at his son as though he is concerned about the competition and is plotting his revenge. The shears he is holding are symbols of castration. They are threatening to snip off the prongs of the rake, which subliminally represent the boy's "horns."

As the close-ups in Figure 4.2 on page 153 illustrate, the Lazy Boy ad addresses every element of the Oedipus complex. If it wasn't intended to "activate" oedipal drives, it's hard to understand what the artist was thinking of when he drew the scene.

Creating advertisements that unconsciously appeal to children makes good business sense. An article in *Social Research* explained:

> Motivation researchers are advising American industry to direct much of its advertising to children. It is said that 71 per cent of breakfast cereal is selected by children, 44 per cent of packaged desserts, 35 per cent of milk and dairy products, 32 per cent of toothpaste, and 38 per cent of family vacation sites. *The percentages are greater for* cars, *parlor furniture*, and television sets.

Figure 4.1

>...What is more, some motivation researchers assure us that the
>fixing of these product preferences in childhood will guaran-
>tee consumer loyalty for a lifetime. (Emphasis added.)

The ad is subliminally appealing to Mom as well as Junior. Mom
unconsciously enjoys the fantasy of increasing her intimate connection with
her son. She may deny it, but she also enjoys increasing her power over Dad
by making him feel rejected and left out.

Oedipus in Media

The subliminal satisfaction of oedipally-related drives is very common in
media. The basic plot of the original *Star Wars* trilogy, for example, involves a young man (Luke Skywalker) who sexually pursues his twin sister
(Princess Lea) while he fights against his father (Darth Vader). He also competes with his symbolic older brother/alternate father figure, Han Solo, for
Princess Leah's affections. Han often addresses Luke as "Kid."
Star Wars is also psychologically appealing because, in the end, Luke ac-
quires his father's approval. After Luke helps him to see the error of his
ways, Darth Vader returns to the light side of the Force and bonds with his
son. Just before he dies Vader tells Luke, "You were right."

In the more recent movie *Spider-man,* the hero indirectly causes
the death of his surrogate "good" father, his Uncle Ben. Peter Parker
(Spiderman) has an argument with Uncle Ben in which he demands, "stop
pretending you're my father." Shortly afterwards, he vents his anger at another male authority figure (a fight promoter who takes advantage of him)
by allowing a thief to steal the promoter's money. The thief hijacks Uncle
Ben's car and causes his death. Peter feels so guilty that he commits his life
to crime fighting.

Peter (Spiderman) also causes the death of his surrogate "evil" father, the Green Goblin. Just before he dies, The Green Goblin tells Peter, "I
was like a father to you." The plot resonates with the unconscious conflicts
of the members of *Spiderman*'s young male audience, who secretly would
like to murder their fathers, but would feel horrified if they acknowledged
such feelings.

The movie *Artificial Intelligence* is an elongated oedipal fantasy more
than a real story. It portrays a male robot-child who competes with his human brother and father for his mother's attention. The mother abandons

Figure 4.2

him, and he spends the next two thousand years trying to reunite and bond with her. For much of that time he is trapped in a small spaceship, underwater, staring longingly at a statue that physically resembles his mother. The water, the spaceship, and the statue symbolically represent the womb and prenatal intimacy.

The robot-boy is eventually saved by eunuch-like aliens, who arrange for him to symbolically mate with his mother. The narrator declares that the boy finally has his mother all to himself (because the father and brother have long since died). When the mother awakes from her long sleep, she is wearing an incredibly sexy nightgown. She and her robot son symbolically have intercourse, after which she says "You never forget how, do you?" As she slips back into sleep her son lays beside her, holding her hand.

The consciously perceived two-thousand-year story line of *Artificial Intelligence* seems convoluted and absurd because it is not important. The plot is merely a distraction to obscure the true purpose of the film, which is to present a sexual oedipal fantasy unconsciously appealing to young boys.

These examples illustrate how *stories in media often start with psychological ideas*, which are then translated into scripts. Such an approach increases the likelihood of success at the box office.

Sail Away

On the surface, the Imperial Bank ad in Figure 4.3 portrays a middle-aged man enjoying a well-earned vacation. It's not terribly difficult to figure out, however, that on an unconscious level it portrays a pedophilic fantasy.

The man and the young girl are posed in awkward positions. The man is pulling the girl towards him, but she seems to be resisting as her feet are further away from him than her torso. Suggestively, his hand is in his pocket, and the girl looks squeamish. Since they are different races, they are not likely to be related. The text promotes the fantasy by proclaiming, "You really can go wherever you want to."

Sail away.

Today Catalina. Tomorrow Hawaii.

There are so many places to see. So many wonderful things to do. You can make your next vacation very special.

Cruise the Mediterranean, drive to British Columbia, fly to Rio, backpack through Glacier National Park, or discover more about California. You've thought of it, now plan on it by saving with an IMPERIAL FREEDOM ACCOUNT.

You really can go wherever you want to.

IMPERIAL SAVINGS

"Have we got 🄱's for you." Member FSLIC

A wholly owned subsidiary of over $4 billion Imperial Corporation of America

Figure 4.3

Dish On Demand

The Dish On Demand ad in Figure 4.4, which appeared in the *San Francisco Chronicle* in 2002, is even more provocative. The caption "The Whole Family Is Happier Since Dad Started Getting It" is obviously ambiguous; it proclaims the benefits of satellite TV, and it refers to Dad's sexual relationship with his wife. Even on a conscious level, the innuendo is somewhat shocking.

The subliminal meaning of the ad, however, is considerably more disturbing. The caption doesn't refer to Dad's sexual relationship with Mom, but with his *daughter*. (That's why he just "started" getting it.) His daughter is seductively pressed against him, and his hand is on her breast. As an added touch, his hand has been blurred to make it look like it is moving.

Oblivious to the Obvious

The forgoing examples demonstrate that subliminal ads that violate powerful taboos, such as child abuse, can be extremely obvious and still not understood consciously. This is because the filter recognizes how unsettling the "secret" meanings are, and works harder to repress them.

Figure 4.4

Free Swim

The ad in Figure 4.6 on page 159 appears to portray an incestuous, forcible, act of child molestation. It depicts a lewd, unattractive middle-aged man holding a young girl (presumably his daughter) very close to him in a pool. If you look at the close-up in Figure 4.5 (below), you will see the little girl is upset and about to cry. She is trying to push her father away, but he won't let her.

The man has well developed breasts, as well as an enormous subliminal erection. It is reddish colored, almost horizontal, and clearly visible in the reflections in the water just in front of the child. A second, smaller penis faces upwards, pushing into the little girl. The water dripping down the man's stomach resembles blood, reinforcing the violence subliminally implied in the picture.

Figure 4.5

Figure 4.6

If you look back at the entire ad, the man's wife seems either oblivious or in denial as to what her husband is doing. The little girl's young sister, to the left, apprehensively waits her turn. Older, sexually mature sisters are symbolically caged on the raised porch. Their faces are partially hidden by shadows, making it difficult to interpret their expressions.

Disclaimer

I cannot say for certain that the creators of the previous three ads (or any of the ads in this book, for that matter) consciously intended them to have the subliminal effect that I have postulated. Perhaps it is only a coincidence that they seem to relate to child abuse and incest. Perhaps the man in the pool ad is the owner of the company, and those are his kids, and they were in a bad mood because the photographer took too many pictures.

Personally, I think it is likely they were created deliberately. They represent a common subliminal technique with dire social consequences.

Even if they were not created intentionally, they have the *effect* of inspiring unconscious pedophilic fantasies in susceptible individuals. The true meaning of media like this must be acknowledged, if society is to avoid inadvertently encouraging criminal activities.

The Psycho Slayer

At first glance, the *Playgirl* cover in Figure 4.7 appears to portray a happy couple sensually embracing in bed.

When you study it, however, it becomes apparent that the woman is *dead.* Her neck is twisted and appears to have been broken. Her body is as limp as a mannequin. Her eyes are pointing in different directions and are not focusing on anything. She isn't really wearing her nightgown – it's draped around her as though she were a Barbie doll.

The woman's departure from the living has apparently inspired her partner, who appears to be a deranged, murderous necrophiliac. The diagonal, yellow stripe at the bottom of the page represents a yellow police ribbon at a murder scene.

Playgirl, although a woman's magazine, is popular with male homosexuals because it features pictures of nude men. Males with deviant sexual proclivities might be stimulated by the captions "How your Mother's Sex Life Shaped Yours," and "Outrageous Ways to Get A …Raise…."

The cover is even more emotionally powerful to women. It unconsciously activates feelings of being abused, raped, and assaulted. Stimulating such emotions increases the desire of female readers to bond with each other – which the editors hope they will do by buying the magazine.

Figure 4.7

The Jailer

The angry man in Figure 4.8, which appeared in *Playboy*, has enslaved his girlfriend. Her bent elbows reveal that her arms are tied behind her back. Her white collar looks suffocating, and her red jacket fits oddly as though it were a straightjacket. She is enclosed in a glass room, and the reflected bars beneath the horizontal bar across her chest suggest she is imprisoned. Her expression is sad and disturbed. Her callous captor has his open hand on her genitals, inferring he can force himself upon her whenever he wants.

Figure 4.8

Figure 4.9

Susan and Paul

What's this? Is Paul Newman strangling his daughter?

Rough Research

The Ruffo Research ad in Figure 4.10 appeared in *Vogue* in 2001, and presents another murder. The woman has been attacked and killed, her body left on the stairs. The knit item around her waist forms the shape of a mask and represents blood from a stab wound. The nipple of her right breast is partially exposed, as though her dress had been torn open during the assault. As in the *Playgirl* cover, her eyes are dead looking and not focused on anything.

Figure 4.10

RUFFO RESEARCH

NEW YORK // Tel 212.5820042
MILAN // VIA DELLA SPIGA 48
photo MARCELO KRASILCIC

The Attack   Figure 4.11

When you look at Figure 4.11, can you see how the smoke billowing out of the World Trade Center after it was viciously attacked forms a cartoonish monster? The *head* of the monster is looking directly at the camera and is formed by the circular ball of smoke on the far left side of the photograph (to the left of the building). The creature's right eye (the left as you look at it) is a small dark area that touches the edge of the picture. Its left eye (the right as you look at it) is a dark area towards the upper center of the circular ball. The mouth is a larger, dark area, and the bottom center of the ball.

The cloud of smoke in the upper/center of the picture forms a giant *hand* about to snap off the top of the Empire State Building. The small amount of smoke visible on the left side of the tower forms the monster's thumb. Light colored portions of the smoke on the right side of the tower form the creature's fingers. Its hand is connected to an arm that is connected to its body. The creature's shoulder is hidden from view by the building.

We all felt extremely *vulnerable* after 9/11 and worried about terrorist attacks that might occur in the future. The subliminal content of the photo reinforces these emotions. It makes the picture seem even more dramatic and threatening, without our realizing why.

It doesn't stretch the imagination to think that a suggestion of the monster may have appeared by coincidence, and then may have been creatively enhanced.* News reporting agencies have strict rules prohibiting the adulteration of news photos, but individual photographers are highly motivated to create pictures that are as provocative as possible. The fact that the subject matter of the photo is consciously very disturbing is irrelevant. A disturbing picture *with* an upsetting embed must be more dramatic than a disturbing picture *without* an embed. If one accepts the idea that subliminal techniques are often used in advertising, it is illogical to conclude they are never incorporated into news presentations. As with all the illustrations in this book, I am merely proposing a hypothesis based solely on the appearance of the picture. This issue is discussed further in the Notes and at the end of Chapter 6.

Sleep Easy

Figure 4.12

The mortgage company ad in Figure 4.12 is an Internet banner ad that was popular on America Online in 2001. It portrays a woman sleeping restfully with her infant child.

The eye of the child, however, also looks like either a vagina or an anus! The caption provocatively promises "Your Closing *Date* Is Guaranteed!"

*See page 261.

Chapter 5:
THE SECRET SELF
REFLECTIONS IN THE SUBLIMINAL MIRROR

The flip side of the *Secret Sales Pitch* is *The Secret Self*. The real reason the use of subliminals isn't universally acknowledged is that *we don't want to accept the truth* about ourselves.

Human beings are just beginning to wake up to the idea that we are driven by emotions we are not aware of. Freud published his seminal work, *The Interpretation of Dreams*, only a century ago in 1900, and his theories did not become widely accepted for many decades. Psychology didn't become popular in mass culture until after World War II, and wasn't seriously applied to advertising until the 1950s.

Acknowledging our unconscious motivations has taken such a long time because we are dismayed by them. We like to think of ourselves as sensitive, mature, and empathetic. We like to believe we navigate life's complexities by making logical decisions. We are understandably reluctant to admit we are driven by "secret" emotions that are selfish and depraved.

Most people are paradoxically aware of the unconscious, and at the same time ignorant of it. They have little difficulty perceiving its influence in other people, but they can't "see" it in themselves. Researchers have noted that when you ask people why *they* bought a new car, they will offer consciously acceptable reasons for their purchase – such as "it's well made, it's a great buy," etc. If you ask them why their *neighbor* bought a new car, on the other hand, they will give you a more truthful answer – they will tell you the neighbor is trying to enhance his or her social status. The reason for the dichotomy is obvious: understanding the unconscious influences of others is not as threatening as understanding our own. *The phenomena of perceptual distortion, denial, and repression that block awareness of the subliminal content of advertisements also block awareness of the true nature of our minds.*

When you study the ads in this book it becomes patently obvious that we are all a lot nuttier than we realize. We reinforce each other's delusions that we are "normal" and well adjusted, when in fact society is inherently emotionally disturbed. The violence and discord engulfing the planet are clues that our self-perceptions are fundamentally misguided.

Seeing Distortions in the Mirror

The collective distortions we engage in clearly inhibit our thought processes. Intelligence has two components: *hardware* and *software*. Our *hardware* is the *physical* structure of our minds, and our *software* is the *program* we use to process and analyze data. Even extremely intelligent people (who have terrific hardware and perform well on tests) exercise horrendous judgement when their software is influenced by emotional factors.

This was illustrated in an amusing study in which a distinguished looking *actor* was asked to address a group of professional educators. He was introduced as "Dr. Myron Fox, an authority on the application of mathematics in human behavior." "Dr. Fox" gave a lecture and conducted a question and answer period on the subject of "game theory," about which he knew *nothing.* Although he appeared confident, his presentation was built around contradictory statements, nonsensical words, and meaningless references to unrelated topics. Remarkably, the teachers and administrators in the audience were unable to see through Dr. Fox's façade. Since they were predisposed to believe he was a renowned expert, they did not become consciously aware of the many cues that pointed to his real identity. They rated him favorably in eight categories, including "organization of materials," "arousal of interest," and "use of examples."

We are all aware of how similar distortions occur in "real" life, and how they often have disastrous consequences. Prior to its collapse, for example, investors in the energy company Enron may not have been entirely receptive to cues that contradicted their belief that the firm was well managed.

The operations of the filter are strongly influenced by our desire to *agree* with the viewpoints of those around us. In a study conducted at Harvard University in the 1950s, groups of male college students were assembled around a table and shown two cards similar to those in Figure 5.1. As you can see, the line on the left card is the same length as one of the lines on the right card. The other two lines on the right card are a substantially different length. The participants were asked to individually indicate which of the lines on the right card matched the line on the left card.

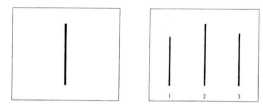

Figure 5.1

Only one of the subjects in each group was an "honest" participant. All the others were confederate researchers posing as fellow volunteers. At first the confederate researchers unanimously picked the correct line. As the experiment progressed, however, they uniformly gave erroneous responses. The study was designed to see if the "honest" participants would be swayed by the majority and give false answers. Remarkably *more than a third did so*, even though they were all intelligent students attending one of the most prestigious universities in the country. Moreover, some of them continued to pick the wrong line after the discrepancy in lengths was increased to *seven inches*!

Taken together, these studies explain how *entire societies* frequently adopt points of view that seem bizarre and irrational when viewed retrospectively. People wish to "see" what everyone around them "sees," and their filter mechanisms adjust their perception of "reality" accordingly. The Salem witch trials and the Holland tulip mania (in which many Dutch citizens lost their life savings investing in tulips) are well known historical examples. Without doubt, many widely held modern day beliefs are similarly irrational. In the future they will become obvious, but in the present our collective distortions make them impossible to accurately discern.

The Subliminal Reflection

Subliminal advertisements are fascinating because they *graphically* reveal how twisted our perception really is. They are *unsanitized* maps of the human psyche. They represent what we *really* dream, not what we *remember* dreaming when we awake. They illustrate unconscious motivations that we may understand intellectually, but emotionally dismiss as far-fetched and theoretical. They turn denial and repression into *tangible* thought processes. For these reasons we are lucky that subliminal advertising exists, and we should study it carefully.

The Id vs. the Ego

We may not realize it, but we are all afflicted with multiple personalities that are constantly at war with each other.

The conscious mind thinks that it is in charge. It has very little awareness of the unconscious, and believes that all the decisions it makes are logical and reasonable.

In reality, the unconscious is often calling the shots. It knows everything the conscious knows. It makes the conscious think it is in charge, but behind the scenes it makes the important decisions. The unconscious "cons" the conscious by distorting and withholding information the conscious has access to. If the conscious becomes aware of this, it has the ultimate authority and the ability to take control. This rarely happens, however, because the decisions it makes are based on false information, intentionally fed to it by the unconscious. The situation is like a television situation comedy in which the wife is secretly in charge of the family. She manipulates her husband's ego and makes him think he is in charge, while in reality she gets him to do everything she wants.

Here's an amusing, real life example of how this interplay unfolds. Imagine a hypothetical male who falls in love with a beautiful, but cold, woman. The man's *unconscious* wants the man to marry the woman because the woman reminds it of "their" mother. If the *conscious* discovers the real reason for the attraction, it will be repulsed and terminate the relationship. The *unconscious* avoids this by blocking awareness of the mother association, and by distorting the perception of the woman. It leads the man to consciously conclude she is not really cold, but warm and kind, with just a few understandable weaknesses. Successfully misled by the unconscious, the man marries the woman, and lives *un*-happily ever after. (He doesn't realize it, but he never really liked his mother in the first place!)

Multiple Selves

The conflict between the conscious and the unconscious is clearly apparent in individuals who suffer from multiple personality syndromes. People with this condition form separate, distinct personalities as a defense against psychological traumas. The opposing selves usually have different strengths and weaknesses, which allow the individual to cope with a variety of situations. Interestingly, in some cases the personalities know about each other, and in other cases they do not.

In the late 1800s, for example, a preacher named Ansel Bourne abruptly disappeared from Rhode Island. Two months later he woke up in Pennsylvania, and was astonished to discover that for that entire period he had acquired an alternate identity known as A.J. Brown. Mr. Brown had become a shopkeeper and had set up a small store selling candies, fruit, and stationary. Remarkably, Mr. Bourne knew nothing of Mr. Brown, and apparently, Mr. Brown knew nothing of Mr. Bourne. The conflicting selves were uncovered through hypnosis. They existed independently of each other, and alternately took over and blotted out the other's existence.

Eve White, a modest, retiring 25-year-old housewife and devoted mother, had a similar revelation. She consulted a psychiatrist because she suffered from headaches and blackouts. Although she had no history of psychological illness, the psychiatrist discovered a separate and distinct personality was secretly sharing her body. Known as "Eve Black," the alter ego was sensual, playful, wild and carefree. Eve Black knew everything about Eve White, but Eve White knew nothing about Eve Black. On one occasion, Eve Black ordered a slinky evening dress through the mail, and when it arrived Eve White had no idea why it was being delivered.

As the two Eves' treatment progressed, a third personality emerged. Her name was Jane. She knew about both Eves, but for the most part only had access to memories that occurred *after* she was formed and the psychiatric treatment had begun. Jane apparently represented a composite personality that embodied the positive characteristics of both Eve White and Eve Black.

Researchers have noted that, to a degree, even "normal" people have separate personalities that are activated in response to different situations.

When we are threatened and become angry for example, we temporarily acquire a more aggressive and violent personality than we have under normal circumstances. Our alternating selves can be viewed as behavior templates that take over in response to different situations. Although each of our conflicting personalities has access to all of our memories, each emphasizes the importance of particular past events when deciding what behavior is appropriate.

Eminent Domain

"Eminent domain" is a legal process by which the government appropriates private property for a reasonable price. It is commonly used by cities and states to make way for roads and civic projects.

    The government should exercise *eminent domain* and require advertisers to reveal the research they conducted more than forty years ago. Advertisers have spent billions of dollars studying subliminal perception and psychology since the 1950s, and have accumulated volumes of illuminating insights into the human psyche. Exercising eminent domain over their research would be fair, because they acquired the data by *experimenting* on the public. Appropriating only dated material would minimize the embarrassment of the firms involved.

The Subliminal Influence

Most people believe they are not personally affected by media. They don't pay much attention to advertising, and they do not feel it unduly influences them.

    If you look at the big picture, however, the impact of media is clearly pervasive. The developed world in general, and the United States in particular, is maniacally materialistic. Most of us are obsessed with the acquisition of things, and the things we acquire determine our position in society. Many of the social interactions we engage in involve comparing our possessions with the possessions of others. At parties when we inquire, "What do you do?" what we really mean is, "How much do you make?" The cars we drive and the clothes we wear are all intended to impress others with our wealth and social status. *It is not a coincidence* that these materialistic obsessions are precisely the inclinations advertisers have struggled to instill within us.

Materialism obviously has undesirable side effects. It makes us feel that no matter how much we have, it is never enough. It fosters feelings of inadequacy and competitiveness. It makes us feel alienated from each other. If we somehow became less materialistic – if we all agreed that it was socially acceptable to wear casual clothes and drive old cars, we wouldn't have to work as hard and the quality of our lives would improve. Ironically, many of the problems we struggle with every day are problems we ourselves have created.

The negative consequences of media would be ameliorated if we were more aware of the psychological techniques it employs. Just as a person with a skeptical attitude is less likely to be taken in by a con artist, a person who is wary of media's subliminal influences is less likely to be unknowingly manipulated by them. Ironically, the more we appreciate how persuasive advertising really is, the less persuasive it will become.

Similarly, the more we stare into the subliminal mirror and become cognizant of our secret unconscious impulses, the more those impulses will mature and the less we will be effected by them.

Chapter 6:
HAVE IT YOUR WAY
HOW TO USE SUBLIMINAL TECHNIQUES

Subliminal Advertising Is Generally Not Illegal

Contrary to what many people think, subliminal advertising is generally *not* illegal in the United States. The use of *flash frames* on television is clearly prohibited, but the use of other subliminal techniques is either lawful or unregulated.

To explain more precisely, the Federal *Trade* Commission (FTC) regulates advertising nationally, and is responsible for enforcing a Federal law which states, "*Unfair and deceptive acts* or practices in commerce are declared unlawful." (Emphasis added). The FTC has never addressed the issue of whether using subliminal embeds and related techniques is "unfair and deceptive" within the meaning of the statute. Although Wilson Bryan Key presented the Commission with innumerable examples of subliminal techniques years ago, the Commission declined to take any action against the alleged perpetrators.

Another bureaucracy, the Federal *Communications* Commission (FCC) is responsible for granting *broadcasting licenses* to radio and television stations. In 1974, a Christmas television commercial for a children's game utilized a subliminal *flash frame* that commanded "Get It!" In response, the Commission declared:

> We believe the use of *subliminal perception* is not consistent with the obligations of the licensee, and therefore we take this occasion to make clear that broadcasts employing *such techniques* are contrary to the public interests. Whether effective or not, such broadcasts are intended to be deceptive. (Emphasis added.)

The FCC's declaration apparently referred *only* to the use of *flash frames*. The FCC (like the FTC) has never prosecuted anyone for using embeds, figure- ground illusions, or other *non-flash-frame* subliminal devices.

Yet another federal agency, the Bureau of Alcohol, Tobacco, and Firearms (ATF), regulates Alcohol, Tobacco, and Firearm advertising. In August, 1984, the Bureau published the following illuminating comments following public hearings regarding the prohibition of subliminal techniques in liquor ads:

> Subliminal or similar techniques can take many forms in advertising. These forms include placing a frame in a film which appears at a speed at which the observer cannot consciously perceive its presence, but subconsciously, the word, phrase, or scene is registered. *Another, and more prevalent, form is the insertion of words or body forms (embeds) by the use of shadows or shading, or the substitution of forms and shapes generally associated with the body.* (Emphasis added.)

Although the ATF's comments clearly encompass subliminal *embeds*, the three (beer, wine, and hard liquor) regulations it actually passed referred only to *flash frames*. All three of these laws state:

> *Deceptive advertising techniques.* Subliminal or similar techniques are prohibited. "Subliminal or similar techniques," as used in this part, refers to any device or technique that is used to convey, or attempts to convey, a message to a person by means of images or sounds <u>of a very brief nature</u> that cannot be perceived at a normal level of awareness. (Underline emphasis added.)

Since the *comments* contradict the plain language of the regulations, it is not clear whether the regulations prohibit the use of embeds. The meaning of the three laws has not been clarified by the Courts, because the ATF has apparently never accused anyone of violating them.

In conclusion, the legality of subliminal advertising in the United States can be summarized as follows:

> * Flash frames on TV *are* prohibited. Flash frames for all liquor advertisements *are* prohibited. Flash frames in movies are *not* prohibited (unless they advertise liquor).

> * The use of embeds *may* be illegal in *alcohol* advertising, but the law is unclear and no one has ever been prosecuted for violating it.

> * "Unfair and deceptive acts" are illegal in all advertising, but no one has ever been prosecuted for using *non-flash-frame* subliminals on the grounds that they are unfair and deceptive.

It therefore appears that the use of *embeds* and related *non-flash-frame* subliminals in *print* media, *other* than for *alcohol* ads, *is legal* (at least as far as the laws are currently interpreted).

Looking the Other Way

The FTC, the FCC, and the ATF have good reasons for not prosecuting advertisers who use embeds. The public would undoubtedly be very upset if it was officially informed that television commercials and magazine ads often contain subliminal pornography. Not only would the issue be very "hot" politically, the economic consequences would be severe.

Moreover, although the issue has never been legally tested, prohibiting embeds and other *non-flash-frame* subliminals is probably unconstitutional. The Supreme Court has held that in order for a statute to be valid, it must *not* be *vague* or *overbroad*. The "vagueness" standard requires that the statute be clear enough so that people generally understand what it prohibits. The "overbroad" standard requires that the statute not inadvertently restrict a constitutionally protected right.

Prohibiting *flash frames* probably *is* constitutional. The ATF regulation that outlaws "images …of a very brief nature that cannot be perceived at a normal level of awareness," is easily understood, and does not unduly suppress free speech. On the other hand, *if* the ATF *comments* (which prohibit the "insertion of words or body forms [embeds] by the use of shadows or shading, or the substitution of forms and shapes generally associated with the body") became law, the law would probably be *unconstitutional.* The phrase is so convoluted and unclear that people would not be able to interpret it. Furthermore, it seems to outlaw artistic techniques (such as "shading," and the use of body parts) that are protected by the free speech provisions of the First Amendment.

Subliminal Advertising Is Psychologically Harmful

Many forms of subliminal advertising are psychologically harmful. After all, they are intended to stimulate drives and fantasies that are repressed because they are morally and consciously reprehensible. The emotions that are activated sometimes include the desire to murder, rape, and commit pedophilia.

In a literal sense, exposure to media is a form of *reverse* therapy, designed to make us emotionally disturbed and therefore better consumers. The effect of looking at any particular subliminal ad may be small, but the cumulative effect of looking at millions of them is undoubtedly considerable. Children receive the largest "dose" because they spend the most time watching TV.

It is not possible to determine how much of the emotional illness and destructive behavior in society is the result of subliminal manipulation, but certainly some of it is. Subliminal ads are targeted at specific psychological weaknesses of particularly vulnerable people. They must exert a dangerous influence on borderline personalities, who even under ordinary circumstances are unable to control their unconscious fantasies. Advertisements aimed at these individuals must occasionally push them "over the edge" and cause them to either harm themselves or commit horrible crimes.

"Drive activation" studies conducted on "normal" people confirm this concern. Five out of eighty hospital *employees* had "pathological reactions" when they were subliminally shown a picture of a nude woman's genital area, from the waist to the knees. Two of them became paranoid, one started scratching himself, one suddenly attacked the test verbally, and one became dizzy. Researchers have noted that "psychopathological" reactions to subliminal stimuli occur when: "1. . . .the stimulus makes contact with a drive that is *unacceptable* to the individual, thus producing a conflict, and 2. the individual lacks the "ego strength" to handle the conflict in a non-pathological manner." Since subliminal advertisements in mass media are perceived by hundreds of millions of people, the personalities of at least some viewers must satisfy both these criteria.

Subliminal Advertising Cannot Be Eliminated

Despite its pernicious effects, however, subliminal advertising cannot be legislatively enjoined. Like pornography, it is too difficult to define to effectively regulate. Subliminals are a form of art. A statute that outlawed "ambiguous phrases or embedded images" would not only be constitutionally invalid, it would be impossible to enforce. One can hardly imagine lawyers, judges, and juries seriously debating whether "In-N-Out Burger" refers to sex or fast food, or whether the Benson ad depicts a backbone or a penis. As discussed above, although *flash frames* can be regulated, the techniques used in the advertisements in this book cannot be practically or legally prohibited.

This should not disturb us. The real problem with subliminal advertising is not that advertisers engage in it, but that society is in denial about it. If subliminal techniques were studied in schools, and people better understood how media really manipulates the mind, the frequency and effectiveness of subliminal advertising would diminish. *Advertisers would cease using extremely disturbing techniques, especially those directed towards children, because they would be afraid of getting caught.* The marketplace would regulate the problem more effectively than the government ever could, and artistic freedom would be preserved.

Using Subliminal Techniques

Since subliminal persuasion is a part of life, it makes sense to learn as much about it as possible, and to examine it from all angles. The flip side of understanding how subliminals influence you is understanding how you can use them to influence others. The following section reviews principles previously discussed, but presents them from a practical "how to" perspective. Many of the applications are useful in a variety of creative contexts, and completely harmless.

The Ambiguity Principle

The essence of subliminal advertising is *ambiguity*. Subliminal messages are most often "delivered" with words or pictures that have more than one meaning. Both meanings are perceived unconsciously, but if one of them is psychologically threatening, it is repressed. The viewer is only aware of the nonthreatening interpretation.

The use of double exposures and embedded optical illusions is a subsection of this concept. An optical illusion is an image with two visual interpretations (i.e. a penis and a backbone), only one of which (the backbone) is perceived consciously.

This principle can be appropriately labeled *The Ambiguity Principle*. It applies to all the advertisements in this book. The Smirnoff (drink-in-the-face) ad, for example, uses a picture with a dual meaning (pleasant party vs. argument) in conjunction with ambiguous text ("the wine sat there..."). The first Benson ad uses dual meanings (sexy embrace v. sexual anxiety), ambiguous text (crushed in the clinch), and an ambiguous optical illusion (penis/backbone). Some ads, such as the Jameson Irish (severed head) illustration, rely primarily on ambiguous illusions, while others, such as the Lazy Boy ad, emphasize the use of dual meanings. In any event, ambiguity is the basis of the subliminal "punch" in all of them.

Ambiguity is the most common, but not the only way to present a subliminal message. Subliminals can also be delivered through the use of flash frames in moving pictures, or sub-audible whispers that are only heard unconsciously.

Presenting the Ambiguity

Constructing ambiguous *text* is self-explanatory, and endlessly challenging. Ideally, the secret meaning should be sexual, and below the threshold of awareness. "Jiffy Lube" is a good example. It is a better name than "Midas Mufflers" because it incorporates sexual associations the viewer might not be aware of.

Pictures with *dual meanings* can be created by:

1. *Hiding the face* (or part of the face) to make it more difficult to tell what the model is feeling. (Dad in the Lazy Boy ad.)

2. Making the model's expression fall precisely in *between two conflicting emotions*, such as fear and smugness. (The Benson ads in Figure 1.2 and Figure 3.1 are good examples of this.)
3. Providing only subtle *incidental cues* regarding the true meaning of the picture that only the unconscious will pick up. (The poorly fitting nightgown in the *Playgirl* necrophilia ad and the blurred hand in the Dish on Demand ad illustrate this technique.)

Subliminal content can be presented through <u>optical illusions</u> in the following ways:

1. Through *embeds* (as in the penis/ backbone ad);
2. Through manipulations of *figure-ground* (as in the demon in the Nightmare ad);
3. Through application of any of the other Gestalt principles (as in the Naturalizer ad);
4. Through faint *double exposures* (as in the third Belair penis ad).

Sometimes, if the picture is sufficiently threatening, the "filter" will block its meaning even though it is not ambiguous, and not hidden. (This was illustrated by the Health and Fitness cover in Figure 2.12.)

The Content of the "Secret" Message

There are two approaches to constructing the *content* of the subliminal message:

1. The hidden message can fulfill unconscious *fantasies* (as in the Smirnoff drink-in-the-face ad or the Wallpaper cover), or
2. The hidden message can activate maladaptive behaviors by stimulating unconscious *anxieties* (as in the Jameson Irish severed-head ad).

The two methodologies frequently overlap. For example, the Sauza Stay Pure ads stimulate latent homosexual inclinations, thus fulfilling unconscious fantasies and, at the same time, generating sexual anxieties.

Unconscious emotions that are often stimulated by advertising include:

1. Men's fears of impotency and castration;
2. Women's fears of rape or being violated;
3. Women's hostility towards men;
4. Men's hostility towards women;
5. The desire to dominate and subjugate the opposite gender;
6. Repressed homosexual inclinations (in both sexes);
7. Resentment of children and the confinements of family and marriage;
8. Feelings of self-destruction, suicide, and hopelessness.

Obviously, these are just a few examples. The possibilities are unlimited, and can include much more disturbing impulses.

An Exercise

The following exercise illustrates how the *Ambiguity Principle* might be applied to a real life situation. See if you can solve the "problem" yourself, before you read the possible "solution."

The Problem: You are an art director of an agency that has just been assigned the task of creating a magazine ad for Monument Cigars. Your research department has discovered that the product is consumed by men, who unconsciously smoke in order to dominate and irritate their wives.

A Possible Solution: Your ad portrays a group of men drinking beer, smoking cigars, and watching a football game on a TV in the background. They are laughing and yelling, and appear to be having a great time. The wife of the most prominent male is offering everyone a cigar from a box, clearly revealing the sponsor's brand. The wife's face is partially obscured by her hair and by shadows, making it difficult to tell what she is thinking. Upon close inspection, however, she appears to be somewhat distressed.

The meaning of the picture is ambiguous. On a conscious level, the reader will perceive the wife as happily condoning her husband's cigar smoking. The men will appear to be excited about the football game on TV.

Unconsciously, however, male viewers will perceive the men in the picture as being jubilant because they have forced the woman to provide them with cigars, despite the fact that she would prefer they didn't smoke.

An ambiguous phrase that reinforces both the subliminal and consciously perceived interpretations of the picture would complete the effect. "Score With Monument Cigars" might be appropriate because it has three meanings. It refers to "scoring" in the football game, to "scoring" in the sense of having sex, and to "scoring" in the sense that the man in the picture has defeated his wife and forced her to support his smoking habit.

An additional enhancement might involve embedding a sexual graphic in the ad (such as a penis in one of the cigars) that would make the husband seem more virile and masculine.

"Monument," by the way, subliminally refers to "gravestones," and activates the viewer's self-destructive smoking tendencies.

If you enjoyed this exercise, more are included in Appendix A. As in the foregoing example, they are all based on actual motivational research.

Subliminal Salesmanship

When I was in law school, I briefly worked as a trainee car salesman for a major automaker. The first thing they taught us was to "qualify" our customers – to act like we were being friendly and engaging in polite conversation, while we secretly tried to uncover the motivations and emotional "triggers" that would lead to a sale. We were shown videotapes categorizing prospective customers according to their psychological orientations, and suggesting techniques we might use to "sell" them. An example was a middle-aged man looking for a family car, who secretly wanted a sports car to compensate for his anxieties about growing older. The way to "sell" him would be to suggest a "family car" that was smaller and snappier than average, and emphasize its speed and sports-car like handling.

My experience illustrates that all businesses, and all advertising, use "subliminal techniques" to some degree, although we don't often think of it in that way. By "qualifying" the customer, I was supposed to figure out what his unconscious motivations were. When "selling" the customer, I was supposed to pretend to address his consciously acceptable feelings (the need for a family car) while secretly satisfying his unconscious impulses (the desire for sexual rejuvenation). Many talented business people intuitively understand these techniques, and use them all the time, without realizing that they are "subliminal."

The ads in this book are extreme examples of principles we all are familiar with. Clarifying what "subliminal salesmanship" is can help anyone become a better salesperson.

In a similar way, we all unconsciously use "subliminal techniques" when engaging in ordinary social interactions. When we want someone to like us, for example, we lean forward when they are talking, and act interested in what they are saying. We laugh at their jokes, and find ways to compliment them. We may not fully understand what we are doing, but we are emitting and they are receiving "subliminal cues" that influence our relationship. This is an example of "implicit knowledge" that is acquired and applied unconsciously. Many of these ideas were pointed out in 1936 by Dale Carnegie in *How to Win Friends and Influence People*. Mr. Carnegie was not psychologically oriented and did not use the word "subliminal" in his book, but he clarified consciously what we all understand intuitively. His insights remain popular to the present day.

The Ambiguity Principle in Other Contexts

The ambiguity principle plays an important role in many contexts other than advertising.

Fictional characters in literature and movies, for example, are often given an ambiguous name whose "secret" meaning is consistent with the person's role in the story. We think of this as a literary technique, but it really is an example of how subliminals can be used to enhance art. The dual meaning of the name is perceived unconsciously, and influences the reader's perception of the character.

Silas Marner is an example I learned about in high school. The classic novel is about a miserly weaver who becomes isolated and withdrawn after being falsely accused of stealing. The weaver's name "Silas Marner" is unconsciously interpreted to mean "Silent Mourner."

Similarly, in *Star Wars* the principle evil character "Darth Vader" subliminally means "Dark Raider."

"James Bond" is a secret agent who couples or "bonds" with his female companions after destroying his male competitors.

In the popular 1987 film *Wall Street*, Michael Douglas' character is named "Gordon Gekko," a financier who takes over companies and liquidates them for profit. "Gekko" subliminally means "Get Co.," or "Get Companies." His younger protégé, played by Charlie Sheen, is named "Bud Fox." "Bud Fox" means "budding fox," or a fox coming of age. "Bud" also refers to "Buddy," or "friend." Sheen's character becomes a "friendly fox" at the end of the movie, when he outwits Gekko and re-connects with his real father.

People that are not religious generally do not consciously realize that "Peter, Paul, and Mary" are all names from the Bible.

Real names that become popular and have a pleasant "feel" to them often have a subliminal meaning people are not generally aware of. For example, everyone realizes that the "Tiger" in "Tiger Woods" refers to a lithe jungle animal. But have you ever considered that "woods" refers to both a forest (where tigers hang out) and a "woody," a type of golf club? Mr. Woods did not pick his name, but its pleasant and congruent unconscious associations contribute to his popularity.

Famous, successful women often have a feminine first name and a masculine last name, making them seem strong and feminine at the same time. "Barbara Walters," "Julia Roberts," and "Martha Stewart" are all examples of this. Again, none of these women created their name, but they were fortunate to be born with one that subliminally facilitated their careers. If you are a female writer or performer contemplating a pen or stage name, you might consider making use of the ambiguity principle.

A man with a masculine first name and a feminine last name usually conveys an effeminate impression, which often, but not always, is undesirable. Having two masculine names, on the other hand, makes the person seem very manly, as in the case of John Wayne, Michael Douglas, and Rod Stewart.

The ambiguity principle plays a role in *politics*. "Al Gore" is an example of a terrible name with unpleasant associations, because the word "gore" reminds one of a bloody attack. Since the 2000 presidential election was such a close race, Mr. Gore might have won if he had a name with more positive associations, such as "Don Goodwin" or "Franklin C. Wright." Franklin C. Wright, by the way, is an imaginary character who was kind enough to provide an endorsement for the back cover of this book. "Frank" means "straightforward and sincere," and "C. Wright" means "view correctly."

The ambiguity principle also applies to *titles*. In Hemingway's *A Farewell to Arms*, for example, a soldier and a beautiful woman escape the ravages of World War II and find sanctuary in Switzerland. The woman later dies of natural causes. The title refers to both the man's departure from the war, and the tragic loss of the loving "arms" of his partner.

Similarly, *The Bridges of Madison County* is about life's transitions as well as elevated roadways.

All the Presidents Men is a book and movie about Richard M. Nixon's criminal subordinates. The title also reminds us of the nursery rhyme *Humpty Dumpty*, who "had a great fall" and couldn't be put back "together again."

When the *plot* of a story suggests multiple meanings, we think of it as having depth and being artistically developed. *The Old Man and The Sea,* as a simplistic example, is both the tale of a frustrated fisherman and an allegory of life. Our peripheral awareness of the allegory makes the story seem more interesting. When the hidden meaning of the plot is more subliminal, so that we are completely unaware of it or have to think about it to "get it," we appreciate the story even more. Great literary works of art are often built around story lines that have layers of subliminally perceived insights.

"What's the difference between a lawyer and a bottom fish? One is a *bloodsucking bottom feeder* and the other has gills." This joke illustrates that *humor* is also related to the ambiguity principle. No one knows exactly what makes something funny, but often funny things involve an ambiguity interpreted in a suprising manner. Perhaps the jolt of amusement we feel when we hear a joke results from the fact that we unconsciously understand the secondary meaning of the punch line before we consciously become aware of it.

Creating Audio Subliminals

Audio subliminals can be created by reducing the loudness of a sound so that the listener is not aware of it consciously. Just as faint visual images are perceived unconsciously, softly whispered audio messages also make a subliminal impact.

Awareness of a stimulus is strongly influenced by where the listener's attention is directed. If you play a recording of a verbal message, and gradually turn down the volume, the listener will be able to hear the message at a much lower intensity than if you secretly played it so that the listener was not aware of it in the first place. Similarly, a listener is less likely to be aware of a verbal message if it is recorded over music. Naturally, audio subliminals can also be created through the use of words with ambiguous meanings.

Judas Priest

Some people believe some rock and roll records contain embedded backward verbal messages that are perceived on a subliminal level. In 1990, Judas Priest was sued in Nevada state court because the rock group had allegedly embedded the backwards message "Do It!" in the song "Better By You, Better Than Me" on the album *Stained Class*. The suit was brought by the families of two teenagers who had spent the day drinking beer, smoking marijuana, and listening to the album before they shot themselves in a nearby park. One of the youths died instantly, and the other passed away three years later as a result of his injuries. The album cover featured a psychedelic picture of a metal spike piercing a human head.

Judas Priest prevailed at the conclusion of the trial. The defense showed that one of the boys had contemplated suicide prior to the day in question, and that both of them had emotional and drug problems. Observers in the courtroom reported that the alleged audio embed was not very convincing. The plaintiffs' attorneys were probably willing to proceed to trial, despite the weakness of their case, because they hoped to force a lucrative settlement. The victory for the defense did not resolve the issue of whether subliminals in rock music are intentionally created, or whether backwards recordings adversely affect listeners.

The Subliminal Perception of Backwards Speech

It is *unlikely* that *backwards* verbal messages are understood unconsciously. Backwards speech does not occur in nature, and there is no reason for the unconscious to have developed the ability to comprehend it.

A study conducted by Volkey and Read tentatively seems to confirm this. Subjects first listened to *backward* phrases containing *homophones* (ambiguous words with two spellings) such as "Climbing a mountain is a remarkable *feat*." They were then *read* a list of homophones and asked to spell them. The spellings they gave were *not* influenced by the backward recordings, suggesting they did not comprehend them on a subliminal level.

Needless to say, further study in this controversial area is clearly warranted. If you are a serious researcher, you might be interested in the experiments suggested in Appendix B.

The Walrus Is Paul

Although backward recordings may not have a subliminal influence, they probably *are* intentionally created. The Beatles may have initiated the idea when they implanted "Paul is Dead" "clues" in their records. If you turn up the volume of "Strawberry Fields" on *Magical Mystery Tour,* at the very end of the song, on the left track, you will hear John say "I buried Paul." On the *White Album*, the lyrics to Lennon's song "Glass Onion," "declare "Here's another clue for you all: the Walrus is Paul." It seems likely that the Beatles were being playful, and later came to appreciate how the hidden "Paul is dead" references enhanced the aura of mystery surrounding their music.

It is logical to conclude that other recording artists, aware of the free publicity the Beatles generated, may have deliberately implanted backwards messages in their records. Fans discovering the messages told other fans, and the mystery enhanced the musicians cult-like appeal. For example, one can hear the phrase, "I sing because I live with Satan! The Lord turns me off!" when the song "Stairway to Heaven," by Led Zeppelin, is played backwards. The backwards message occurs at precisely the moment the forward singer exclaims "There's still time to change the road you're on," and is consistent with the theme of the album. The cover features satanic symbols and imagery, and the song itself describes followers of an evil "pied piper."

Although backward masking may not subliminally manipulate listeners, *sub-audible* whispers *are* perceived subliminally. Moreover, they are more difficult to detect and less expensive to create. It is likely, therefore, that much of the commercial music we listen to contains low volume messages designed to affect our mood by "activating" unconscious thought processes.

Subliminals in Visual Art

Subliminal illusions can enhance the emotional impact of visual art. If you paint a picture of a beach on a rainy day, for example, and you embed the image of a sad face in the clouds, the embedded face will make your painting "feel" sadder.

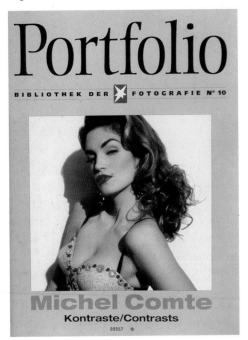

A simple, but very effective variation of that idea appears in the book cover depicted in Figure 6.1. "Portfolio" is a collection of photographs by Michel Comte, an extremely talented fashion and war photographer, and presumably the same "Michel Comte" who created the Nightmare ad in Figure 2.40.*

Please study the cover for a moment before reading further. It portrays a provocative, sexy picture of Cindy Crawford.

Figure 6.1

Did you notice that the shadow behind her forms the shape of a man's head? It's just below the threshold of consciousness – most people don't initially "see" it, but easily become aware of it as soon as it is pointed out.

The masculine shadow makes Ms. Crawford seem more interesting and intense. It is congruent with the title of the book, which is "Contrasts."

*See page 265.

The painting by Jurgen Peters in Figure 6.2 is another example of subliminal art. It hung behind my desk in my law office in San Francisco for many years. Altogether, over fifteen hundred clients were exposed to it. Since the subject fascinates me, I asked many of them what they saw in it.

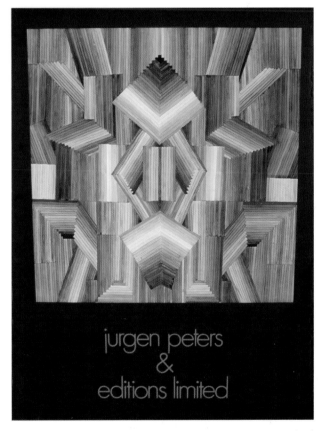

jurgen peters
&
editions limited

Figure 6.2

Not one of them realized it contained the hidden image of a man standing in the middle of the picture. The image is *cubist*, and not at all literal. The colorful diamond shape near the top/center forms his head, and the diagonal lines extending down at approximately 45 degree angles form his arms. The vertical rectangle in the center of the picture forms his torso, and the reddish shapes at the center/bottom (just above the word "Jurgen" and the word "Peters") form his legs and feet.

In the context of this book, the hidden figure is not that subliminal. Some readers may find it fairly easily. In the laboratory of my law practice, however, the image was completely invisible.

Interestingly, even when people become aware of the man, they hardly ever realize that his hands are on his genitals.

The picture illustrates how subliminals can be used to enhance art. The hidden image makes the painting much more interesting than it would be if it were merely a colorful abstract.

A more elaborate and brilliantly executed example of an illusion used in an artistic commercial context appears in the book cover in Figure 6.3. See if you can find it before reading further.

At first glance, the picture appears to portray a woman holding a piece of material, with a small town visible in the background.

The town and the material, however, form the shape of a *demonic infant*. The illusion is more visible from a distance, and easier to see in the reduction in Figure 6.4 on page 193. It may take a little effort to "find" it, but you will appreciate it when you do. Switch your figure-ground and concentrate on the *dark* space, not the light space, between the woman and the right side of the page. The child's teeth are formed by the words "A Novel." Its eyes, nose, and other ghoulish facial features are formed by the buildings. The curve of the material, behind the woman's fingers, forms the infant's arm.

The artwork in the *Mirabilis* cover is creative and ingenious, and the subliminal monster child is consistent with the story line of the novel.*

Hidden images are inspiring in at least two ways. When the viewer is not aware of them, they subliminally enhance the appeal of the artwork. If the viewer happens to discover them, they make the artwork even more interesting.

One media executive I interviewed suggested that, in the past, subliminal techniques were for the most part employed exclusively by big agencies, because only they had the resources to develop them. Modern computer programs now make it possible for anyone to create sophisticated double exposures and embedded illusions digitally. The use of subliminal techniques is therefore likely to become much more widespread in the future.

*See page 266.

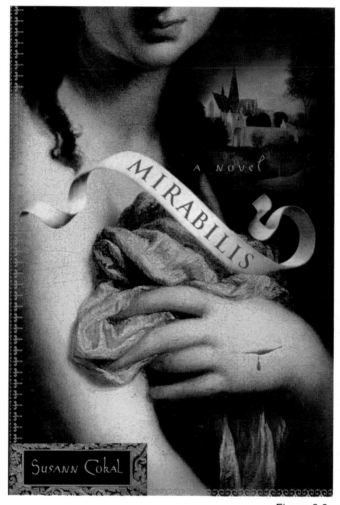

Figure 6.3

The Unconscious Creation of Subliminals

Artists don't have to know what they are doing when they create something unconsciously inspiring. Indeed, often their objective is to simply relax and let the words or images flow freely from their unconscious into the medium they are working on. Abstract painters often remark that embedded images sometimes emerge, quite unintentionally, in their work. Artists who understand subliminal perception can capitalize on such spontaneously appearing ambiguities.

As a personal example, song writing is my avocation. A few years ago I wrote a love song to an imaginary woman named Christine, and came up with the following lyrics:

> Christy lay your heaven down on me
> Show me your love and set me free

Suddenly I realized that "Christy" is ambiguous. It is not just a woman's name, it is also a reference to *Christ*. I had unconsciously woven religious imagery into a romantic love song. I had not intended the duality initially, but I capitalized on it by adding the lines "Show me your miracles" and "Forgive me for my sins." Although people listening to the song are generally not aware of the ambiguity, the subliminal meaning enhances the emotional impact of the verse.

If you are a visual artist, you can easily make use of this technique. Try switching your figure ground and viewing the projects you are working on from different perspectives. Occasionally, you will discover embedded materials that are emotionally consistent with your work. When you do, you can capitalize on the subliminal effect by enhancing them. Through experimentation, you can determine how "far you can go" and still retain the images' hidden character.

On Purpose or Not

Logically, there are three possibilities regarding each of the illustrations in this book:

1. The artist *deliberately* created the subliminals to psychologically manipulate the viewer;
2. The artist *unconsciously* created the subliminals without realizing that she or he was doing so; or
3. The appearance of the subliminals is entirely *coincidental.*

Figure 6.4

It is likely that the subliminals in many of the ads, such as the Benson penis/backbone, were deliberately created. The scene had to be set up, the text had to be written, and the photographer, the copywriter, and the art director all had to work together to produce the subliminal effect.

Other illustrations, such as the Rough Murder (Figure 4.10) or the World Trade Center attack (Figure 4.11) are harder to characterize because they contain only one layer of ambiguity. The artist who made the Rough Murder ad conceivably could have taken many pictures in different poses, and simply picked the one that looked the most dramatic. The monster in the smoke billowing out of the World Trade Center conceivably could be just a coincidence. The photographers may have created and selected the pictures in question for unconscious reasons.

In my opinion, it is more likely that the subliminals in both circumstances were created consciously. It is illogical to think that people in media use subliminals in many circumstances, but not when the subject matter is particularly disturbing. It is important to note, however, that *it really doesn't matter.*

Both illustrations incorporate content that is perceived only on a subliminal level. Both have a subliminal effect, *regardless of whether the artist that created them intended them to.*

The materials in this book explain *why* the pictures are so dramatic.

The ambiguity principle clarifies an artistic process some artists have applied and understood only on an intuitive level.

Once you understand the ambiguity principle, you can use it to create subliminal effects consciously, and to capitalize on subliminal effects that occur by chance.

Chapter 7
FROM LA BAMBA TO THE INTERNET
BRINGING IT ALL HOME

On the Signpost Up Ahead

Rod Serling could not have come up with a more intriguing episode of *The Twilight Zone* than what has been going on in the "real" world. A giant, secret experiment has been underway in which all of us have been exposed to millions of subliminal messages, intended to stimulate unconscious anxiety and make us insecure and materialistic. To some extent the messages can be detected if you know how to look for them, but the concept is so disturbing that most people avoid thinking about it. If they do stumble on a subliminal, they conclude it is a coincidence, or minimize its significance without ever putting the big picture together. This may sound like a science fiction story, but if you look at all the evidence, you have to conclude it's true.

The "experiment" has been going on for a very long time. The Budweiser ad in Figure 7.1 appeared in *Life* magazine in August, 1959, when Eisenhower was President, Ritchie Valens' "La Bamba" was a big hit, and I was six years old. I may have perused it wearing my Davy Crockett coonskin cap.

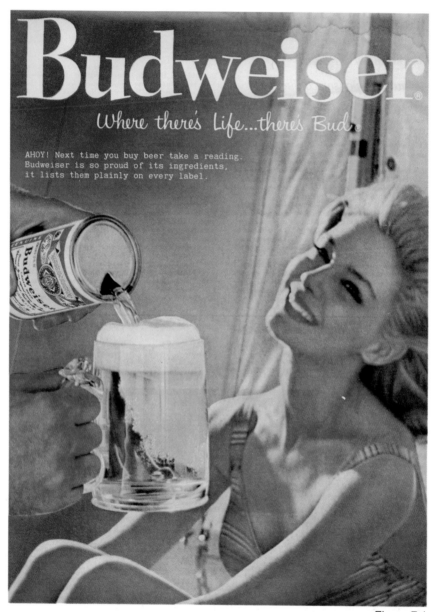

Figure 7.1

It came out just eleven months after James Vicary held his famous press conference in New York, announcing the formation of the "Subliminal Projection Corporation" and his plans to sell subliminal ads to major corporations. It appeared just five months after *Life* magazine ran a major story entitled "Hidden Sell Technique Is Almost Here." The article chronicled the intense controversy raging at the time, and revealed that subliminal techniques had been incorporated into at least two Hollywood horror films. It included the picture of a skull and the word "Blood," shown in Figure 1.2(b), being subliminally flashed behind the lead actress in *My World Dies Screaming.*

The article revealed that a psychologist name Robert E. Corrigan had been employed as a consultant for the studio that made the movie. He and a partner had formed the "Preconscious Process and Equipment Corporation," which competed with Vicary's company and had the same goal of selling subliminal techniques. The article indicated Corrigan and his partner had performed "extensive experiments in subliminal perception since 1950," and that subliminal devices could be used to "magnify" emotions other than horror. Motherly love, for example, could be expressed subliminally by the drawing of a baby, or the need for help could be expressed by hands clasped in prayer. Corrigan believed the use of subliminals represented "an authentic and honest approach" that could "increase the entertainment impact of motion picture art."

Given this background, it is not suprising that subliminal techniques seem to have been incorporated into the Budweiser ad. Ostensibly, it portrays a pretty lady in a bathing suit, smiling suggestively as a man pours her a beer. The woman's seductive attention seems to be split between the viewer and the unseen beer holder.

Hidden within the glass, however, is an erotic, surrealistic image of the woman performing fellatio on her male companion. The man is naked and standing with his back against the glass, facing to the right side of the picture. The dark hair on his chest is clearly visible.

The "woman" is also naked, and kneeling with her back to the camera. Her buttocks are provocatively positioned near the center of the bottom of the glass.

The impressionistic image illustrates the sexual fantasies inspired by the photo. It is outlined in Figure 7.2 (a) on page 197.

The woman's back is also an erect penis. Its testicles are formed by her buttocks, and the tip can be found just below her "hair."

Figure 7.2(a-c)

The yellow bubbles in the glass form the profile of a head of a man smiling and looking down on the orgasmic scene. The head is looking towards the left side of the picture, and represents the viewer, who is either voyeuristically watching the couple or about to join them. His lips are almost kissing the head of the penis embedded in the fellatio woman's back. It is outlined in black in Figure 7.2(c).

The ad probably marks the beginning of Madison Avenue's serious efforts to incorporate subliminal devices into print advertisements. Ironically, the industry energetically attempted to assure the public it had lost all interest in the techniques, at the same time it secretly began using them.

In and Out Burger

If you fast forward to the present, it appears that subliminal techniques seem to have been incorporated into every aspect of modern society, affecting us no matter where we go and what we do on a daily basis. Imagining yourself meandering through a typical day will illustrate this point.

You begin with lunch at "In-N-Out Burger," a popular fast food chain on the west coast of the U.S. Even before reading this book you probably realized that the name, "In-N-Out," refers to sex as well as the speed with which the company's hamburgers are provided. There is, however, a much deeper, more provocative meaning to the name that you have probably never thought of.

"In" refers to eating and taking food in.

"Out" refers to *defecating.*

Before you throw this book across the room in disgust, please give this idea a moment's deliberation.

To a breast-feeding infant, food is intensely gratifying in many ways. Mommy's milk is warm and satisfying, and being held and nurtured while eating is also euphoric.

At some point after he or she is done, Baby defecates. This is again extremely gratifying in different ways. The release of warm, soft fecal matter, which is pleasant in itself, leads to lots of love and attention as Baby is cleaned, patted, powdered, and played with. Babies are generally much happier after their diapers are changed, and, I suppose, with good reason.

Although we may have forgotten these experiences on a conscious level, we remember them unconsciously, and seek out food as a nurturing "love substitute" as adults. The name, "In-N-Out Burger" brilliantly capitalizes on this. Burgers go in, and naturally, burgers come out, "activating" unconscious fantasies of being nurtured and held.

These infantile associations are reinforced inside the restaurant in very creative ways. The aprons worn by the employees are fastened in the back by enormous safety pins, which become visible to the customers when the employees turn to fill orders. The apron and safety pin together unmistakably resemble diapers (Figure 7.3(a)). The ketchup dispensers in Figure 7.3(b) look remarkably like toilets.

The logo in Figure 7.3(c) is also very clever. The bent yellow arrow not only represents an erection, but also the movement of food through the intestinal track. The tip of the arrow falls directly over the letter "U," which forms the shape of a toilet-like container. The term "Company Store" (as opposed to "restaurant,") refers to a place where "company," or "companionship" is "stored" and therefore for sale and available. And finally, an "In-n" is a place where one seeks lodging and shelter from the world.

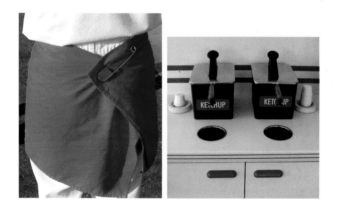

Figure 7.3(a-c)

Macy's Biggie

Imagine that, after lunch, you drop by Macy's Department Store to buy some jogging shorts. You discover the picture appearing in Figure 7.4 is prominently displayed in the sports department. It's about two feet wide and attached to the wall without any text or accompanying explanation.

When I chanced upon it in the Fall of 2001, I almost fell over. I couldn't "see" anything in the picture except an erect penis sticking through the fly of someone's pants, with the word "Biggie" tattooed on it.

The image is extremely disturbing because it's impossible to look at it and not imagine a tattoo needle painfully piercing one's genitals.

Furthermore, the red snake forming a question mark behind the word, "Biggie" poses the challenging query: "Is it really that big?"

The day I stumbled on the Biggie, I got so excited I immediately ran home to get my camera. After taking a few shots, I interviewed two different shoppers in the store and asked them what they thought was portrayed in the picture. They both looked at me in absolute disgust, as if I were a horrible pervert, and walked away without saying a word. This mystified me. If they thought it looked like a penis, why would they be upset with me? If they thought it was something innocuous, why didn't they just tell me what they saw? I can only guess that awareness of the phallus started to enter their consciousness and caused them to feel anxious.

Shortly afterwards, a young saleswoman happened by. I pointed to the picture and told her I would like to take a look at "the clothing item featured in that ad." "Oh, we don't sell those," she responded, "I don't even know what those are." When I asked her what the purpose of the picture was, she told me she wasn't sure, but it had "always been there." When I went back a month later, the sign was gone. I don't know if our conversation had anything to do with its disappearance.

The Biggie ad is one of my favorite illustrations in this book because it's so controversial. For the most part, although people are willing to accept the existence of subliminal penises in magazine ads, they have a much harder time accepting the idea that they pop up in department stores.

There is no logic to this viewpoint. If subliminal embeds inspire sales you would expect to find them everywhere, not just in certain venues.

People react to the "Biggie" sign in fascinating ways. Many immediately see it for what it is. Others "confabulate" seemingly "rational" explanations that are obviously illogical when you analyze them.

Figure 7.4

Some suggest the picture portrays a man's chest covered by a jacket. This cannot be because there are no breasts, no cleavage, no muscles, and nothing else to indicate you are looking at a torso. Furthermore, there is no reason for shadows to appear on either side of the person's body.

Others claim the picture depicts a man's calf in a pant leg. This is equally illogical because the garment is closed at the bottom and open at the top. The "leg" would have to be upside down, pointing up, for the picture to make sense. If it were, however, the Nike logo would be upside down.

Even if the garment were zippered closed at the bottom *and* the top, so that it bulged open in the middle, the appendage inside couldn't possibly be a leg or an arm. It is as smooth and as cylindrical as a tootsie roll, with nary a hint of muscular curvature.

Too Much Pleasure

While meandering through a bookstore in the mall, you come across The Haagan-Dazs ad (shown in Figure 7.5) in a magazine. It is a perfect illustration of the "Ambiguity Principle."

The picture portrays a handsome young man eating ice cream beneath a tag line which declares "Thank God she's late."

On a conscious level, the reader concludes the man is grateful that his girlfriend has been delayed because he gets to eat all her ice cream.

On a subliminal level, however, "Thank God she's late" means "Thank God her period is late." The ad associates the product with the desire to be fertile and impregnate females.

Although many men are consciously terrified of getting their girlfriends pregnant, on a primal, unconscious level they yearn to do so in order to sow their seed and duplicate their DNA. The fantasy of impregnation is secretly gratifying, notwithstanding conscious aversion to the idea.

Lifting Me Higher

Driving home in the car, you turn on your favorite "oldies" station, and enjoy listening to the classic "*Higher and Higher" by Jackie Wilson. You can't help singing along to the lively lyrics:

> You know your love
> Is lifting me higher
> Than I have ever
> Been lifted before
> So keep it up
> Quenching my desire
> And I'll be at your side
> For ever more

Literally millions of people, of all different ages, are listening to the song along with you. Hardly any of them realize that while the singer is ostensibly thanking his girlfriend for *uplifting his spirits*, in a very graphic manner he is secretly applauding her for generating his *erections*.

The other verses confirm the singer is rejoicing because he has been cured of his impotency problems:

Figure 7.5

Now once I was **down**hearted
Disappointment was my closest friend
But then you **came** and it soon departed
And you know **he** never
Showed **his** face again

I'm so glad I've finally found you
Yes that one in a million girls
And I **whip** my loving arms around you
I can **stand up**, and face the world. (Emphasis added)

The song is another entertaining example of the ambiguity principle. I know many musicians who have played it in bands for years, without ever becoming aware of its subliminal meaning.

Beat Your Husband

Back at home you go on the Internet to check movie listings, and come across the K-Mart "All Tents On Sale" banner ad depicted in Figure 7.6. It tells an amusing story with a highly motivating theme.

The ad portrays a couple, probably married, playing cards while camping in a tent.

The shadow falling across the husband forms the profile of the head of a crocodile, complete with jagged teeth. Its jaws are about to snap off the man's hands and soda can, which from a distance are suggestive of his genitals.

The man looks happy and oblivious to his fate. The woman's expression is more ambiguous; is she merely concentrating on her hand, or is she irritated and determined? She seems to be hitting the crocodile on the head, encouraging it to consume her spouse's private parts for dinner.

The secret message of the ad is "Win the game and castrate your husband (that irritating nerd) by shopping till you drop at K-Mart!"

Figure 7.6

Dialing Down the Center

When you are finished surfing the Net, you relax for a few minutes by watching TV. Between the six o'clock news and a situation comedy, you are secretly inspired by a thirty-second telephone commercial. Carrot-Top, a well-known comedian, is comically portrayed as a policeman interrogating a sexy blonde woman with prominent breasts (Figure 7.7(a)). "Miss Lewis!" he commands, "Can you tell me again how you use 1-800 Call ATT for collect calls?" "Well, I just dial down the center," she replies sensually. "With what?, Miss Lewis. With *what?*" Carrot-Top angrily slaps a picture of a phone in a phone booth on the table, and demonstrates how to "dial down the center" with his finger (Figure 7.7(d)). Remarkably, Miss Lewis' naked breasts are reflected in the background, in the metallic part of the phone. You do not become consciously aware of them because they are only shown for about two seconds. The "center" of her *cleavage* is adjacent to the right vertical row of the phone's buttons. Her *left* breast (the one on the right as you look at them) is outlined by shadows on the right bottom of the photo. Her nipple is cut off by the right edge of the picture. Her *right* breast (the left one as you look at them) is *behind* the left vertical row of buttons. Her nipple is obscured by the star symbol. Her armpit is formed by the vertical shadows on the left side of the picture. Her breasts are incredibly erotic, and almost beg the male viewer to "reach out and touch" them.

The Dial-Down-the-Center commercial subliminally presents a voyeuristic bondage fantasy, simultaneously observed by millions of small children. In the beginning of the interrogation, Carrot-Top excitedly murmurs "Yes!" when he confirms that Miss Lewis is single. He briefly appears to hit her in the head as he does so (Figure 7.7(b)). Miss Lewis is extremely submissive, and clearly enjoys being abused. Her hands are subliminally tied to her chair (Figure 7.7(f)). Her nude breasts represent the male viewer's unconscious fantasy of forcibly stripping her naked, sexually overpowering and satiating her, while other men look on with envy. Predictably, Miss Lewis sighs contentedly when Carrot-Top is done. He stares into the one-way mirror and brags to the other cops who have been watching, "God, I'm good!"

Figure 7.7(a-g)

Cast Away

Off to the movies, you discover the poster for the film *Cast Away* featured in Figure 7.8. This illustration was taken from a magazine, but the same picture was also used in billboards and even stand-up displays in video stores. It portrays Tom Hanks yelling joyfully because, after much hard work, he has created a fire by rubbing two sticks together.

If you take a long look at the fire, however, you'll find there is more for him to be yelling about. It contains a cartoonish image of a naked, beautiful, large-breasted woman. She is standing with her back and side to the viewer and looking at Tom. His eyes are fixed on her genitals. The blonde's most prominent feature is a horizontal, extremely erotic orange breast, pointed slightly upwards, just above the level of Mr. Hanks' eyes. It is revealing to note that fire doesn't generally burn *sideways*.

The blonde has a sex partner: a male, subliminal demon creature drawn in the grass between the orange flames and Hanks' head. Its arms are extended upward, its legs are spread, and it is facing the fiery maiden. It has an erect penis, formed as a white, horizontal bar, protruding into her vaginal area.

An African, "Zulu warrior" type person can be found at the maiden's feet, staring up her. Many more faces, creatures, and genitalia can be found hidden in the flames and grass throughout the picture, although the ones I have discussed are the most dramatic. The primary figures are outlined in Figure 7.9 on page 211.

Cast Away, by the way, is an ambiguous title. It refers not only to the protagonist's status as a person marooned on an island, but also as a rejected lover, which is the central theme of the story.

Sweet Dreams

When the movie is over you go home and go to bed. After such a satisfying day of subliminal stimulation, if you're a man, you contentedly dream that the "good mother of childhood" breast feeds you, changes your diapers, tells you how big and strong you are, congratulates you for impregnating her, and consumes you with fiery sexual passion. If you are a woman, your sleeping fantasies are similarly galvanized by the day's invisible provocations.

Figure 7.8

The Subliminal Sex™ Story

Whenever I give live presentations of the materials in this book, people want to know how I became interested in subliminal advertising, and how the SEX design (the floral illusion on the cover) was developed. The following is my personal story.

When I was nineteen I went on a fantastic adventure. I spent a year traveling by trains and buses from Morocco to the southern tip of India. The world was enormous then. There were no fax machines, no Internet, and very few phones. Many of the places I visited were wild, anarchistic, and fascinating. The men in Afghanistan carried curved swords and wore billowing white shirts with sequined vests. The people in India celebrated religious holidays by joyfully carrying purple porcelain elephant Gods, bedecked in flashing Christmas-tree lights, in chaotic street processions. Monkeys jumped joyfully from rooftop to rooftop in Katmandu, which was an unspoiled village. Dinners cost a dime and consisted of piles of rice and spicy hot potatoes, served in dirt-floored sheds by barefoot children. At night rats congregated under my bed, searching for crumbs of food. I constantly felt exhilarated.

When I returned home I was overcome with culture shock. In a way, America seemed far more bizarre than the bazaars of Tunis or Marrakech. *Everything was strangely interesting.* Cars, freeways, microwave ovens, and electric garage door-openers fascinated me. I was mesmerized by television, but even more so by television commercials. Shopping in the supermarkets was like visiting Disneyland. I was amazed not only by the astounding quantity of food products, but by the fact that so often they were packaged in brightly colored, artistically designed containers. In a strange way I fully appreciated the creative efforts behind products like "Cheer!" "Rice Krispies," and "Uncle Ben's Minute Rice."

This sense of estrangement made me receptive to the idea of subliminal advertising. When I stumbled on a copy of *Subliminal Seduction* in a bookstore in San Francisco in 1975, I immediately became mesmerized by the subject. I started collecting examples of my own and put on slide shows at colleges and coffee shops in Northern California. I began working on this book, and flew to Madison Avenue in New York to interview airbrushers.

I had an inspiring and disconcerting experience during my trip to New York. Through a friend of a friend, I managed to convince the owner of an ad agency in Manhattan to let me interview him "for ten minutes." As

Figure 7.9(a-b)

soon as I showed him a few ads from my portfolio, he became extremely agitated. He told his secretary to hold all his calls, and physically threatened me by saying, "You better be careful because you might get hurt." He raved and ranted endlessly, and then took me into the creative department and introduced me to the employees who physically made the ads. He said something like "Mr. Bullock is writing a book on 'subliminal advertising' – tell him its all a bunch of crap." As they dutifully informed me my "interpretations" were fanciful, I sensed that they felt guilty and distressed. I wondered if the owner was responsible for one of the ads in my portfolio, and was worried about the bad publicity he might receive when my book was published.

I abruptly realized how naïve I was; millions of dollars were at stake, and getting rid of an unknown, unpublished person (like myself) would not be very difficult. Accordingly, I pretended to be persuaded by their arguments and left promising to reconsider my views. I tried to make them think I wasn't serious about writing a book, and was just "playing around" by interviewing people. When I got out on the street and looked at my watch, I was astonished to discover it was three in the afternoon! The interview had lasted *six hours!* I sincerely hope that those people are either no longer in business, or have grown somewhat calmer over the years.

When I returned to California, a newspaper reporter wrote a review of my slide presentation in which he stated, "Bullock's show is startling....the overall impact is convincing." He reproduced copies of the Smirnoff (drink-in-the-face) and the *People* penis-cover, as shown in Figure 7.10.

I mailed a copy of the review to Wilson Bryan Key and he graciously invited me to visit him at his home. We became friends, and with my permission he used my SEX design both in his live lectures and as an illustration in his fourth book, *The Age of Manipulation*.

The SEX design was originally developed as a cover illustration for *The Secret Sales Pitch*. I thought that a sexy (but not offensive) illusion would illustrate the concept of subliminal advertising in an interesting and meaningful way. I happened to mention my idea to Nelson Carrick, someone I met at a party. By sheer coincidence Nelson was a talented artist with a particular interest in optical illusions. A few days later he created the Subliminal Sex™ flower design, which is gradually becoming recognized around the world. (It recently was featured in a psychological text published by W.W. Norton.) A picture of Nelson and me, taken in 1979, appears in Figure 7.11.

Figure 7.10

All my friends were fascinated by Nelson's creation. I took lots of photographs of it to see if the illusion "worked" in black-and-white and reduced in size. A photo of a friend holding the drawing against her chest inspired me to print the design on T-shirts. I called them "Subliminal Sex™ T-Shirts" and sold them with an amusing booklet discussing subliminal perception. The booklet joked that they "endowed the wearer with mysterious powers of persuasion." The first printing sold out instantly. Within a year, Subliminal Sex™ T-shirts were available in Macy's Department Stores across the United States. I also started a mail-order business by advertising in *Rolling Stone* magazine.

Unfortunately, the shirts were subject to a "secret" flaw. When they first appeared in Macy's, they were very popular because the sales personnel showed them to all the customers. When the clerks became accustomed to them, however, sales declined. The Internet eventually solved this problem, but at the time I was unable to devise a way to "demonstrate" the illusion properly. I decided to go to law school, which wasn't nearly as much fun.

The Secret Sales Pitch was relegated to a large box in my attic until several years ago, when I stumbled upon it and listened to a live tape recording of one of my slide shows. It was an eerie experience, hearing a message from My-self-of-the-past to My-self-of-the-present. My-self-of-the-past convinced me it was important to complete this project without delay. I wish I could send a message back in time saying, "Thanks for the inspiration."

Frasier Sane

Society has matured considerably in the last few decades. When I first began researching subliminals and showing them to people, they often became agitated and defensive. They would say things like "You're imagining things!" or "That can't be!" Today, even extremely conservative people are receptive to the concept of unconsciously perceived illusions. Although few have "seen" an embed or know what one is, they accept the existence of them when they are pointed out.

One advertiser I discussed this with pointed out that the public's perception of the unconscious has also matured. Freudian psychology was very

August Bullock and Nelson Carrick, circa 1979   Figure 7.11

unpopular in the sixties and seventies. People were involved with spiritual and personal growth, but not into examining the darker side of human nature. Today, society is much more comfortable with psychoanalytic theory. The success of the television show *Frasier* illustrates how accepted and less threatening the topic has become.

The American Home Series

The central themes of *The Secret Sales Pitch* are colorfully illustrated by *The American Home* series, beginning with Figure 7.12 on page 216.

Magazines are complete packages that present complete personalities. The cover attracts the viewer's attention, and the editorial content appeals to the reader's unconscious fantasies. The sole purpose of the art and text is to provide a platform for the ads, which provide the income to support the enterprise.

The cover of this issue portrays a beautiful woman wearing a devilishly red outfit, and a handsome, dark haired man. The woman is aloof, cold, and obviously in control. The man seems to be babbling that he loves her and would do anything for her. The picture seems to be directed at women who fantasize about having power in their relationships.

Figure 7.12

Figure 7.13 depicts an article from the inside of the magazine. The caption says "The Bedroom Life— More Than For Sleeping." The picture is very similar to the cover, and could portray the same couple. The woman is also wearing red, and looks very cold and indifferent. She is selfishly consuming the man's wine; her wine sits untouched on the left side of the picture. The man doesn't seem to mind. He appears to be worshiping her, and a fuzzy, warm, subliminal puppy is embedded on his chest.

Figure 7.13(a-b)

The article in Figure 7.14 appeared in another part of the magazine. It declares, "Why We Have No Children. A married couple reasons that for their own happiness there is no reason to have children in this day and age." One has to wonder why such an article is featured in a magazine marketed to families with children.

Figure 7.14

Magazines often present an "ego ideal," a fictitious person the reader identifies with. The ego ideal of *Playboy*, for example, is an affluent bachelor who drives a fast car, has a big round bed, owns the latest stereo and electronic gadgets, and has sex with lots of beautiful women. The ego ideal of *American Home* magazine is the Emerging Woman, portrayed in this issue as Leith Klauber, a 32-year-old housewife who just inherited a cattle ranch from her father. She is holding the family spurs in Figure 7.15.

On the lower left corner of that same page, she is shown interacting with her children. It is interesting to note that no one is smiling. The child on the left is staring into space. The child on the right could be about to burst into tears. Why would the editor pick such an unpleasant photo?

Please turn the page and look at Figure 7.16.

THE EMERGING WOMAN

AT HOME ON THE RANGE

Can a former radical student protester find happiness outside the urban scene raising children and Black Angus cattle? Leith Klauber thinks so.

Leith Klauber's passport papers list her occupation as "cattle breeder."

"It sounds a hell of a lot more interesting than 'housewife,'" she laughs. But raising cattle is no joke for 32-year-old Leith, who started building her herd of hand-picked Black Angus and hardy Mexican cattle when she inherited the "JL," an Arizona ranch, on the death of her father. Comprising about 20,000 acres, owned and government-leased, it's a business she intends to pass on to her children.

The only difference between Leith and all other 32-year-old women ranchers is that she controls the entire operation by long-distance telephone from Connecticut.

Disguised "as a housewife," she runs a large house near the University of Connecticut, where her husband, George, is a pediatric urologist; copes, aided by part-time *(continued on page 96)*
70

Figure 7.15

Could it be that Leith Klauber, the Emerging Woman, the ego ideal of millions of *American Home* readers, is heartlessly crushing her innocent offspring in the trunk of her station wagon?

What is the look on her face as she commits this terrible deed? Is it remorse? Is it despair? No! It's absolute exaltation. She seems to be enjoying nearly orgasmic pleasure as she murders her children and stuffs their mangled little bodies in her car.

Remarkably, although she is a competent business owner and efficient housewife, being photographed by a top-notch photographer for a nationally distributed magazine, she has in her frenetic joy neglected to button her sweater correctly.

In her left arm she holds a coiled snake.

The photograph at the upper right is even more revealing. The text indicates Leith is "taking care" of her older son. There is no comb in her hand; she appears to be grabbing him around the neck with her left hand and beating him over the head with her right. Her husband, George, a urologist, is standing by with clenched fists.

The son is valiantly attempting to defend himself. If you look at the close-up in Figure 7.17 you will see that, amazingly, he is crying and stabbing at his mother's vaginal area with a peeled banana. A face has been subliminally drawn on her skirt, the mouth of which is about to receive the fruit.

On the bottom center of the full page, in Figure 7.16, a much more relaxed Leith is seductively meeting with her farm manager in the barn. Her hand is in her pocket, and her family is gratefully absent.

Why We Have No Children. Indeed!

Bringing It All Home

The *American Home Series* illustrates perfectly what *The Secret Sales Pitch* is all about. It vividly demonstrates how media covertly appeals to unconscious impulses we are scarcely aware of.

The true meaning of the series, that "The Emerging Woman" wants to murder her children, becomes obvious once it is pointed out. Until that moment, however, your unconscious "filter" prevents you from becoming aware of it. You see a woman loading her kids into the car, not crushing them in the trunk. The revelation you experience when the filter breaks

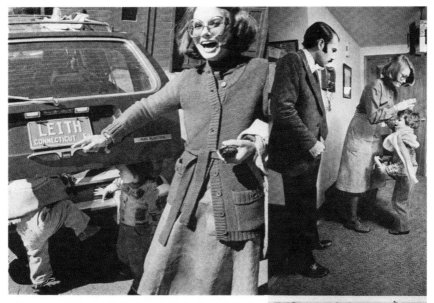

A young Connecticut housewife and mother, Leith Klauber, moonlights—and often daylights as well—as an Arizona lady cattle rancher. Since she took over her late father's ranch, the "JL," cattle raising has altered a great part of her lifestyle. Leith's reading matter (far left) is more likely to include literature on cattle than the latest best seller or cookbook. Memorabilia such as her father's spurs (left), embossed with the "JL" brand, can be found all around her home. Her unusual mixture of ranch and housewifely duties include (clockwise from top) chauffeuring twin daughters Blake and Rachel; taking care of husband George and son Adam; family shopping in Farmington, Conn.; talking over business with her farm manager; inspecting with the twins her "beef on the hoof" and coping at home with their youngsters' energetic escapades.

Figure 7.16(a-e)

down is very much like the revelation you have when a sudden insight, or a subliminal embed, "jolts" into your consciousness. The information feels familiar because you were already unconsciously aware of it.

People often joke about wanting to get rid of their children. They say things like, "I wouldn't trade them for a million dollars, but on the right day offer me a dime." They are peripherally aware of their submerged hostility, but don't think of it as real. As the series makes clear, such feelings are very real, but they are repressed. The human mind is a morass of conflicting emotions. Only the emotions that are socially acceptable are allowed past the filter; the rest reside in our unconscious and influence us without our realizing it.

Sometimes repressed emotions can cause neurosis in otherwise well-adjusted individuals. In other words, if normal mothers are aware that on some level they want to murder their kids, the impulse is probably not very harmful. If they are extremely disturbed by the idea, however, and deny having such thoughts, their "secret" feelings can be more dangerous. They sometimes wind up suffering emotional and health problems that seem to be unrelated to conflicts involving their children.

Society's reluctance to acknowledge the pervasiveness of subliminal advertising poses a similar threat. As long as we are in denial about it, it can cause us serious harm. The second we acknowledge it, however, society will change for the better. The subliminal content in ads will become more innocuous, because advertisers will fear being exposed. Media will become less influential, because the public will be more skeptical of it, and more wary of its power. On a personal level, we will all become slightly more comfortable with our multiple selves, and the unconscious processes that secretly drive us. Instead of wasting our energy fighting or pretending we don't have such impulses, we will direct them towards positive goals.

It's easy to imagine society accepting the existence of subliminal advertising. Advertisers engage in it to be competitive. They lie about it because they have to to stay in business. Magazines, newspapers, and television shows ignore it because their sponsors want them to. Individuals avoid recognizing it because it's psychologically unsettling. The whole world is in denial about it, and yet it's as obvious as the penis in the Benson ad or the SEX in the Subliminal Sex™ design. With just a little push, the whole interlocking system of truth avoidance could collapse upon itself.

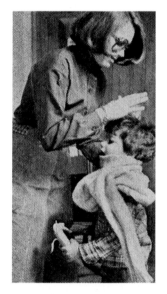

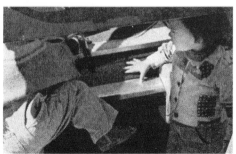

Figure 7.17

AFTER WORDS

If you have any comments about this book, I'd enjoy hearing from you. My e-mail address is ABullock@SubliminalSex.com.

If you thought the *Secret Sales Pitch* was interesting, please tell your friends about it.

If you are a student, please share it with your teachers.

If you are a teacher, please consider assigning it in your classes.

Visit our web site at SubliminalSex.com in order to:

> * purchase additional copies of *The Secret Sales Pitch* (wholesale or retail);
> * purchase Subliminal T-shirts;
> * inquire about our live multi-media presentations; and
> * check out the latest news regarding the subliminal controversy.

Many thanks,

August Bullock

Appendix A
PROJECTS AND EXPERIMENTS

If you are interested in sharpening your subliminal skills, apply the *Ambiguity Principle* and create unconsciously appealing names and advertisements for the products described below. Make sure your work is consistent with the actual motivational research that is provided. An example is provided on page 181.

1. A *device that kills cockroaches* by trapping them on a sticky surface. Women unconsciously associate cockroaches with men who have mistreated them in the past.

2. An *antiseptic cream* to which a chemical has been intentionally added to make it sting. The irritant provides mothers with an opportunity to comfort their children.

3. An *antacid.* Consumers unconsciously consider indigestion a status symbol.

4. A *greeting card company.* Greeting cards are unconsciously appealing because they enable the sender to avoid directly expressing emotion.

5. A *hair coloring targeted at both mothers and their daughters.* A test ad featuring a mother and daughter with identical hairdos and the tag line "A Double Header For Dad" was unsuccessful because it made mothers feel they were competing with their daughters for their husbands' affection.

6. A *low-cost department store.* Consumers who shop at thrift stores are "bargain hunters" who wish to outsmart others. Bargain hunters unconsciously are expressing hostility toward their mothers, whom they view as cold and refusing.

7. *Shortening.* Shortening is unconsciously associated with purity and fluffiness.

8. *Candy.* Consumers have exaggerated ideas about how unhealthy candy is. During childhood, parents use candy as a reward and as a punishment. Adults unconsciously consider candy to be an immoral indulgence.

9. A *laxative.* Consumers who use laxatives psychosomatically make themselves constipated, in order to express their unconscious desire to withhold from the world.

MORE FUN

10. Find a very odd looking ad and analyze its subliminal content.

11. Find five ads with copy that is secretly ambiguous in a way you wouldn't have recognized before reading this book.

13. Show the Benson penis/backbone ad in figure 1.2 to people not familiar with this book and instruct them: "This ad contains an optical illusion. See if you can find it." Determine:

    a. how long they look at the picture before giving up;

    b. whether they are able to find the embed, and

    c. if they are able to find the embed, how long it takes them.

Repeat the experiment with different subjects. This time, offer them a monetary reward if they are able to find the embed. Determine if the reward offer:

    a. causes them to spend more time looking at the ad before they give up;

    b. makes it more difficult or less difficult for them to find the embed; and

    c. if they are able to find the embed, whether it takes them more time or less time than the subjects in the first part of the experiment.

The reward offer paradoxically might make it *more* difficult for subjects to find the illusion. The incentive to work harder consciously might make it more difficult for the unconscious to relax the filter. The experiment could also be conducted using the SEX design on the cover.

14. Show either the Benson penis/backbone ad in Figure 1.2, the Smirnoff drink-in-the-face ad in Figure 2.20, the Naturalizer "Rock Star" ad in Figure 2.24, or the Nightmare ad in Figure 2.40 to people not familiar with this book. Ask them to make up a story about what is happening in the picture. See if the stories they create are influenced by the subliminal content of the pictures.

You can also create a control ad for the Naturalizer ad by cropping the "rock star" out of the picture. See if the stories for the control ad differ from the stories for the complete ad.

If you have computer graphic skills, you can create a neutral control stimulus for the Benson ad by airbrushing the phallus out of the backbone. See if the stories for the control differ from the stories for the original ad.

15. Replicate Poetzl's dream experiments by showing the Nightmare ad in Figure 2.40 to a friend for one second. Ask the friend to describe what she saw, and record her response. Provide the friend with a pen and paper, and ask her to write down what she dreamed about as soon as she wakes up the following morning. Analyze her dream, and try to determine if it was symbolically influenced by what was she did not report "seeing" in the ad.

16. Test the effect of prior verbal instructions by photocopying the Duck/Tree illusion in Figure 2.1. Tell ten people who are not familiar with it "I am going to show you a picture of a duck" and let them look at it for one second. Record how many of the subjects consciously "see" the duck hidden in the tree. Repeat the process by telling ten other people "I am going to show you a picture of a tree."

Perform the experiment again using the SEX design on the cover of this book. The SEX design is considerably more hidden than the duck, and most people will have a harder time "finding" it. Conscious perception of the SEX is influenced by many variables, the most important of which is the distance from which the design is first perceived. Make sure the subjects in your experiment are the same distance from the design when they first perceive it. If you want you can experiment wearing a Subliminal Sex™ T-shirt (available on our website).

17. Show the SEX design (on the cover) for one second to someone who is not familiar with it. Ask the person to draw a nature scene and label its parts. See if the drawing contains sexual imagery.

Repeat the experiment on different subjects. This time, cut off the bottom of the picture (where the SEX is hidden). Analyze the drawings of the two groups of subjects to see if they are significantly different.

18. Find a poem that is not well known, but was written by a famous poet. Ask people to read it and evaluate its artistic merit on a one-to-ten scale. Before you do so, tell them:

    a. it was written by the famous poet, or

    b. it was written by a college student, or

    c. it was written by a homeless person selling original poems to buy food.

Determine if the identity of the supposed author influences the subjects' impressions of the poem.

In a second part of the experiment, tell conservative people the poem was written by a famous radical (like Abby Hoffman), and tell liberal people it was written by a famous conservative (like Newt Gingrich), and vice versa. Analyze the results.

19. Interview individuals who saw the film *The Exorcist* more than six months ago. Determine:

      a. when they saw the film;

      b. whether they saw the original or DVD version;

      c. if they remember seeing a fleeting death mask in the film;

      d. at what point in the film they think the death mask(s) appeared; and

      e. what they think the death mask(s) looked like.

Next, observe their reactions as you show them the picture of the mask (in Figure 3.17). Ask them if the actual mask is more disturbing than their memories of it.

Hypothetically, many people who saw the film will not remember the death masks, and if they do, they will remember a sanitized version of what they saw. Analyze the data and determine whether it confirms to refutes the hypothesis. Note that the DVD version contains several more death masks than the original video.

20. Show individual subjects the movie preview contained on the DVD version of *The Exorcist*. Immediately following the presentation, determine:

      a. if they saw a fleeting death mask in the film;

      b. at what point in the preview it appeared; and

      c. what it looked like if they saw it.

Finally, show them the actual death mask and record their responses, as in the preceding experiment.

Repeat the forgoing procedure on different subjects, but do not ask them any questions (or show them the actual death-mask) until *twenty-four hours* after showing them the preview.

Repeat the forgoing procedure on new subjects one more time, but do not ask them any questions (or show them the actual death-mask) until *one week* after showing them the preview.

Hypothetically, subjects who watched the preview one week in the past will be more inclined to not remember the mask, or to remember a less frightening version of it, than the subjects who watched the preview more recently. Analyze the data and determine whether it confirms or refutes this hypothesis.

I would very much appreciate hearing the results of your research. Please contact me at ABullock@SubliminalSex.com.

Appendix B
SERIOUS RESEARCH

The following suggestions are provided for serious researchers who wish to investigate the influence of subliminals.

The Penis in the Backbone: Use a computer to eliminate all the text and product references in the Benson penis/backbone ad in Figure 1.2. Crop the photo just above "Benson and Hedges 100s" and cover up "If You Got Crushed In The Clinch With Your Soft Pack, Try Our New Hard Pack" with neutral tan coloring. Make two copies of the finished picture.

Create a control stimulus by eliminating the penis from the backbone in one of the pictures (as in the Kilbourne "Marlboro Lights penis/rock" experiment). Monitor the skin conductance (and other responses) of subjects to see if they react differently to the original and modified ads.

In the alternative, start by taking a completely new photograph of a different couple in a similar pose. Create the experimental stimulus by digitally altering the woman's backbone to make it look like the penis in the Benson ad. Use the original, unaltered photograph, as a control. This procedure is more difficult, but would eliminate any possibility that the subjects had been previously exposed to the stimuli.

The Naturalizer: As in the preceding suggestion, eliminate the text and product references in the Naturalizer "rock star" in Figure 2.24. Create a control stimulus by cropping the rock star out of one of the pictures. Show the photos to different groups of subjects, and monitor their physiological reactions.

Revealing Stories: Show the penis/backbone and Naturalizer experimental and control stimuli (described above) to subjects and ask them to make up a story about what is happening in the pictures. Determine if the subliminal content of the pictures emerges in the stories the subjects make up.

Ruth and Mostache utilized an interesting and effective variation of this technique. They told the subjects the purpose of the experiment was to test their memories. They showed them a series of numbers, and then asked them to perform a "distracter task" designed to force them to think about something other than the numbers. When they were done, they asked them to recall as many of the numbers as possible.

The "distracter task" the subjects were asked to perform was actually the true purpose of the experiment. It required them to look at a picture and make up a story about it. Misleading the subjects in this manner caused them to be to be more spontaneous and less self-conscious. As a result, the stories they made up more accurately reflected their unconscious emotions. The study is cited in the Notes, (referenced to pg. 230).

Personality Tests: Administer personality tests to construct a personality profile of each of the subjects prior to the experiment(s). Use the data to determine if subliminals are more influential when they are targeted at a subject's individual sensitivities (such as fears of impotency or latent homosexual inclinations).

Flashing the Drink-in-the-face: Show female subjects who drink heavily and resent males the Smirnoff drink-in-the-face ad at subliminal speeds. Show them a similar but neutral party scene as a control. Measure their skin conductance, ask them to make up stories, and monitor their alcohol cravings. Presenting the stimuli tachistoscopically should make it easier to create a suitable control ad. The same technique could be used with the Jameson Irish severed-head ad, with a glass of water used as a control.

More Than Meets the Eye: Use the "Three's A Crowd" *People* magazine cover in Figure 2.16 as an experimental stimulus. Create a control stimulus by using a computer to remove the penis from Mr. Ritter's mouth. Show the two pictures to different subjects, and track their eye movements to determine how the embed affects them.

Replicate Leeper: Replicate Leeper's experiments in which verbal and perceptual cues were given prior to the presentation of the young/woman old/woman drawing, using 1. Simple cues such as OLD WOMAN and 2. More complete descriptions (as suggested above) and 3. Pictures of old people in retirement homes, which would unconsciously activate thoughts associated with old women. Refer to the footnotes for a complete discussion. If it's difficult to find subjects who have not seen the drawing on prior occasions, you may wish to consider using adolescents.

I Sing Because I Live With Satan: Utilizing the following procedure, determine if *backwards speech* is perceived unconsciously:

> a. create a variety of audio subliminal (*forward* played) whisper messages that are emotionally *disturbing.*

    b. create a variety of audio subliminal (*forward* played) whisper messages that are emotionally *neutral*.

    c. using a computer, create versions of both the disturbing and neutral sub-audible messages that are played *backwards*.

    d. make *loud* copies of the *backwards* versions, so that the subjects can hear the messages but can not understand them because they are played backwards.

Monitor the skin conductance levels of a series of subjects as they listen to both the *forward* played subliminal whisper messages described in Section a and b, and the *backwards* subliminal whisper messages described in Section c.

Some of the subjects are likely to react to the sub-audible forward played disturbing whispers. If backwards speech is understood unconsciously, the individuals who react to the *forward* disturbing sub-audible messages should also react to the *backwards* disturbing sub-audible messages. Conversely, subjects who do not react to the forward disturbing messages, should not react to the backwards disturbing messages.

In a second phase of the experiment, expose all the subjects to the louder disturbing and neutral backwards messages described in Section d. The results in the second phase of the experiment should be consistent with the results in the first.

* * *

These are just some rough ideas that I hope will inspire you. If you undertake any experiments relevant to the materials in this book I would very much appreciate hearing about your work. You can e-mail me at ABullock@SubliminalSex.com.

A.B.

ACKNOWLEDGMENTS

This project would not have been possible without the help of the following people, who are listed more or less in order of their assistance:

Sharon Goodwin, whose many outstanding contributions included discovering the Naturalizer ad, discovering the Happy Dad ad, making the illustration "keys" for the Budweiser and several other ads, and sharing the third In-and-Out Burger epiphany while we were having lunch.

Giovanni Vaz Del Bello, Emily Loufek, Dean Woerner, Patricia Stearns, and Lynn M. Raadik were tremendously helpful "content" editors who read the manuscript in its formative stages.

Joan Kruckewitt, author of *The Death of Ben Linder*, and Richard Lange, also a writer, were my excellent professional editors, who provided many valuable insights and corrections. Joan also took the photograph of me on the back cover.

Julie Bones graciously posed for the face on the front cover. Inci Ak posed for the key for the "old/woman young/woman" illustration.

Robert Pimm, an attorney in San Francisco, California, consulted with me regarding the legal issues.

Pete Masterson, with the Aeonix Publishing Group, was my publishing and production advisor.

Christopher A. Bergman, Ph.D., RPA and anthropologist currently in Cincinnati, Ohio, helped me understand the evolutionary development of consciousness.

Richard Curtis did an excellent job creating the cover design.

As noted in the text, my good friend Nelson Carrick was the gifted illusionist who created the Subliminal Sex™ design. Sadly, he passed away in 1999.

Bob and Lynn Dress, life long friends, encouraged and supported in regard to most of my creative endeavors over the years.

The illusions in this book were tested on fellow attorneys, clients, and scores of complete strangers while they were waiting for their Court hearings. If you are one of them, I thank you for your help.

Finally, I wish to thank my relatives, whose relentless criticisms inspired me to do a better job than I would have otherwise.

CREDITS

The Subliminal Sex™ Flower Design on the cover © August Bullock 1979. All rights reserved. Artwork by Nelson Carrick. Please contact ABullock @SubliminalSex.com to request permission to reproduce it.
Cover design by Richard Curtis. © 2004 by August Bullock. All rights reserved.
The endorsements by Dr. Dixon and Steve Hart on the back cover are used with their permission.
"Franklin C. Wright" is an imaginary character who was also kind enough to endorse my work. "Frank" subliminally means "straightforward and sincere," and "C. Wright" means "view correctly."
Figure 1.1(a): Hungry? Eat Popcorn!: Photo by Walter Doran. Time Life Pictures/ Getty Images. Used with permission.
Figure 1.1(b): "Blood" photo: Photo by OMECC Productions.
Figure 2.1 - 2.2: Trees: Eagle, M, Wolitzky, D.L., and Klein, G.S. (1966). Imagery: Effect of a concealed figure in a stimulus. *Science*. 151(3712): 837-839.
Figure 2.6: *My Wife and Mother In Law*: created by cartoonist W.E. Hill. It first appeared in *Puck Magazine* in 1915. It was first brought to the attention of psychologists by Edwin Boring in 1930. (Boring, E. (1930). A new ambiguous figure. *American Journal of Psychology*. (42); pg. 444-445).
Figure 2.9: Gestalt Chart: Inspired by Wilke, William L. (1994). *Consumer Behavior*. First published 1986. Third Ed. NY: John Wiley and Sons.
Figure 2.11: Aames room: Photo by William Vanderbilt.
Figure 2.23: *Immaculate Conception* by Bartolome Esteban Murillo (1617-1682). Photo by Scala/ Art Resource, NY. Used with permission.
Figure 2.39: Pen/Knee illustration: Shevrin, H. and Fisher, C. (1967). Changes in the effects of a waking subliminal stimulus as a function of dreaming and non dreaming sleep. *Journal of Abnormal Psychology*. 72(4): pg. 362-8.
Figure 4.11: Attack ad: I regretfully am unable to credit the photo because I don't know who the author is. I found it on the Internet (by searching Yahoo/news/photos) shortly after 9/11.)

Figure 6.1: Portfolio cover: *Portfolio* includes a collection of photographs by the talented, world famous photographer Michel Comte. *Michel Comte: Kontraste/Contrasts Portfolio* (Stern Portfolio Library). Available on Amazon.com and elsewhere.© All rights reserved.

Figure 6.2: Peter Jurgens artwork: Offset litho poster from an original watercolor by Jurgen Peters. Published by Editions Limited, 4090 Halleck Street, Emeryville, CA 94608. http://ww.editionslimited.com. Used with permission.

Figure 6.3: *Mirabilis* cover: Jacket design and imaging by Honi Werner Mirabilis © 2001 by Susann Cokal. G.P. Putnam's sons; a member of Penguin Putnam Inc. All rights reserved. Available on Amazon.com and elsewhere.

Song lyrics on pages 202-203: Your Love Keeps Lifting Me Higher and Higher. Jackson, Smith, Miner (P) 1967. *Brusnwick Records Corp. Under license from Columbia Special Products, A Service of CBS Records, A Division of CBS Inc.* Protected by US copyright. All rights reserved.

Figure 7.10: Newspaper article: Courtesy of Santa Rosa Press Democrat. Used with permission.

Figure 7.11: Picture of the author and Nelson Carrick: Photo by Dale Martin; Courtesy of Ukiah Daily Journal. Used with permission.

The illustrations in this book are published in accordance with 17 U.S.C.§107, which states in pertinent part:

[T]he fair use of a copyrighted work…for purposes such as criticism, comment, news reporting, teaching…, scholarship, or research, is *not* an infringement of copyright. (Emphasis added.)

ANNOTATED NOTES AND REFERENCES

DISCLAIMER

My analyses of all the illustrations in this book are based solely on the appearance of the pictures. I can only speculate as to how the creators of the illustrations intended them to be perceived. Furthermore, I am not inferring in any way that the models portrayed in the pictures had any knowledge or understanding of the "secret" meanings articulated in my hypotheses.

Opposite Title Page:

Reference to Advertising Textbook: Weir, Walter. Another look at subliminal "facts." *Advertising Age.* October 15, 1984. pg. 46. The author states, "If subliminal advertising did exist, there certainly would be textbooks available on how to practice it."

pg. 7: Chapter One:
HUNGRY? EAT POPCORN!
THE HISTORY OF SUBLIMINAL PERSUASION

Motivational research: Packard, Vance. (1957). *The Hidden Persuaders*. New York: Penguin Books.

Hypnoidal trances in supermarkets: Packard, Vance. (1957). State of the question: The mass manipulation of human behavior. *America,* (December 14), pg. 342-344.

Cigar study: Weiss, Edward H. (1954). *How motivation studies may be used by creative people to improve advertising,* Advertising Conference, Contributed Papers, University of Michigan, Bureau of Business Research May 7. Discussed in Hepner, Harry W. (1964) *Advertising: Creative Communication with Consumers* (New York: McGraw Hill 4th edition, pg. 147-153. Also discussed in Britt, Steuart H. (Ed.) (1966). *Consumer Behavior and The Behavioral Sciences: Theories And Applications.* New York: John Wiley and Sons, pg. 105-106.

Billion dollars a year on motivational research, ten billion dollars a year on advertising: Rose, Alvin W. (1958). Motivation research and subliminal advertising. *Social Research.* Fall (25): pg. 271-284. Reference on pg. 272-273. The author states: "Motivational research in the United States is a billion dollar per year business; nearly every major industry in the country is employing psychologists to pierce the mind of the consumer..."

The Hidden Persuaders: Packard, Vance. (1957). (Cited above).

pg. 9: Hungry? Eat Popcorn:

Vicary's press conference: Westin, Alan F. (1968). *Privacy and freedom.* In *Tampering With the Unconscious.* New York: Antheum. pg. 279-297. Reference on pg. 279.

1/300 second: Press reports from the period indicate Vicary allegedly flashed the subliminal messages at 1/3000 of a second. This is probably an error. Most of the studies discussed in Chapter Two (of this book) utilized presentations in the 1/300 of a second range.

Picnic: Picnic © 1956 Columbia Pictures.

My World Dies Screaming: © 1958.

Vicary's claims exaggerated: Rogers, Stuart. (1992-1993). (Winter). How a publicity blitz created the myth of subliminal advertising. *Public Relations Quarterly.* (37)(4): pg.12-17.

See also: Weir, Walter. (1984). Another look at subliminal "facts." *Advertising Age.* October 15, pg. 46.

Whisper ads on radio: *Advertising Age.* December 17, 1957. pg. 93. Reported in *Privacy and Freedom*, cited above, at pg. 283-284.

KTLA contract: *Advertising Age*, January 27, 1958, pg. 107. Reported in *Privacy and Freedom*, cited above.

Life magazine horror film article:.(1958) 'Hidden sell' technique is almost here. *Life* March 31, 1958 at pg. 102.

New Yorker: Talk of the Town, *The New Yorker*, Sept 21, 1957.

Newsday: Newsday (Garden City, N.Y.) referred to in the *Christian Science Monitor*, January 6, 1958.

Letter from prominent businessman: See Brooks, John. (1958). The little ad that isn't there. *Consumer Reports.* January, pg. 7. See also Rose, Alvin W. (1958). Motivation research and subliminal advertising. *Social Research.* Fall (25): 271-284, pg. 277.

The poll: Haber, Ralph N. (1959). Public Opinions regarding subliminal advertising. *Public Opinion Quarterly.* (Summer) (23): pg. 291-293.

Ad industry reversal/ CBS announcement: *New York Times* December 4, 1957. Also discussed in Westin, Alan F. (1968) *Privacy and Freedom*. (Cited above).

No bills passed: Westin, Alan F. (1968). *Privacy and Freedom.* pg. 292. (Cited above).

FCC pronouncement: Westin, Alan F. (1968). *Privacy and Freedom.* pg. 292. (Cited above).

Christian Science Monitor article: Ad firms ponder success of invisible commercials. *Christian Science Monitor.* January 6, 1958.

Subliminals left the news: Packard, Vance (1977). *The People Shapers.* Boston: Little, Brown, and Co. pg. 136. Also, I conducted a computer search that revealed very few subliminal articles for that time period.

pg. 11: Subliminal Seduction:

Subliminal Seduction: Key, Wilson Bryan. (1973). *Subliminal Seduction: Ad Media's Manipulation of a Not So Innocent America.* New York: Signet.

pg. 12: Try Our Hard Pack:

Current cost of full page ad: From a telephone interview with *Time's* headquarters, in reference to figures quoted on their web site, September 18, 2002.

pg. 13: The Not So Soft Sell:

(15): Father of motivational research: Dichter, Ernest. 1979). *Getting Motivated, The Secret Behind Individual Motivations by the Man Who was Not Afraid To Ask "Why?"* From: About the author, pg. 198. New York: Pergamon Press.

Dichter quote: Dichter, Ernest. (1964). *Handbook of Consumer Motivations: The Psychology of the World of Objects.* Mc Graw Hill.

pg. 15: The Secret Sales Pitch:
Other books Key wrote subsequently:
Key, Wilson Bryan. (1977). *Media Sexploitation.* New York: Signet.
—(1981). *The Clam-Plate Orgy and Other Techniques for Manipulating Your Behavior.* New York: Signet.
—(1993) *The Age of Manipulation: The Con in Confidence; the Sin in Sincere.* New York: Madison Books. (Originally published by New York: H. Holt in 1989).
Key's influence on public opinion: Rogers, M. and Smith, K. (1993). Public perceptions of subliminal advertising: Why practitioners shouldn't ignore this issue. *Journal of Advertising Research.* March-April. 33(2): pg. 10.
Pop psychology: Moore, Timothy E. (1982). Subliminal advertising: What you see is what you get. *Journal of Marketing.* Spring. (46) 38-47. At pg. 45, the author states: "Key provides no documentation for the effects that he attributes to embedded stimuli…Key appears to invent whatever features of perception and memory would be necessary to achieve the results imputed to embedded stimuli."
See also Rogers, Smith. (1993). Public perceptions of subliminal advertising: Why practitioners shouldn't ignore this issue. *Journal of Advertising Research.* March- April. 33(2): pg. 10-19. "Key's theories have been widely discredited by academicians who have examined marketing applications scientifically…"
For a comprehensive criticism of Dr. Key's work (and presumably my own) see also Haberstroh, Jack. (1994). *Ice Cube Sex: The Truth About Subliminal Advertising.* Notre Dame, IN: Cross Cultural Publications.

pg. 17: Chapter Two:
MOMMY AND I ARE ONE
THE SCIENCE OF THE SECRET SALES PITCH:

Hundreds of experiments: As early as 1962, a commentator noted: "Experiments are no longer simply directed toward establishing subliminal perception as an empirical phenomenon, but incline more toward exhibiting its influence upon a variety of behavioral contexts." Bevan, W. (1962). Subliminal stimulation: A pervasive problem for psychology. *Psychological Bulletin.* 61(2): pg. 81-99. Quote at pg. 84.
See also: Bornstein, Robert F. and Masling, Joseph M. (Eds.) (1998). *Empirical Perspectives on the Psychoanalytic Unconscious.* New York: American Psychological Association. At pg. xvii the authors state: "During the 1980s, there were dozens of published papers questioning the existence of unconscious perception and memory. Since 1990, there has not been a single article in a mainstream psychology journal challenging the existence of these phenomena."
pg. 18: The Holes Between Things:
Duck Tree Experiment: Eagle, M., Wolitzky, D.L., and Klein, G.S. (1966). Imagery: Effect of a concealed figure in a stimulus. *Science.* 151(3712): pg. 837-839.
Dixon quote: Dixon, N.F. (1971). *Subliminal Perception: The Nature of a Controversy* London, McGraw Hill. Quote at pg. 124-125.

The unconscious perception of both the figure and the ground in a figure-ground draw-ing was also documented by Fisher and Paul in: Fisher, Charles and Paul, I.H. (1959). The effect of subliminal visual stimulation on images and dreams: A validation study. *American Psychoanalytic Association Journal.* (7): pg. 35-85. Subjects were sublimi-nally shown a simplified figure-ground picture, consisting of the profile of two heads facing each other. After the drawing was presented for 1/100 of a second, so that it was perceived subliminally, many of the subjects created drawings that involved *dual* ele-ments. One subject remarked, "I am reminded…of a boy and girl kissing. Their noses seem to be attached." (pg. 36). When the drawing was shown for a longer time period, no subject realized that it consisted of two alternating profiles until it was shown for a full second. Most required five seconds to become consciously aware of both faces. (pg. 49). The study revealed that the two figures were *unconsciously* perceived (in 1/100 second), even though only one figure was *consciously* perceived (after a one sec-ond exposure).

pg. 19: The Unconscious Perception of Embeds:

Kilbourne Study: Kilbourne, William E., Painton, Scott, and Ridley, Danny. (1985). The effect of sexual embedding on responses to magazine advertisements. *Journal of Ad-vertising.* 14(2): pg. 48-56. I have not commented on the first part of this study, which involved showing the stimuli to subjects and asking them to evaluate how the ads made them feel. (Reactions to the Marlboro ad were significant; but reactions to the Chivas ad were neutral.) I have emphasized the skin conductance part of the study because the results are more objective. The GSR response to the Marlboro Lights penis/rock was quite significant - the readings were 16.9 to 20% higher for both sexes.

pg. 20: The Unconscious Perception of Faint Images: Miller Study: Miller,

James G. (1939). Discrimination without awareness. *American Journal of Psychology.* (52): pg. 562-578. Quote at pg. 567-568.

pg. 21: The Corners of Our Minds:

Matrix study: Somekh, D.E. (1976). The effect of embedded words in a brief visual display. *British Journal Of Psychology.* 67(4): pg. 529-535.

pg. 23: The Filter Mechanism and the Pyramid of Perception:

Filter mechanism: The term "filter" was first proposed by D.E. Broadbent. (Broadbent, D.E. (1958). *Perception And Communication.* London. Pergamon Press.) He used it in a somewhat different context than I have, relating it to the manner in which conscious *attention* is directed towards specific information, as opposed to the manner in which data is unconsciously processed and distorted.

See also Treisman, Anne M. (1969). Strategies and Models of Selective Attention. *Psy-chological Review.* 76(3): pg. 282-299, which discusses Broadbent's theories. The au-thor states at pg. 282, "In 1958 Broadbent summarized a large area of research and attempted to provide a unified explanation of his "filter" theory of selective attention. He assumed that, when several messages reach the senses, they are initially processed in parallel, but must at some central stage converge on a perceptual or decision channel of limited capacity. To reduce the load ..[on the]system, *a selective filter* blocks irrel-evant messages before they reach the bottleneck. (Emphasis added.)

See also Duetsch, J.A. and Deutsch, D. (1963). Attention: Some theoretical considerations. *Psychological Review.* (70)(1) pg. 80-90. At pg. 81 the author notes that analysis of a stimulus occurs unconsciously *before* it reaches the filter. He concludes that the content of competing messages "is analyzed *prior to* the rejection of one and the acceptance of the other." (Emphasis added.)

See also: Norman, Donald A. (1968). Toward a theory of memory and attention. *Psychological Review.* 75(6) 522-536. The author notes that information blocked by the filter continues to influence behavior. At pg. 528 he states: "The theory presented so far has behavioral consequences. For one, all sensory inputs, whether attended to or not, excite their representation in primary memory. This means that subjects should retain in primary storage material which has been presented to them, even if not attended to at the time of presentation."

pg. 25: The Unconscious Perception of Visual Ambiguity:

My Wife and Mother in Law: *My Wife and Mother in Law* was created by the cartoonist W.E. Hill and first appeared in *Puck* magazine in 1915. It was first brought to the attention of psychologists by Edwin Boring in 1930.(Boring, E. (1930). A new ambiguous figure. *American Journal of Psychology.* (42): pg.444-445. On the initial exposure, 65% of viewers see the old woman, and 35% see the young woman. (Leeper, R. (1935) A study of the neglected portion of the field of learning — the development of sensory organization. *Journal of Genetic Psychology.* (46): pg. 41-75.

pg. 26: Filtering Based On Context:

Context and clouds: Leeper, R. (1935). A study of the neglected portion of the field of learning— the development of sensory organization. *Journal of Genetic Psychology.* (46): pg. 41-75. Leeper experimented with the presentation of two ambiguous drawings — the old woman/young woman and a picture that could be seen as either a pirate or a rabbit. The subjects were shown the drawings in three experimental conditions: 1. with no prior explanation or commentaries; 2. with a prior perceptual cue; 3. with a prior verbal description (i.e. the central feature of the next drawing is a rabbit...)

They were then asked to describe what they had seen. When no prior explanation was given, 65% saw the old woman and 35 % saw the young woman. 73% saw the pirate, 12% saw the rabbit, and 12 % were aware of both images. When perceptual cues were given, the subjects were significantly more likely to see the image that had been cued. When the verbal cues were given, the subjects shown the pirate/rabbit image were more likely to see the image that had been verbally cued. For some reason this was not the case with the old woman/ young woman.

The fact that the verbal cues did not influence perception of the old woman/ young woman may be due to a statistical anomaly, or a flaw in the experiment. Verbal cues did affect perception of the pirate/rabbit image, as one would expect. I have shown the SEX design (on the cover) to thousands of individuals, and I have subjectively observed that verbally cueing the viewer (i.e. "you are probably aware of only flowers as you look at this beautiful design") significantly affects how the illusion is perceived. Leeper's verbal cues also may have been too lengthy and convoluted. It would be interesting to replicate his experiments using simple cues such as "OLD WOMAN" and "YOUNG WOMAN."

In any event, the many studies and examples discussed in this chapter make it clear that 1. Both interpretations of ambiguous images are analyzed unconsciously, and 2. Context helps the filter decide which interpretation is most appropriate. The Gestalt "B" = "13" example in Figure 2.8 illustrates this effectively. The fact that the viewer is aware of *only* a "B" or a "13" (depending on the context) indicates that both ambiguities must be analyzed pre-consciously— if they were not the viewer would sometimes "see" the "wrong" interpretation.

pg. 27: Filtering Based On Gestalt Principles: Filter operations: The Gestalt chart and discussion of Gestalt principles were inspired by Wilke, William L. (1994). *Consumer Behavior.* First published 1986. Third Ed. New York: John Wiley and Sons. Figure–ground: From Hartmann, George W. (1935) *Gestalt Psychology.* New York. The Ronald Press Company. pg. 24-25.
Gestalt: Katz, David (1950). *Gestalt Psychology: Its nature and significance.* The Ronald Press Company.
See also: Encyclopedia Americana (1999) "Gestalt psychology."
See also: Dixon, N.F. (1971). *Subliminal Perception: The Nature of a Controversy.* London, McGraw Hill. The author states on pg. 125: "As Fisher suggested, this effect of embedded figures presented below the threshold of awareness implies that Gestalt processes of organization affect incoming sensory information beyond that at which this information has access to memory trace systems."

pg. 29: The Filtering of Discordant Information:
Discordant playing card study: Bruner, J. and Postman, L. (1949). On the perception of incongruity: A paradigm. *Journal of Personality.* No. 18, September. Reprinted in Bruner, J. and Postman, L. (1973). *Beyond The Information Given: Studies In The Psychology Of Knowing.* Chapter 4, pg. 69-83. New York: W.W. Norton. The authors state at pg. 70: "...for as long as possible and by whatever means available, the organism will ward off the perception of the unexpected, those things which do not fit his prevailing set." The repression of *discordant* information is closely related to the Gestalt principle of *context*, discussed above.

pg. 30: The Filtering of Emotionally Disturbing Information:
Dirty Word Experiments: McGinnies, E. (1949). Emotionality and perceptual defense. *Psychological Review.* (56): pg. 244-251. McGinnies wrote: "It is well established, then, that the perceptual 'filtering' of visual stimuli serves, in many instances, to protect the observer for as long as possible from an awareness of objects which have unpleasant emotional significance for him."
Dixon split vision study: Dixon, N.F. (1958). Apparent changes in the visual threshold as a function of subliminal stimulation. *Quarterly Journal of Experimental Psychology.* November (10): pg. 211-219.
See also Dixon, N.F. and Haider, M. (1961). Changes in visual threshold as a function of subception. *Quarterly Journal Of Experimental Psychology.* (13): pg. 229-235
See also: Lazarus, R.S., and McCleary, R.A. (1951). Autonomic discrimination without awareness: A study of subception. *Psychological Review.* (58): pg. 113-122. (Subjects first shown nonsense syllables for one second, some of which were paired with an electric shock. Subjects then shown syllables at subliminal speeds, while their GSRs (skin

conductance levels) were measured. The subjects' GSRs were higher for the "shock" syllables, causing the authors to conclude: "There seems to be little doubt that subjects can make autonomic discriminations when they are unable to report conscious recognition."

Stroop Test: MacLeod, Colin. (1962). Anxiety and the selective processing of emotional information: Mediating roles of awareness, trait and state variables, and personal relevance of stimulus materials. *Behaviour Research & Therapy*. September. 30(5): pg. 479-491.

Distorted Room and Glasses Experiments: Wittreich, Warren J. (1959). Visual Perception and Personality. *Scientific American*. April, (200): pg. 56-60.

pg. 33: Psychoanalytic Theory:

Psychoanalytic theory: To be more precise, Freud proposed that there are three parts to the mind: the id, the ego, and the superego. I have simplified his theories to avoid getting bogged down in psychological jargon. For the same reason I have exclusively used the term "*un*-conscious" and not the term "*sub*-conscious." ("*Un*-conscious" refers to information the subject is usually completely unaware of, whereas "*sub*-conscious" refers to mental activities just below the threshold of consciousness –which the subject may have some access to). (Merriam-Webster's Dictionary.)

For an easily understood overview of Freud's theories see: Lande, Nathaniel. (1976). Psychoanalysis/Sigmund Freud (1856-1939) in *Mindstyles/Lifestyles*. Los Angeles: Price/Stern/Sloan; and

Fishman, L. Lescano, C. and Torgeson, I. (1997). *The Stimulating World of Psychology:* Study Sidekick - 1st Edition..The Standard Deviants/Cerebellum Corporation 1997. (This is a simplified overview written in an amusing manner.)

Freud's seminal work: Freud, S. (1975) The interpretation of dreams. *In The Standard Edition of the Complete Psychological Works of Sigmund Freud (Vols. 4 & 5)*. London: Hogarth. (Original work published 1900). pg. 34: Sybil: *Sybil* ©1977 Lorimar Productions, Inc. Starring Sally Field and Joanne Woodward. Some commentators have suggested the Sybil story may have been over dramatized. Nonetheless it illustrates the point I am making.

Bornstein quote: Bornstein, R.F. (1990). Subliminal mere exposure and psychodynamic activation effects: Implications for the psychoanalytic theory of conscious and unconscious mental processes. In J. Masling (Ed.), *Empirical Studies Of Psychoanalytic Theories* (Vol. 3, pg. 55-88). Hillsdale, NJ: Erlbaum. (Quote at pg. 59).

pg. 34: The Social Façade:

Stanford prison experiiment: Zimbardo, Philip G. Information taken from the web site at http//www.prisonorg/index.html on October 16, 2002.

pg. 35: The Evolutionary Perspective:

Consciousness is a recent development: Western, Drew. (1998). Unconscious thought, feeling and motivation: The end of a long debate. In Bornstein, R.F. and Masling, J.M. (Eds.) *Empirical Perspectives on the Psychoanalytic Unconscious*. New York: American Psychological Association. The author states at pg.11: "From an evolutionary perspective, consciousness, at least in its human form, appears to be a relatively recent development superimposed on an information processing system that worked relatively well for millions of years." Citing Reber, A. (1992). The cognitive unconscious: An evolutionary perspective. *Consciousness and Cognition.* (1): pg. 93-133.

It is impossible to determine for certain when consciousness and/or a sense of morality developed. The 200,000 to 500,000 years ago estimate was posited by Christopher A. Bergman, Ph.D., RPA, a pre-historian in Cincinnati, Ohio, during a phone interview. An article in the *New York Times* (February 26, 2002, Debate is fueled on when humans became human) noted that humans "began to manifest creative and symbolic thinking" as evidenced by cave drawings and the creation of ornaments 40,000-70,000 years ago. Whatever the actual date, it is clear that consciousness is a *relatively* recent development because it emerged thousands, and not millions, of years ago.

The Evolutionary Basis of Attention: Multi-tasking as a law professor: This discussion was adapted from ideas presented by Drew Western in: Western, D. (1998) Unconscious thought, feeling and motivation: the end of a long debate. In Bornstein, R.F. and Masling, J.M. (Eds.) *Empirical Perspectives on the Psychoanalytic Unconscious.* New York: American Psychological Association. (pg. 11).

Another researcher has explained: "Unconscious processing is usually said to be fast, parallel, effortless, and efficient; and conscious processing is usually said to be slow, serial, effortful, and inefficient…. the routine of our lives is said to be governed by intelligent but insensible agencies, whereas consciousness itself shows up for a modest try when there is novelty to be handled, problems to be solved, or troubles to be shot. Dulaney, Donelson E. (1997). Consciousness in the Explicit (Deliberative) and Implicit (Evocative). In Cohen, J.D. & Schooler, J.W. (Eds.) *Scientific Approaches to Consciousness.* Mahway, NJ: Lawrence Erlbaum and Associates.) pg.179-212. Quote at pg.181.

Evolutionary Basis of Thought Repression: As far as I know, this is my own hypothesis.

Only the First Page: Age of pyramids/life of sun: Encyclopedia Americana (1999). Danbury Connecticut: Grolier Incorporated.

Beginning of the evolutionary process: Currently, the human species is probably not evolving, because intelligent people do not bear more offspring than unintelligent people. In the future, however, advances in genetic engineering will likely exponentially advance our development.

Easier to understand: It's also easier to understand why the primary preoccupation of the human species continues to be warfare.

Philosophical note: The filter also performs the following functions, which have philosophical ramifications: 1. It makes the Universe *less* beautiful, so that we are not incapacitated by our sense of awe. 2. It suppresses awareness of the fact that we exist for a very short time, and could cease to exist at any moment. (We may realize this intellectually, but we rarely feel it emotionally.) 3. It distorts our sense of priorities. It makes us believe that the details of day to day life are important, whereas what is going on in the Universe as whole, or what will be happening a billion years from now, is irrelevant. Arguably, the opposite is true. The "big picture" is what really matters because it provides the reason, if there is one, for us to exist at all.

pg. 45: Ambiguity in Text:

Selected from alternative candidates: Marcel, T. (1980). Conscious and preconscious recognition of polysemous words: Locating the selective effects of prior verbal context. In R.S. Nickerson (Ed.) *Attention and Performance VIII*. Hillsdale, NJ: Erlbaum. See also Marcel, T.J. (1983) Conscious and preconscious recognition of polysemous words: Locating the selective effects of prior verbal context. *Cognitive Psychology*. (15): pg. 197-237.

In the early 1970s, researchers presented subjects with two words, one after the other, and asked them to determine as quickly as possible if the second word was taken from the English language. The researchers discovered that the subjects could make the determination much more quickly if the *meaning* of the second word was related to the *meaning* of the first word. In other words, if the subjects were shown the word "NURSE" and then the word "DOCTOR," they could determine that "DOCTOR" was an English word more quickly than if they were shown the word "BREAD" then "DOCTOR." Apparently, presentation of the word "NURSE" activated nurse *associations* and allowed the viewer to process subsequent words in the same subject category more quickly.

In 1983, T.J. Marcel elegantly applied this technique to *polysemous* words. Polysemous words are words with two meanings, such as "PALM," which can refer either to a part of the hand or a tree. Dr. Marcel discovered that when polysemous words are presented subliminally, *they activate associations related to both meanings*. In other words, the subliminal presentation of the word "PALM" enables the viewer to more quickly identify words whose meanings are related to *both* the word "TREE" *and* the word "HAND." Dr. Marcel concluded that on an unconscious level the presentation of a polysemous word accesses all semantic interpretations associated with *each* meaning. At page 437 he states:

> Recent reviews of ambiguity, its resolution, and the effects of context have invoked the theoretical distinctions between preconscious and conscious processes (Citations). Thus, although we may only be aware of one meaning, it may be that multiple meanings have been computed nonconsciously....
>
> There is much evidence that what receives our attention and becomes conscious is only what is selected from alternative candidates.

Researcher Philip M. Mericle has further elaborated: "...in the absence of conscious awareness, the multiple meanings of a stimulus are automatically activated." Merickle, Philip M. (1998). Psychological investigations of unconscious perception. *Journal of Consciousness Studies*. 5(1): pg.5-18. (Quote at pg. 13.)

pg. 50: Distortion of Meaning:

Cartoon ridiculing bigotry: Cooper, C. and Jahoda, M. (1947). The evasion of propaganda: How prejudiced people respond to anti-prejudice propaganda. *The Journal of Psychology* (23): pg. 15-25.

Malamud and Linder: Malamud, W., and Linder Forrest E. (1931). Dreams and their relationship to recent impressions. *Archives of Neurology and Psychiatry*. (25): pg. 1081- 1099.

pg. 52: The Law of Exclusion:

See also the notes referring to "Dreaming of Demons" towards the end of this chapter. Poetzl studies and Fisher replications: An excellent review of Poetzl's work and Fisher's replications can be found at: Shevrin, Howard: (1986). Subliminal perception and dreaming. *The Journal of Mind and Behavior.* Spring and Summer. 7(2-3): pg. 379[249]-396[266].

Subjects who ordinarily did not dream while sleeping could process subliminal data while they were awake. Fisher, Charles and Paul, I.H. (1959). The effect of subliminal visual stimulation on images and dreams: A validation study. *American Psychoanalytic Association Journal.* (7): pg. 35-85.

"Stood the test of time" quote: In Shevrin, Howard (1986) cited above, Dr. Shevrin states at pg. 393[263]: On the whole, it can be said that Poetzl's original findings have been borne out and amplified... a subliminal stimulus registers and is recovered in dreams.... He further notes "perceptual registration is always greater than immediate consciousness reveals." See also Shevrin, Howard (1990). Subliminal perception and repression. In Singer, Jerome (Ed.) *Repression and Dissociation.* Chicago: University of Chicago Press. pg. 103-119. Dr Shevrin similarly states at page 109: ..the basic finding of these early studies have stood the test of time: much more of the stimulus registers during a brief flash than can be consciously reported; moreover, what is not reported can be recovered in dreams as well as in other forms.

Not suprisingly, Fisher found that the viewer's psychological sensitivities and life's experiences influenced how the information in the picture was repressed, transformed and recovered. A woman who had spent five years in a concentration camp, for example, misperceived a swastika as a Star of David. Fisher interpreted the transformation as a "wish fulfilling denial." Reported in Shevrin (1986). Cited above, at pg. 388 [258].

1/1000 second: Shevrin, Howard (1986). Cited above. Page 393.

The more threatening a stimulus is the more likely it is to be repressed, and the greater impact it has on a subliminal level: Shevrin, Howard (1990). Cited above. At pg. 109, the author states:

>...the more items recovered in the dream, the more unpleasant the dream was rated by the judges, suggesting that the recovered items became part of some anxiety-arousing defensive operation...subjects with a higher threshold for recognizing the subliminal stimulus recovered more of the stimulus in their dreams.

pg. 52: Evidence of the Unconscious Through Hypnosis:

Hypnosis played an important role: Stross, Lawrence and Shevrin, Howard. (1969). Hypnosis as a method for investigating unconscious thought processes: A review of research. *American Psychoanalytical Association Journal.* January-April (17): pg. 100-135.

pg. 53:Dream Theory: Freud's dream theory: The manner in which the mind sanitizes unconscious material was discussed in: Bornstein, Robert F. (1990) Subliminal mere exposure and psychodynamic effects: Implications for the psychoanalytic theory of conscious and unconscious mental processes. In Masling, J.M., (Ed) *Empirical Studies of Psychoanalytic Theories.* The Analytic Press. At page 61, Dr. Bornstein states:

Unconscious material is distorted primarily by ego defenses (e.g., displacement, projection, splitting) which alter the unconscious material in order to disguise its unacceptable content. Thus the material that eventually emerges in consciousness is "detoxified," and seldom in its original, repressed form. When unconscious material does manage to find its way undisguised into consciousness, as it does in nightmares, it is typically associated with a considerable anxiety....

pg. 53: Roffenstein study: Roffenstein, G. (1924). Experiments on symbolization in dreams. In Rapaport, D. (Ed.) (1951). *Organization and Pathology of Thought.* New York: Columbia University Press. pg. 249 -256. Discussed in Stross, Lawrence and Shevrin, Howard. Hypnosis as a method for investigating unconscious thought processes: A review of research. *American Psychoanalytical Association Journal.* January-April (17): pg.100-135. The snake quote is at pg. 116.

Farber and Fisher "pleasant hill" dream experiment: Farber, L.H. & Fisher, C. (1943) An experimental approach to dream psychology through the use of hypnosis. *Psychoanalytic Quart*erly. (12): pg. 202-216.

pg. 54: Inducting Neurosis: Luria "artificial neurosis" study: Luria, A.R. (1932). *The Nature of Human Conflicts*, New York: Liveright. Discussed in Stross, Lawrence and Shevrin, Howard (1969). (Cited above).

Artificially generated psychosomatic illnesses: Stross, Lawrence and Shevrin, Howard. (1969). Cited above.

(54):Rationalizing Behavior: Umbrella confabulation: Stross, Lawrence and Shevrin, Howard, (1969). (Cited above). Quote at pg. 101. The authors quote Freud, S. (1964). *Some Elementary Lessons In Psycho-Analysis.* (1940 [1938]). Standard Edition, (23): pg. 279-286. London: Hogarth Press.

pg. 55: Brain Waves and Psychoanalysis:

Shevrin brain wave/psychoanalysis study: Shevrin, H.K., Bond, J.A., Brakel, L.A., Hertel, R.K., and Williams, W.J. (1996). *Conscious and Unconscious Processes.* Guilford Press.

In another study, Dr. Shevrin measured the brain wave patterns of subjects suffering from phobias. He found that when words relating to the phobias were presented subliminally, they were processed within 4/10 of a second after exposure. When they were presented so the viewer was aware of them, however, they were processed *later* – 4/10 to 7/10 of a second after exposure. He concluded that the subliminal words were processed earlier because the viewer never became aware of them, and defensive perceptual processes were never activated. When the viewer was aware of them, the delay between exposure and processing was longer because the filter had to search for associates that were not "anxiety arousing." (Shevrin, H. [1990]. Subliminal perception and repression. In Singer, Jerome [Ed.] *Repression and Dissociation*. Chicago Press.)

See also: Shevrin, Howard. (2001) Event-related markers of unconscious processes. *International Journal of Psychophysiology.* October (42)(2): pg.115-124. This study measured the brain wave patterns of subjects adversely conditioned by subliminal stimuli.

pg. 61: Staying Pure:

pg. 62: Looks like a homosexual: A few readers have suggested it is not entirely politically correct to suggest someone can "look like a homosexual," since it is often impossible to determine a person's sexual orientation from their appearance. I have struggled to rewrite the sentence but can't think of any other way to make the point. The ad taken from a magazine marketed to *heterosexual* men; yet it seems to portray *homosexuals* engaging in sexual activities. I apologize if I have inadvertently offended anyone.

pg. 66: Subliminal Influences on Attitudes:

Chinese symbols/ subliminal face study: Murphy, S.T. and Zajonc, R. (1993). Affect, cognition, and awareness: Affective priming with optimal and suboptimal stimulus exposures. *Journal of Personality and Social Psychology.* (64): pg. 773-779.

See also: Smith, J.W., Spence, D.P., and Klein, G.S. (1959). Subliminal effects of verbal stimuli. *Journal Of Abnormal And Social Psychology.* September. Vols. 58-59: pg. 167-176. The words "happy" and "angry" when subliminally presented influenced the conscious perception of an expressionless face.

Honest/nasty/biography study: Erdley, Cynthia and D'Agostino, Paul R.D. (1988). Cognitive and affective components of automatic priming effects. *Journal of Personality and Social Psychology.* 54(5): pg. 741-747.

pg. 68: Unconscious Learning:

Amnesiac study: Kirsner, K., Speelman, C., Maybery, M., O'Biren-Malone, A., Anderson, M., and MacLeod, C. (1998). *Implicit and Explicit Mental Processes.* London: Lawrence Erlbaum Associates. (Reference. in Introduction and Overview at page 5).

Musically untrained subjects study: Western, Drew. (1998). Unconscious thought, feeling and motivation: The end of a long debate. In Bornstein, R.F. and Masling, J.M. (Eds.) *Empirical Perspectives on the Psychoanalytic Unconscious.* New York: American Psychological Association. Citing: Holyoak, K. and Spellman, B. (1993). Thinking. *Annual Review of Psychology.* (44): pg. 265-315.

Complex mathmatical formula: Lewickim P., Czyzewska, M., and Hill, T. (1997). Cognitive mechanisms for acquiring "experience": The dissociation between conscious and nonconscious cognition. In Cohen, J.D. and Schooler, J.W. (Eds.). *Scientific Approaches to Consciousness.* Mahway, NJ: Lawrence Erlbaum and Associates. pg. 161-179. Reference at page 170.

pg. 69): Unconscious Conditioning:

Rats/anesthesia study: Weinberg, N.M., Gold, P.E., and Sternberg, D.B. (1984). Epinephrine enables Pavlovian fear conditioning under anesthesia. *Science* (223): pg. 409-418.

Subliminal face/shock study: Bunce, S.C., Bernat E., Wong P.S., Shevrin H. (1999). Further evidence for unconscious learning: preliminary support for the conditioning of facial EMP to subliminal stimuli. *Journal of Psychiatric Research.* (33): pg. 341-347.

Snakes and spiders study: Ohman, A., and Soares, J.J.F. (1998). Emotional conditioning to masked stimuli: expectancies for aversive outcomes following nonrecognized fear-relevant stimuli. *Journal of Experimental Psychology:* General. (127): pg. 69-82. See also: Esteves, F., Dimberg, U., and Ohman, A. (1994). Nonconscious associative learning: Pavlovian conditioning of skin conductance responses to masked fear-relevant facial stimuli. *Psychophysiology.* (31): pg. 375-385.

Mmm-mmhs study: Greenspoon, J. (1955). The reinforcing effect of two spoken sounds on the frequency of two responses. *American Journal of Psychology.* (68): pg. 409-416.

Coca-Cola Pavlov quote: Koten, John. Coca-Cola Turns to Pavlov…Car Buyers…90-second ads. *Wall Street Journal.* January 19, 1984.

pg. 70: Conditioning in a Marketing Context:

Gorn conditioning study: Gorn, Gerald. (1982). The effects of music in advertising on choice behavior: A classical conditioning approach. *Journal of Marketing.* 46(1): pg. 94-101.

pg. 71: Not "Random" Choices:

"Birth order" interviewer study: Lewicki, P. (1985). Nonconscious biasing effects of single instances on subsequent judgments. *Journal of Personality and Social Psychology.* (48): pg. 563-574.

Strive/affiliation study: Western, Drew. (1998). Unconscious thought, feeling and motivation: The end of a long debate. In Bornstein, R.F. and Masling, J.M. (Eds.) *Empirical Perspectives on the Psychoanalytic Unconscious.* New York: American Psychological Association. (Ref. at page 33).

These studies also demonstrate that a very mild stimulus can have a significant effect on behavior, when the subject is forced to select from alternative choices that are more or less equally appealing. In the "birth order interviewer" study, for example, the subjects wre required to choose between two eaually available researchers. The logically irrelevant and seemingly insignificant fact that one of the researchers physically resembled an interviewer the subjects had just had an unpleasant encounter with was enough to "tip the scales" and influence their decisions. Similarly, when a consumer has to choose between two brands of vodka that he or she finds equally appealing, subliminal advertising that is only mildly influential can significantly affect the selection process.

pg. 72: The Cumulative Effect:

See: Oshikawa, Sadaomi. (1970). Learning and behavior without awareness: Their implications to consumer behavior and sovereignty. *California Management Review.* Summer. Vol XII, No 4: pg. 61-69. . The author states at page 68:

> …a person gradually forms a new attitude and learns a new verbal behavior by unconscious stimuli. One is led to conclude that the influence of one unit of subliminal stimulus is minute and negligible, *but its effect may be cumulative.* (Emphasis added.)

pg. 72: Subliminal Staying Power:

Levinson anesthesia study: Levinson, B.W. (1965). States of awareness during general anesthesia. *British Journal of Anesthesia.* (37): pg. 544-546. Discussed in Merikle, Philip M. (1998). Psychological Investigations of Unconscious Perception. *Journal of Consciousness Studies.* 5(1): pg. 5-18.

pg. 72: Drive Activation:

Stutterers: Silverman, L.H., Klinger, H., Lustbader, L., Farrell, J, and Martin, A.D. (1972). The effects of subliminal drive stimulation on the speech of stutterers. *Journal of Nervous and Mental Disease.* (155): pg.14-21. (Quote at pg. 14).

See also Silverman, L.H. (1976). The reports of my death are greatly exaggerated. *American Psychologist.* 31(9): pg. 621-637, for an illuminating and easily understood review of this area of research. Other studies achieved similar results using a picture of a man defecating accompanied by the phrase "GO SHIT" as the stimulus.

Schizophrenics: Silverman, L.H. and Spiro, R.H. (1968). The effects of subliminal, supraliminal, and vocalized aggressions on the ego functioning of schizophrenics. *Journal of Nervous and Mental Disease*. 46(1): pg. 53-61.

Suicidal patients: Rutstein, E.H. and Goldberger. The effects of aggressive stimulation on suicidal patients: An experimental study of the psychoanalytic theory of suicide. In Rubenstein , Benjamin J. (Ed.) (1973). *Psychoanalysis and Contemporary Science, Vol. Two*. New York: MacMillan. pg. 157-174.

Homosexuals: Silverman, L.H., Kwawer, J.S., Wolitzsky, C. and Coron, M. (1973). An experimental study of the aspects of the psychoanalytic theory of male homosexuality. *Journal of Abnormal Psychology*. 82(1): pg.178-188.

See also Silverman, L.H. (1983). The subliminal psychodynamic activation method: overview and comprehensive listing of studies. In Masling, J. (Ed.), *Empirical Studies Of Psychoanalytic Theories*, Vol. 3. Hillsdale, NJ: Erlbaum. pg. 55-88. This is an exhaustive review of Dr. Silverman's work. He notes that 50 studies had validated his research. Although not all of them confirmed his hypotheses, the ratio of supportive to non-supportive studies is greater than 3:1.

Note: none of these studies prove Freud was correct; they merely prove the subjects were sensitive to the subliminal images being presented. In other words, the defecation studies do not prove that stuttering is *caused* by toilet training, but they do prove that stutters are psychologically sensitive to defecation images. See Silverman, L.H. (1976). The reports of my death are greatly exaggerated. *American Psychologist*. 31(9): 621-637, at pg. 623.

pg. 74: Relevant Subliminals Are More Effective:

Switched stimuli ineffective: Silverman, L.H. (1983). (Cited immediately above.). Ref. at pages 73-74.

See also Silverman, L.H., Bornstein, A., and Mendelsohn, E. (1976). The further use of the subliminal psychodynamic activation method for the experimental study of the clinical theory of psychoanalysis. *Psychotherapy: Theory, Research, and Practice*. (13): pg. 2-16.

pg. 75: The 20/80 Rule:
Wilkie, William L. (1994). *Consumer Behavior*. Third Edition. New York: John Wiley and Sons, Inc. First published 1996. Ref. at pg. 107.

pg. 82: Regressing to Infancy:

Dichter quote: Dichter, Ernest. (1964). *Handbook of Consumer Motivations: The Psychology of the World of Objects*. Mc Graw Hill.

Oral fantasy study: Spence, Donald P., and Gordon, Carol M. (1967). Activation and measurement of an early oral fantasy: An exploratory study. *Journal of the American Psychoanalytic Association*. (15): pg. 99-129.

pg. (86): Anxiety, Depression, and Addiction:

Half of heavy drinkers have psychiatric disorders: Zack, M. and Toneatto, T. (1999). Implicit activation of alcohol concepts by negative affective cues distinguishes between problem drinkers with high and low psychiatric distress. *Journal of Abnormal Psychology*. 108(3): 518-531. Ref. at page 518.

Depressed anxious people smoke and drink more, and drinkers and smokers more likely to be anxious and depressed: Stewart, S.H., Karp, J., Pihl, R.O., and Peterson, R.A.

(1997). Anxiety sensitivity and self reported reasons for drug use. *Journal of Substance Abuse. (9): pg. 223-240.*

See also Bacona, E., Vazques, F., Fuentes, M.J., and Lorenzo, Md.C.(1998). Anxiety, affect, depression, and cigarette consumption. *Personality and Individual Differences.* January 1; 26(1): pg. 112-119. "Results of our study confirm a relationship between depression, negative affect, and cigarette consumption, especially, in the subjects with a consumption of 31 or more cigarettes a day."

See also: Comeau, N., Stewart, S.H., and Loba, P. (2001). *Addictive behaviors.* (26): pg. 803-825. Anxious people are more likely to smoke and smokers are more likely to be anxious.

See also: Kandel, D.B., Huang, F-Y, and Davies, M. (2001). Comorbidity between patterns of substance use dependence and psychiatric syndromes. *Drug and Alcohol Dependence.* (64): pg. 233-241 …. "drug-dependent individuals have higher rates of psychiatric symptoms."

See also: Escobedo, L.G., Kirch, D.G., and Anda, R.F. (1996). Depression and smoking initiation among U.S. Latinos. *Addiction.* 91(1): pg. 113-119. The authors state at page 118: "The incidence of smoking initiation at all developmental stages had been generally higher among adults at interview who had depressed mood or a history of major depression."

See also: Johnson, J.G., Cohen, P., Pine, D.S.,. Klein, D.F., Kasen, S., and Brook, J.S. (2000). Association between cigarette smoking and anxiety disorders during adolescence and early adulthood. *JAMA: Journal of the American Medical Association.* November. 284(18): pg. 2348-2351.

Schizophrenics and smoking: Herran, A., de Santiago, A., Sandoya, M., Fernandez, M.J., Diez-Manrique, J.F., and Vazqyes-Barquero, J.L. (2000). Determinants of smoking behavior in outpatients with schizophrenia. *Schizophrenia Research.* (41): pg. 373-381. (Among schizophrenics, the number of cigarettes smoked per day is correlated with state anxiety, trait anxiety, and neuroticism.)

Conditionability and anxiety: Zack, M., Toneatto, T., and MacLeod, Colin M. (2000) Anxiety and explicit alcohol-related memory in problem drinkers. *Addictive Behaviors.* (27): pg. 331-343. The authors state at page 332: "'Conditionability,' a personality dimension strongly related to clinical anxiety …reflects the ease with which an individual can be conditioned." Citing Gershuny, B.S. and Sher, K.J. (1998). The relation between personality and anxiety: Findings from a 3-year prospective study. *Journal of Abnormal Psychology.* (107): pg. 252-262, and Eysenck H.J. and Eysenck S.B. (1969). *Personality Structure and Measurement.* San Diego: Knapp.

Heavy drinkers drink when depressed: Zack (cited immediately above) at page 520: "Unlike social drinkers, problem drinkers tend to drink more often in negative than in positive affective states, a bias that increases with levels of alcohol dependence."

Negative mood inducers increase alcohol cravings: Zack (cited immediately above) at page 520: "Cue exposure research with dependant drinkers shows that negative mood induction can increase desire to drink even when physical alcohol cues (e.g., smell of alcohol) are absent. (citing Litt, M.D., Cooney, N.L., Kadden, R.M., & Gaupg., L.

(1990). Reactivity to alcohol cues and induced moods in alcoholics. *Addictive behaviors*. (15): pg.137-146.

Drinking associated with depression: Zack (cited above) at page 519: "The reliable and frequent pairing of negative affect [mood] and heavy drinking in problem drinkers with high PD [psychiatric distress] would provide an opportunity for conditioned associations to develop between negative affect and alcohol use."

Imaging negative scripts increases cigarette cravings: Tiffany York, S.T., and Drobes, D.J. (1990). Imagery and smoking urges: the manipulation of affective content. *Addictive Behaviors*. 15(6): pg. 531-539.

Trauma words increased cravings in Vietnam Veterans: Beckham, J.C., Lytle, B.L., Vrana, S.R., Hertzberg, MA, Feldman, M.E., Shipley, R.H.(1996). Smoking withdrawal symptoms in response to a trauma-related stressor among Vietnam combat veterans with posttraumatic stress disorder. *Addictive Behaviors*. 21(1): pg. 93-101.

Smokers consume more cigarettes before speaking publicly: Schachter, S. (1978). Pharmacological and psychological determinants of smoking. *Annals of Internal Medicine*. (88): pg. 104-114.

pg. 88: Drive Activation In Every Day Life:
Drive Activation In Every Day Life: Silverman, Lloyd H. (1972). Drive stimulation and psychopathology: On the conditions under which drive related external events evoke pathological reactions. In Holt, R.R. and Peterfreund (Eds.) *Psychoanalysis and Contemporary Science* (Vol.1). New York: Macmillian. pg. 307-326. Ref. at pg. 310-312.

pg. 89: Therapeutic Uses of Subliminals:
Beating Dad is OK/ Mommy and I are one: Reviewed in: Silverman, L.H. (1983). The subliminal psychodynamic activation method: Overview and comprehensive listing of studies. In Masling, J. (Ed.) *Empirical Studies Of Psychoanalytic Theories*. Vol. 3. Hillsdale, NJ: Erlbaum. pg. 55-88.

See also: Siegal, P. and Weinberger, J. (1998). Capturing the "mommy and I are one" merger fantasy: The oneness motive. In *Empirical Perspectives on the Psychoanalytic Unconscious*. New York: American Psychological Association. pg. 71-98.

NO ONE LOVES ME: Masling, J., Bornstein, R., Poynton, F., Reed, S., & Katkin, E. (1991). Perception without awareness and electrodermal responding: A strong test of subliminal psychodynamic activation effects. *The Journal of Mind and Behavior Winter*. 12(1): pg. 33-48.

pg. 92: Perceptual Vigilance:
Disturbing subliminals "stand out:" Blume, G.S. (1954). An experimental reunion of psychoanalytic theory with perceptual vigilance and defense. *Journal of Abnormal and Social Psychology*. (49): pg. 94-98.

Phobics/fear relevant word study: Foa, E.B., and McNally, R.J. (1986). Sensitivity to feared stimuli in obsessive-compulsives: a dichotic listening analysis. *Cognitive Therapy & Research*. (10): pg. 477-486.

Anxious mothers study: Parkinson, L. and Rachman, S. (1981). Speed of recovery from an uncontrived stress. *Advances in Behavior Research and Therapy*. (3): pg. 119-123.

See also: MacLeod, Colin and Rutherford, Elizabeth. (1998). Automatic and strategic cognitive biases in anxiety and depression. In *Implicit and Explicit Mental Processes.* London: Lawrence Erlbaum Associates. pg.233-254.

More difficult to "see" the phallus: Many studies have demonstrated viewers have a much harder time recognizing a threatening stimulus than a neutral one, and that a threatening subliminal stimulus has a greater effect on behavior. For example, see Silverman, Lloyd H. (1964). A clinical experimental approach to the study of subliminal manipulation: The effects of a drive related stimulus upon Rorschach responses. *Journal of Abnormal Psychology.* 69(2): pg. 158-172. ("Normal" subjects" who had a high threshold for a picture of female genitalia exhibited pathological reactions following subliminal exposure.) Discussed in reference to "Subliminal Advertising is Psychologically Harmful," in Chapter 6.

pg. 93: Banishing the "White Bear":

White Bear Studies: Wegner, Daniel M. (1989) *White Bears and Other Unwanted Thoughts: Suppression, Obsession, and the Psychology of Mental Control.* New York: Penguin Books.

Similar study in which thoughts of sex were suppressed: Wegner, Daniel M., Shortt, Joann W., Blake, Anne W., and Page, Michelle S. (1990). The suppression of exciting thoughts. *Journal of Personality and Social Psychology.* 38(3): pg. 409-418.

Faked Sawmill study: Koriat, A., Melkman, R., Averil, J.A.., and Lazarus, R.S. (1972). The self-control of emotional reactions to a stressful film. *Journal of Personality.* (40): pg. 601-619.

Parent/Sex study: Martin, Barclay. (1964). Expression and inhibition of sex motive arousal in college males. *Journal of Abnormal and Social Psychology:* (68): 307-312.

Subjects who are inclined to *forget* briefly-flashed tachistoscopic images are more likely to *dream* about them, and more likely to have *bad dreams*: Luborsky, Lester and Shevrin, Howard. (1962). Forgetting of Tachistoscopic Exposures as a function of repression. *Perceptual and Motor Skills.* (14): pg. 189-190.

pg. 94: The Nature of the Unconscious:

Seething cauldron of sexual and aggressive drives: Quote from page 3 in Western, Drew. (1998). Unconscious thought, feeling and motivation: The end of a long debate. In Bornstein, R.F. and Masling, J.M. (Eds.) *Empirical Perspectives on the Psychoanalytic Unconscious.* New York: American Psychological Association. pg. 1-43.

It can write poetry, and it makes long term plans. Bornstein, Robert F. and Masling, Joseph M. (1998). Introduction: The psychoanalytic unconscious. In Bornstein, R.F. and Masling, J.M. (Eds.) *Empirical Perspectives on the Psychoanalytic Unconscious.* New York: American Psychological Association. At page xx the authors state: "It now appears that the unconscious is 'smarter' than first thought, capable of processing complex verbal and visual information and even anticipating (and planning for) future events. (Citations).

(94): The unconscious is a parallel processor: Dulaney, Donelson E. (1997). Consciousness in the explicit (deliberative) and implicit (evocative). In Cohen, J.D. and Schooler, J.W. (Eds.). *Scientific Approaches to Consciousness.* Mahway, NJ: Lawrence Erlbaum and Associates. pg. 179-212. At page 181 the author states: "unconscious

processing is usually said to be fast, parallel, effortless, and efficient; and conscious processing is usually said to be slow, serial, effortful, and inefficient...."

Unconscious associations "fan out:" Pen/knee discussion: Shevrin, H. and Fisher, C. (1967). Changes in the effects of a waking subliminal stimulus as a function of dreaming and non-dreaming sleep. *Journal of Abnormal Psychology.* 72(4): pg. 362-8. The pen/knee drawing is taken from this study.

See also Shevrin, H. and Luborsky. (1961). The rebus technique. *Journal of Nervous and Mental Disease.* (133): pg. 479-88. This was the initial study investigating rebus processing.

See also: Silverman, L.H. and Spiro, R.H.(1968). The effects of subliminal, supraliminal, and vocalized aggression on the ego functioning of schizophrenics. *The Journal of Nervous and Mental Disease.* 146(1): pg. 50-61. The authors state, at Page 59: "one idea can spread more freely through the system than is possible with conscious thinking..." (quoting Spence, D.P. and Holland B.(1962). The restricting effects of awareness: A paradox and an explanation. *Journal of Abnormal Psychology.* (64): pg. 163-174.

(95): The unconscious is Freudian: Dixon quote: Dixon, N.F. (1971). *Subliminal Perception: The Nature of a Controversy* London: McGraw Hill. Ref. at pg. 124.

See also: Bach, S. (1959). The symbolic effects of words in subliminal, supraliminal, and incidental presentations. Unpublished Doct. Dissert. New York University.

See also: Pine, F. (1960) Incidental stimulation: a study of preconscious transformations. *Journal of Abnormal Social Psychology.* (60): pg. 68-75.

See also: Pine, F. (1961) Incidental vs. focal presentation of drive related stimuli. *Journal of Abnormal Social Psychology.* (62): pg. 482-490.

See also: Pine, F. (1964) The bearing of psychoanalytic theory on selected issues in research on marginal stimuli. Journal of Nervous and Mental Disease. 138(3): pg. 205-222.

(96): The unconscious is creative: Automatic writing and drawing: Kelly, William L. (1991). *Psychology of the Unconscious: Mesmer, Janet, Freud, Jung, and Current issues.* New York: Prometheus Books. Ref. at pg. 177.

pg. 97: Thinking in Reverse:

Lucky Number study: Epstein, S. (1994). Integration of the cognitive and the psychodynamic unconscious. *American Psychologist..* (49): pg. 709-724.

Additional note: The Scientific Method is successful because it overcomes backwards thinking.

pg. 98: The Nightmare in the Magazine

Note: As with all the illustrations in this book, *my analysis is based solely on the appearance of the picture.* I do not know how the creators of the ad intended it to be interpreted, or what they were driving at when they created it. I am also not inferring in any way that the *models* portrayed in the picture had any knowledge of or understanding of any of the "secret" meanings articulated in my hypothesis. This also applies to the *Portfolio* discussion on page 198. The illusions in both instances could have occurred coincidentally.

pg. 103: Dreaming of Demons:

Effect of figure-ground drawings on dreaming: Refer to the footnotes in reference to "The Law of Exclusion," discussed earlier in this chapter.

Poetzl photography analogy: Shevrin, Howard: (1986). Subliminal perception and dreaming. *The Journal of Mind and Behavior*. Spring and Summer. 7(2-3): pg. 379[249]-396[266]. At pg. 382[252], the author states:

> For Poetzl, the visual apparatus was like a photographic darkroom in which the visual perception, like a photographic plate, was developed on the basis of different combinations of "chemicals" at different times. During waking perception, the flashed pictures registered totally on the plate, but only a few elements could be developed and printed (delivered into consciousness)... the remaining elements were developed later and printed in the dream.

See also: Fisher, Charles and Paul, I.H. (1959). The effect of subliminal visual stimulation on images and dreams: A validation study. *American Psychoanalytic Association Journal*. (7): pg. 35-85. (Discussed in footnotes in reference to "The Holes Between Things" in the beginning of this chapter.)

See also: Paul, H and Fisher, C. (1959). Subliminal visual stimulation: A study of its subsequent influence on images and dreams. *Journal of Nervous and Mental Disease* 29(4): pg.315-340.

pg. 103: Vicary Misapplied:

Vicary's claims exaggerated: Rogers, Stuart 1992-1993. How a publicity blitz created the myth of subliminal advertising. *Public Relations Quarterly*. Winter. 37(4): pg.12-17. The author questions whether Vicary's experiments really took place at all.

See also: Weir, Walter. Another look at subliminal "facts." *Advertising Age*, October 15, 1984. pg. 46. The author states, "under questioning, Mr. Vicary admitted he had fabricated the results of his "test" and had done so because his business was failing and he had hoped to revive it."

A review of studies purporting to "prove" subliminal advertising is ineffective and doesn't exist is included in Chapter 3.

pg. 104: The Viewpoint of Psychologists:

"Could possibly be developed" quote: Greenwald, A.G. and Draine, S.C. (1997). Do stimuli enter the mind unnoticed? Tests with a new method. In Cohen, J.D. & Schooler, J.W. (Eds.) *Scientific Approaches to Consciousness*. Mahway, NJ: Lawrence Erlbaum and Associates. pg. 83-108. Quote at page 106.

Dr. Dixon is the author of: Dixon, N.F. (1971). *Subliminal Perception: The Nature of a Controversy* London, McGraw Hill.

Kilbourne's stand: Kilbourne, William E., Painton, Scott, and Ridley, Danny. (1985). The effect of sexual embedding on responses to magazine advertisements. *Journal of Advertising*. 14(2): pg. 48-56. Quote at page 54.

pg. 105: The Private vs. the Public Sector:

More money: One billion dollars a year in 1957: Rose, Alvin W. (1958). Motivation research and subliminal advertising. *Social Research*. Fall (25): pg. 271-284. The author states at pg. 273: "Motivational research in the United States is a billion dollar per year business; nearly every major industry in the country is employing psychologists to pierce the mind of the consumer…"

Advertising and NASA expenditures: Statistical abstract of the United States 2000. The National Data Book. US Department of Commerce. Issued December 2000.

Advertising: No. 937 Advertising - Estimated Expenditures, through medium: 1990 to 1999.

Nasa: No 978, R&D Expenditures: 1960 to 1999.

pg. 107: Chapter 3:
BOPPED DOING THE BUMP/ REBUTTING THE DENIAL

pg. 107: Too Many Coincidences:
Advertisers deny they use subliminal techniques: Kanner, Bernice. (1989). From the subliminal to the ridiculous. *New York* magazine, December 4. pg. 18-20. Prophetically, the author commented: "If subliminals worked, wouldn't there be textbooks on how to practice it?" and "How can showing someone a penis get him to switch, say, from Kent (cigarettes) to Marlboro?"

See also: Weir, Walter. Another Look at Subliminal 'Facts.' *Advertising Age*. October 15, 1984. pg. 46. The author states, "If subliminal advertising did exist, there certainly would be textbooks available on how to practice it."

For an overview of the advertising industry's point of view, see: Haberstroh, Jack. (1994). *Ice Cube Sex: The Truth About Subliminal Advertisi*ng. Notre Dame, Indiana: Cross Cultural Publications.

pg. 120: Advertisers Are Freudians:
Quote from Virginia Slims account executive: Originally reported by W.B. Key: Key, Wilson Bryan. (1981). *The Clam-Plate Orgy and Other Techniques for Manipulating Your Behavior*. New York: Signet at page 26. The quotation was also discussed in Haberstroh, Jack.. (1994). *Ice Cube Sex: The Truth About Subliminal Advertisi*ng. Notre Dame, Indiana: Cross Cultural Publications, at page 49.

1994 marketing text *Consumer Behavior:* Wilkie, William L. (1994). *Consumer Behavior*. Third Edition. New York. John Wiley and Sons, Inc. First published 1996. The "unconscious level" quote is on page 126. The "Combat" campaign is discussed on pages 130-131.

1958 Motivation Research article: Rose, Alvin W. (1958). Motivation research and subliminal advertising. *Social Research*. Fall (25): pg. 271-284. Quote from pg. 275.

Consumer Behavior and Behavioral Sciences 1960s text: Britt, Steuart H. (Ed.) (1966). *Consumer behavior and the Behavioral Sciences: Theories and Applications*. New York: John Wiley and Sons, Inc. Quote from pages 42. At page 103 the text states:

> The pathologic gambler's unconscious wish to lose as punishment for equally unconscious aggression;…bargain hunting as the need to outsmart others and to express aggression toward a substitute of the bad, refusing mother; chronic psychogenic constipation as a symbol of withholding from the world ("not giving"); [and] homosexual and Oedipus tendencies….

pg 123-124: Damned If They Do:

Subliminals are also cost effective because even mild influences can significantly affect choice, when the consumer is choosing between brands that are consciously equally desirable. Refer to the discussion re: pg.71: Not "Random" Choices, above.

pg. 125: The Role of Images:

Visual Persuasion: Massaris, Paul. (1997). *Visual Persuasion: The Role of Images in Advertising*. Thousand Oaks, CA: Sage Publications. Quote from pages 10-13.

pg. 130: Protesting Too Much:

The partner's quote: The partner is responding to a letter by Jack Haberstroh. The dialogue was reported by Haberstroh in Haberstroh, Jack. (1994). *Ice Cube Sex: The Truth About Subliminal Advertisi*ng. Notre Dame, Indiana: Cross Cultural Publications, at pg. 23.

pg. 130: No Gallup to This Poll:

The Answer is No article: Rogers, Martha and Seiler, Christine. (!994). The answer is no: A national survey of advertising industry practitioners and their clients about whether they use subliminal advertising, *Journal Of Advertising Research*. March/April 34(2): pg. 36-45.

pg. 131: Scientific Disinformation:

Moore study: Moore, Timothy E. (1982) Subliminal advertising: What you see is what you get. *Journal of Marketing*. Spring (46): pg. 38-47. Mr. Moore also argues that subliminal advertising is *impractical* because individual thresholds differ. This is obviously erroneous. The subliminal content of most of the illustrations in this book are not consciously perceived by the vast majority of viewers until it is pointed out to them. On page 45 Mr. Moore states, "Key provides no documentation for the effects that he attributes to embedded stimuli…Key appears to invent whatever features of perception and memory would be necessary…." I hope most readers will conclude I have responded to this criticism.

(132):Dummy magazine study: Kelly, Steven J. (1979). Subliminal embeds in print advertising: A challenge to ethics. *Journal Of Advertising* 8(3): pg. 20-22. One can also assume that the author chose the *least* convincing of Key's examples.

Kilbourne (Marlboro Lights penis/rock) experiment: Kilbourne, William E., Painton, Scott, and Ridley, Danny. (1985). The effect of sexual embedding on responses to magazine advertisements. *Journal of Advertising*. 14(2): pg. 48-56.

Other studies often cited by the advertising industry:

1. Hawkins, D. (1970). The effects of subliminal stimulation on drive level and brand preference. *Journal of Marketing Research*. Vol. VII August. pg. 322-326; and Beatty, S.E. and Hawkins D.I. (1989). Subliminal stimulation: Some new data and interpretation. *Journal of Advertising*. Summer. 18(3): pg. 4-9. In the 1970 study, subjects who were exposed to the subliminal messages "COKE" or "DRINK COKE" became more thirsty. The authors concluded "a simple subliminal stimulus can serve to arouse a basic drive." The 1989 study replicated the original experiment, but cast doubt on the conclusions of the first. Both studies used unemotional, psychologically irrelevant commands, and therefore are not very meaningful.

2. Gable, M., Wilkens, H.T., Harris, Lynn, and Feinberg, R. (1987). An evaluation of subliminally embedded sexual stimuli in graphics. *Journal of Advertising.* 16(1): pg. 26-31.

The authors of this study took separate photographs of four products: a camera, a pen, a bottle of beer, and food (consisting of a croissant, cheese and a cup of coffee.) Allegedly, they then created copies of the four pictures and embedded "sexual stimuli" in them. They did not explain what the embedded sexual stimuli consisted of, but they included copies of the pictures when they published their study.

The subjects in the experiment were shown the pictures in pairs. For example, they were shown the picture of the pen containing the embed, and the picture of the pen not containing the embed, at the same time. They were asked which one they *preferred*, and to make their selection in a few seconds.

Considerably more subjects preferred the pen with the embed over the pen without the embed (249 vs.176.) Slightly more subjects preferred the camera with the embed over the camera without the embed (227 vs.198). Men's preference for the pen with the embed was fairly substantial, whereas women's preference for the camera with the embed was slightly negative. (120 vs. 89 vs. 107-109.)

The authors reported that more subjects preferred the beer without the embed (264 vs. 161). They similarly reported that more subjects preferred the food without the embed (280 vs.145.)

The amazing thing about this study is that although one can easily find the word SEX scratched on the camera, (which was preferred) and with a little more difficulty one can find the word SEX in the shadows behind the pen (which also was preferred), it is virtually impossible, however, to find embedded stimuli in the beer or food pictures (which were not preferred).

I showed the pictures to students at San Jose State University and offered them a $5.00 reward if they could find the sexual embeds. They easily located them in the pen and camera pictures, but could not find them at all in the beer and food pictures. The Gable, Wilkens et.al. study therefore seems to be invalid because, contrary to the authors' assertions, the beer and food stimuli do not appear to contain discernible sexual embeds.

Even if the beer and food pictures do contain sexual embeds, and all the students I showed them to and I failed to find them, the study is invalid because the subliminal content of the pictures is not balanced. The embeds in the camera and pen pictures are fairly clear, but the supposed embeds in the beer and food pictures are not. Comparing the subjects' preferences for the camera and pen against their preferences for the beer and food is therefore not productive.

Furthermore, determining which pictures the subjects preferred is not meaningful. The television commercials people *like* the most are not necessarily the ones that produce the most *sales*. Some subjects may have consciously preferred the pictures without embeds, because the pictures with embeds unconsciously made them uncomfortable.

pg. 133: With Their Hands In The Cookie Jar:

Slipped in the Shorts: Stroup, Katherine. Three's company, four's a crowd. *Newsweek*. March 26, 2001. pg.51.

A Dramatic Bedroom Setting: *San Francisco Chronicle*. January 28, 1980. pg. 2.

Rats: The quote is from: Berke, Richard L. The 2000 campaign: The ad campaign: Democrats see, and smell, rats in G.O.P. ad. *New York Times*. September 12, 2000.

See also: Subliminal headache for Mr. Bush. *New York Times*. September 13, 2000.

See also: The 2000 campaign: The Texas Governor; Bush says rats reference in ad was unintentional. *New York Times*. September 13, 2000.

The Lion King: Barclay, Linda. 'Dust-busters' expose animal sex plot. *Toronto Star*. September 9, 1995.

See also: Disney Movies facing offbeat attacks from religious groups. *The Guardian/ The Gazette*. (Montreal). October 25, 1995.

See also: Tran, Mark. Subliminal smut in Disney movies, religious right says. *The Guardian/The Ottawa Citizen*. October 27, 1995.

Russian Imitators: *San Francisco Chronicle*. August 8, 2002.

pg. 136: Serving Themselves:

I'm Your Penis: Subliminal sounds: Kalish, David.(1988). Now you hear it…(subliminal advertising). *Marketing and Media Decisions*. May (23): pg. 32-33. I certainly am not implying in any way that Mr. Palmer creates the type of subliminal sounds I hypothesized; rather, I am suggesting that others may be tempted to experiment with such processes.

The Saintly President: Skenazy, Lenore. Political touch-ups: Special effects benefit Bush. *Advertising Age*. April 18, 1988. pg. 3.

pg. 136: Serving Themselves:

pg. 138: Saturday Night Fever: *Saturday Night Fever* © 1977 Paramount Pictures. All Rights Reserved. *Stayin' Alive* [by the Bee Gees Band from the album "Saturday Night Fever] (P) 1777 RSO Records, Inc.

pg. 137: Cinematic Subliminals:

The Exorcist: *The Exorcist* © 1973 Warner Bros. Re-released as "The version you've never seen." Program content © 2000. Photography © 1973 Warner Bros. All Rights Reserved. Neither Warner Brothers or Mr. Freidkin has endorsed or approved my commentary in any way.

Wilson Bryan Key reported that Warner Brothers admitted using fleeting images: Regarding the fleeting death masks in the *Exorcist*, Wilson Bryan Key reported the following in *Media Sexploitation*, at page 102:

> Warner Brothers, who produced the film, refused to comment about the subliminal cuts but admitted their existence, claiming, "We thought everyone knew." One of Director Friedkin's assistants …conceded, "It's not common knowledge that the film contained subliminal cuts." He denied their use in the *Exorcist* was a secret, however.
> –Key, Wilson Bryan. (1977) *Media Sexploitation*. New York: Signet. (pg. 98-117)

Around the threshold of consciousness: *In Media Sexploitation*, Key reported the Father Karras dream sequence mask was displayed for 1/48 of a second. According to Massaris, Paul. (1997). *Visual Persuasion: The Role of Images in Advertising*. Thousand Oaks, CA: Sage Publications. at pg. 70, the minimum time an image can be displayed in a movie (a single frame) is 1/24 of a second. The minimum time an image can be displayed on television is 1/30 of a second. However long the masks are displayed in *The Exorcist*, they are clearly presented around the threshold of consciousness. Some people are aware of them, and some are not, and whether they become aware of them has a lot to do with whether they are looking for them. Appendix A suggests several experiments exploring this.

(138):Viewers who consciously perceive the death masks often do not realize how disturbing they are, and tend to forget them after exposure: Luborsky, L., and Shevrin, H., (1962). Forgetting of Tachistoscopic Exposures as a function of repression. *Perceptual and Motor Skills*. (14): pg. 189-190. The study found that subjects who rely on the defense of repression (and are therefore more inclined to forget a tachistoscopic display) are more likely to have bad dreams about the material they have repressed.

pg. 140: A Different Sense:

Subliminals in a more artistic sense: The fact that Regan's male voices belonged to other characters in the movie was revealed by Director Freidkin in his comments in the *Exorcist* DVD, released in 2000. He did use the word "subliminal" in his discussion.

pg. 140: Subliminal Sounds In Movies:

Subliminal *audio* techniques in the *Exorcist*: Key reported the following in *Media Sexploitation* (cited above) at page 110: "Freidkin openly admitted he had used several natural sound effects in the movies auditory background. One of these, he explained, was the sound of angry, agitated bees." At page 111, Key stated: "Another auditory archetype mixed subtly into the sound track was the terrified squealing of pigs while they were being slaughtered."

All the President's Men, Alfred Hitchcock, and King Kong: Weis, Elizabeth. (1995). Sync tanks: The art and technique of postproduction sound. *Cineaste*. Winter-spring v. 21 m1-2. pgs.56-62.

Silence of the Lambs: (related article in the same magazine) Creating sound for Demme: Ron Bochar discusses the creation of sound effects in scenes from Jonathan Demme's *Silence of the Lambs* and *Philadelphia*.

pg. 141: Embeds In Moving Pictures:

Tomb Raider: *Lara Croft Tomb Raider* ™ and © 2001 by Paramount Pictures. All Rights Reserved.

Tomb Raider white horse: My analysis is based solely on the appearance of the white horse in the film. I have not discussed the matter with the producers, and they have not endorsed or approved my commentary in any way.

White horses symbolize life and uncontrollable instinctive drives: Jung, Carl G., con Franz, M, Henderson, J, Jacobi, J., Jaffe. *A Man and His Symbols*. (1964). Aldus Books Limited. New York: Doubleday and Company, Inc.

pg. 144: The Subliminal Continuum:

<u>Enchilada Nirvana</u>: Just before going to press, Taco Bell came out with another masturbatory ambiguous slogan: "To experience enchilada nirvana, you've got to think outside the bun." (Emphasis on "you've got.")

<u>Reversal of stereotypical roles</u>: Very few people in the 1950s realized that popular media was extremely unhealthy for little girls, because it usually portrayed females as excessively passive and ineffectual. Today, most people don't realize that the reverse is true: media has become very unhealthy for little boys. While some shows flatter the male gender, most do not. Husbands in Circuit City ads, for example, are often portrayed as ignorant children who lose control when taken to the store. Television shows like *Everyone Loves Raymond* portray the husband as far less intelligent, capable, and commanding than his spouse. The lack of role models for male children may have much to do with their declining academic test scores.

<u>Other common scripts unhealthy in media include</u>: 1. Men kill other men and have sex with women as a reward; and 2. In situation comedies, small lies lead to awkward situations that are finally resolved by telling the truth. These scripts are generally sympathetic to the liar, and do not question the morality of such deceptiveness.

pg. 149: Chapter 4:
DISTURBING TABOOS/ THE COURAGE TO LOOK

pg. 149: How Mom and Lazy Boy Celebrated Fathers Day:

<u>Note</u>: As with all the illustrations in this book, I am merely proposing a hypothesis; *my analysis is based solely on the appearance of the picture.* I do not know how the creators of the ad intended it to be interpreted, or what they were driving at when they created it.

<u>Quote re: selling to children</u>: Rose, Alvin W. (1958). Motivation research and subliminal advertising. *Social Research*. Fall. (25): pg.271-284. Quote from pg. 275.

<u>See also</u>: McMeal, James U. (1994). *Kids as Customers: A Handbook of Marketing to Children.*

New York: Lexington Books. pg.63-69. (Children responsible for 35% of furniture sales, amounting to 1.75 billion dollars annually.)

pg. 152: Oedipus in Media:

<u>Star Wars</u>: *Star Wars* is a federally registered trademark. The film original Star Wars © 1977 Twentieth Century Fox Film Corporation. All Rights Reserved. ™ and © 1977 Lucas Film Ltd.

<u>Spider-Man</u>: *Spider-Man and the Return of the Green Goblin*™ and © 2002 Marvel Characters, Inc. All Rights Reserved.

<u>Artificial Intelligence</u>: *Artificial Intelligence* © 2002 DreamWorks LLC and Warner Bros. All Rights Reserved.

As I go to press, *The Hulk* is another movie based on a comic book that has become remarkably popular with young males. In the film, the Hulk not only engages in mortal combat with his *father*, but the father of the girlfriend of his alter ego is trying to kill him. (General Ross wants to kill the Hulk, whose alter-ego (Bruce Banner) is in love with Betty Ross, the General's daughter.) (*The Hulk* is also a federally registered trademark of Marvel Characters, Inc.)

pg. 154: Sail Away

Note: As with all the illustrations in this book, *my analysis is based solely on the appearance of the picture*. I do not know how the creators of the ad intended it to be interpreted, or what they were driving at when they created it. I am also not inferring in any way that the *models* portrayed in the picture had any knowledge of or understanding of any of the "secret" meanings articulated in my hypothesis.

pg. 156: Dish on Demand:

San Francisco Chronicle April 4, 2002.

Note: As with all the illustrations in this book, *my analysis is based solely on the appearance of the picture*. I do not know how the creators of the ad intended it to be interpreted, or what they were driving at when they created it. I am also not inferring in any way that the *models* portrayed in the picture had any knowledge of or understanding of any of the "secret" meanings articulated in my hypothesis.

pg. 156: Oblivious to the Obvious:

Oblivious To The Obvious: McGinnies, E. (1949). Emotionality and perceptual defense. *Psychological Review* (56): pg. 244-251. McGinnies wrote: "It is well established, then, that the perceptual 'filtering' of visual stimuli serves, in many instances, to protect the observer for as long as possible from an awareness of objects which have unpleasant emotional significance for him."

pg. 159: Free Swim:

I deleted the identity of the manufacturer. My intent is to highlight general practices in advertising, not to comment on the particular practices of particular individuals. As with all the illustrations in this book, *my analysis is based solely on the appearance of the picture*. I do not know how the creators of the ad intended it to be interpreted, or what they were driving at when they created it. I am also not inferring in any way that the *models* portrayed in the picture had any knowledge of or understanding of any of the "secret" meanings articulated in my hypothesis.

Pg. 160: The Psycho Slayer:

Note: As with all the illustrations in this book, *my analysis is based solely on the appearance of the picture*. I do not know how the creators of the picture intended it to be interpreted, or what they were driving at when they created it. I am also not inferring in any way that the *models* portrayed in the picture had any knowledge of or understanding of any of the "secret" meanings articulated in my hypothesis.

pg. 162 The Jailer, and pg. 163: Susan and Paul:

Note: As with all the illustrations in this book, *my analysis is based solely on the appearance of the picture*. I do not know how the creators of the picture intended it to be interpreted, or what they were driving at when they created it. I am also not inferring in any way that the *models* portrayed in the picture had any knowledge of or understanding of any of the "secret" meanings articulated in my hypothesis.

pg. 164: Rough Research:

Note: As with all the illustrations in this book, *my analysis is based solely on the appearance of the picture.* I do not know how the creators of the ad intended it to be interpreted, or what they were driving at when they created it. I am also not inferring in any way that the *models* portrayed in the picture had any knowledge of or understanding of any of the "secret" meanings articulated in my hypothesis.

pg. 165: The Attack:

My *guess* is that a suggestion of the monster may have appeared by coincidence, and then may have been creatively enhanced. I don't have evidence of this – as with all the illustrations in this book *I am merely proposing a hypothesis based on the appearance of the picture.* I have not interviewed the photographer or consulted the agency that released the picture. I have not had the photo analyzed by experts. I have included the illustration because it is an example of how subliminals *may* be used to enhance the emotional impact of photos. This concept is discussed in more detail at the end of Chapter 6.

I regretfully am unable to credit the photo because I don't know who the copyright owner, photographer, or distributor is. I found it on the Internet (by searching Yahoo-news photos) shortly after 9/11. If you are the photographer who took the photograph and you wish to comment on my analysis, I will post your statement on our website.

A news photographer I discussed this with told me that all news reporting agencies have strict policies prohibiting the adulteration of news photos in any way. Photographers are immediately fired if they are caught violating this rule. Some individuals have lost their jobs because they were caught creating *composite* news photos, in which two or more images were combined using PhotoShop®. Since most people are not aware of or looking for subliminal embeds, the likelihood of being exposed for subliminally enhancing a photo is probably considerably less than for creating composite pictures.

News reporting agencies (like Reuters, Associated Press, etc.) work at a fast and furious pace, in a fairly public environment. It would be difficult for them to secretly adulterate photographs without getting caught. Individual photographers also work at a fast pace, but in a much more private manner. They are highly motivated to have their work commercially appreciated. On balance, it is not inconceivable that some individuals working in the news media make use of subliminal enhancements, despite the attendant risks.

An image of the face of the devil in the smoke in the World Trade Center following the attack was also displayed on CNN and other news programs. Most commentators discussed whether the appearance of the face was a religious phenomenon, and not whether it was subliminally perceived. As of this writing an article about the image can be found at the Detroit News website at http: //clickondetroit.com. The photographer denied the picture had been adulterated. When asked about the face, Associated Press noted that it "has a very strict written policy which prohibits the alteration or content of a photo in any way."

It should also be noted that some news photos on the Internet are independently distributed and not disseminated by news reporting agencies.

pg. 167: *Sleep Easy:*
The mortgage company ad in Figure 61(b) is an Internet banner ad that appeared frequently on America Online in 2001. As with all the illustrations in this book, *my analysis is based solely on the appearance of the picture*. I do not know how the creators of the ad intended it to be interpreted, or what they were driving at when they created it. I am also not inferring in any way that the *model* portrayed in the picture had any knowledge of or understanding of any of the "secret" meanings articulated in my hypothesis.

pg. 167: Chapter 5:
THE SECRET SELF/ REFLECTIONS IN THE SUBLIMINAL MIRROR:

Freud's seminal work: Freud, S. (1975). The interpretation of dreams. In *The Standard Edition of the Complete Psychological Works of Sigmund Freud*. (Vols. 4 & 5). London: Hogarth. (Original work published 1900).
See also: Bornstein, Robert F. and Masling, Joseph M. (Eds.) (1998). *Empirical Perspectives on the Psychoanalytic Unconscious*. New York: American Psychological Association. At pg. xvii the authors state: "During the 1980s, there were dozens of published papers questioning the existence of unconscious perception and memory. Since 1990, there has not been a single article in a mainstream psychology journal challenging the existence of these phenomena."
See also: Shevrin, Howard: (1986). Subliminal perception and dreaming. *The Journal of Mind and Behavior*. Spring and Summer. 7(2-3): pg. 379[249]-396[266]. The author states at pg. 379:

> For many years psychology has been dominated by a behaviorist point of view which not only denied the existence of unconscious processes, but denied to consciousness itself any valid place in psychology. The tide has recently been turning as cognitive psychology has refocused interest on the nature of consciousness and finally on the contribution that unconscious processes make to consciousness itself.

pg. 168: *Seeing Distortions in the Mirror:*
Doctor Fox: Naftulin, J., Ware, J., and Donnelly, F. (1973). The doctor fox lecture: A paradigm of educational seduction. *Journal of Medical Education*. (48): pg. 630-635.
People don't want to admit it, but one of the reasons TV police shows dealing with rape and sex crimes are popular is that they enable the viewer to unconsciously fantasize about committing such crimes. Similarly, the secret appeal of the torture scenes in violent movies (such as the torture scene in *Reservoir Dog*) is that they enable the viewer to engage in unconscious sadistic fantasies.
Line study: Asch, Solomon E. (1955). Opinions and social pressure. *Scientific American*. November. 193(5): pg. 31-35.

pg. 171: *Multiple Selves:*
Ansel Bourne: James, W. (1981). *Principles of Psychology*. Cambridge, MA: Harvard University Press. (Original work published 1890).

Debt doesn't matter: A currently widespread belief that may in the future be revealed as delusional is the idea that "debt doesn't matter." Most Americans assume that the U.S. government, its corporations and its citizens can borrow unprecedented amounts of money without experiencing adverse consequences. Another possibility is the idea that "real estate always goes up." The belief that real estate prices are not influenced by the business cycle has become universally popular.

Eve/Jane White/Black: Thigpen, C.H. and Cleckley, H.M. (1954). A case of multiple personality. *Journal of Abnormal and Social Psychology*. (49): pg. 135-151.

See also: Kelly, William L. (1991) *Psychology of the Unconscious: Mesmer, Janet, Freud, Jung, and Current Issues.* New York: Promethius Books. pg. 176.

See also: Kihlstrom, J.F. (1997). Consciousness and Me-ness. In Cohen, J.D. and Schooler, J.W. (Eds.) *Scientific Approaches to Consciousness.* Mahway, NJ: Lawrence Erlbaum and Associates. pg.451-468. Ref. at pg. 461-462.

Normal people have multiple personalities: Kihlstrom, J.F. (1997). (Cited above). Ref. at pg. 464.

pg. 172: Eminent Domain:

Eminent domain: Emmanuel, Steven. (1993). *Constitutional Law*. New Rochelle, N.Y: Emmanuel Law Outlines. First Edition. pg. 154-160. Emmanuel outlines are very well written and easy to understand. See also *Berman v. Parker,* 348 U.S. 26 (1954). (A Supreme Court case discussing eminent domain issues.)

pg. 174: Chapter 6:
HAVE IT YOUR WAY/ HOW TO USE SUBLIMINAL TECHNIQUES

pg. 174: Subliminal Advertising Is Generally Not Illegal:

Law outlawing unfair and deceptive acts: 15 U.S.C. § 45(a)(1).

Key presented innumerable examples: Key, Wilson Bryan. (1981). *The Clam-Plate Orgy and Other Techniques for Manipulating Your Behavior.* New York: Signet. Pg. 132-149.

See also: Haberstroh, Jack. (1994). *Ice Cube Sex: The Truth About Subliminal Advertising.* Notre Dame, IN: Cross Cultural Publications. Pg. 130.

Get It! television commercial: Subliminal ad flap raised. *Advertising Age.* December 24, 1973. Pg. 21.

FCC comments: FCC 74-78, 29 RR 22 395 (January 24, 1974.)

ATF comments: Federal Register. Volume 49, No. 154. August 8, 1984. Page 31670. (The word "embed" was misspelled in the original; it has been corrected it in the text.)

ATF regulations: 27 C.F.R. 4.64(8)(k), 27 C.F.R. 5.65(9)(h), and 27 C.F.R. 7.54(2)(h).

pg. 176: Looking the Other Way:

Overbreadth issue: *Broadrick v. Oklahoma* 413 U.S. 601 (1973).

Vagueness issue: *Connally v. General Construction Co.,* 269 U.S. 385 (1926).

For an intelligent, easily understood overview of these First Amendment Constitutional issues, see: Emmanuel, Steven. (1993). *Constitutional Law.* New Rochelle, N.Y: Emmanuel Law Outlines. First Edition. pg. 448-452.

pg. 177: Subliminal Advertising Is Psychologically Harmful:

Drive activation studies on "normal: people: Silverman, Lloyd H. (1964). A clinical experimental approach to the study of subliminal manipulation: The effects of a drive related stimulus upon Rorschach responses. *Journal of Abnormal Psychology*. 69(2): pg. 158-172. The subjects' reactions to the subliminal genital stimulus were related to how much they psychologically felt threatened by it. This was determined by measuring the amount of time the drawing had to be shown before the subjects could consciously recognize it. (The same method McGinnies used in the "dirty word" experiments.) The subjects who reacted pathologically were also "primed' prior to the subliminal exposure by being read a violent and disturbing passage. The quote is from page 321 of: Silverman, Lloyd H. (1972). Drive stimulation and psychopathology: On the conditions under which drive related external events evoke pathological reactions. *In Psychoanalysis and Contemporary Science* (Vol.1) Holt, R.R. and Peterfreund (Eds.) New York: Macmillan. pg. 307-326.

pg. 182: Subliminal Salesmanship:

Dale Carnegie: Carnegie, Dale. (1964). *How to Win Friends and Influence People.* New York: Simon and Schuster. 1964. (Originally published in 1936.)

pg. 183: The Ambiguity Principle In Other Contexts:

Wall Street: © 1987 by Twentieth Century Fox.

pg. 184: Donald Goodwin: unconsciously means "well done and victorious" (done-good-win).

pg. 185: Franklin C. Wright: As noted in the text and the credits, "Franklin C. Wright" an imaginary character. "Frank" means "straightforward and sincere," and "C. Wright" means "view correctly." The endorsement on the back cover jokingly attributed to Mr. Wright is not totally imaginary. A real sociology instructor commented in a letter to me that that my presentation "entertains as well as informs." However, I was unable to locate him because he moved away.

pg. 186: Creating Audio Subliminals:

Audio subliminals can be created by reducing the loudness of a sound: Fisher, S. (1976). Conditions affecting boundary responses to messages out of awareness. *Journal of Nervous and Mental Disease*. May: 162(5): pg. 313-322. (Sub-audible "whispered" messages conveying either hostility ["hate, kill, push, explode…"] or depression ["... I feel low. I feel low. I feel like crying."] affected the emotional states of listeners.)

See also: Fisher S. (1975). Effects of messages reported to be out of awareness upon the body boundary. *Journal of Nervous and Mental Disease*. (161): pg.90-99.

pg. 186: Judas Priest:

Judas Priest trial: Halford, Rob. (1990). Judas Priest's lead singer testifies. *The New York Times*. August 1, 1990. v. 139. pg. C-12 Col.6.

See also: Band is held not liable in suicides of two fans. *The New York Times*. August 25, 1990. v.139. pg.13(L) Col. 1.

See also: Billard, Mary. Judas Priest defendants of the faith: At the close of the teen suicide trial, the metal rockers await a verdict. *Rolling Stone*. Sept 20, 1980. n 587 p 25(1).

See also: Neely, Kim. Judas Priest gets off the hook. *Rolling Stone*. October 4. 1990. n. 588. pg. 39(1).

See also: Moore, Timothy. Scientific consensus and expert testimony: Lessons from the Judas Priest trial. *Skeptical Inquirer*. Nov-Dec 1966. v.20 n6. p 32-40.

The C.D.: Judas Priest. Stained Class. ©2001 Sony Music Entertainment (UK) Ltd./(P) 2001 Sony MusicEntertainment (UK) Ltd./Manufactured by Columbia Records. All Rights Reserved. Originally recorded 1978.

pg. 187: The Subliminal Perception of Backwards Speech:

Volkey and Read study: Volkey, J.R. and Read, J.D. (1985). Subliminal messages: Between the devil and the media. *American Psychologist*. November. 40(11): pg. 1231-1239.

pg. 187-188: The Walrus Is Paul:

Note: In discussing apparent subliminals and/or backwards recordings in Beatle, Led Zeppelin, and other musical CDs, *I am merely proposing a hypothesis based solely on the sounds that some people hear in these records*. I have not interviewed the musicians or the producers, and have no evidence that anyone associated with these groups deliberately inserted subliminal or backward materials in the recordings.

Beatles White Album: Beatles (P) Original Sound Records made by EMI Records, Ltd. ©1968 EMI Records, Ltd. The Beatles in The Magical Mystery Tour ©1967 EMI Records, Ltd.

Led Zeppelin ©1971 Atlantic Recording Corporation for the United States, and WEA International Inc. for the world outside of the United States. All Rights Reserved.

pg. 188: Subliminals in Visual Art:

Portfolio: The "Portfolio" series includes a collection of photographs by the world famous photographer Michel Comte. Comte, Michel. *Michel Comte: Kontraste/Contrasts Portfolio* (Stern Portfolio Library). The "Nightmare ad" in Figure 2.40 is signed by "Michel Comte," and I assume (but cannot say for certain) that they are the same person.

As with all the illustrations in this book, in presenting my analysis *I am merely proposing a hypothesis based solely on the appearance of the pictures in question*. I have not interviewed Mr. Comte, and I have no knowledge as to what he may or may not have been thinking when he created his book cover or his other artwork. It is possible that the masculine shadow appears simply by coincidence. I have included the illustration as an example of how subliminal techniques *may* be used to enhance artwork. This issue is discussed more thoroughly on pages 192-193.

The foregoing considerations also apply to the discussion of the "Nightmare" ad on pages 98-103. In analyzing the "Nightmare" ad, I am *I am also proposing a hypothesis based solely on the appearance of the picture*. I have not interviewed the artist, and do not know what the artist may or may have been thinking when the artwork was created. This issue is discussed more thoroughly on pages 192-193. The illusions in the "Nightmare" ad could also have occurred coincidentally.

Jurgen Peters: The painting can also be viewed as three dimensional, and the cubist shapes can be seen as having depth. The picture is used with permission, as indicated in the Credits.

Mirabilis cover: As with all the illustrations in this book, in presenting my analysis *I am merely proposing a hypothesis based solely on the appearance of the picture.* I have not interviewed the artist who created the *Mirabilis* cover, and do not know what the artist may or may have been thinking when the artwork was created. This issue is discussed more thoroughly on pages 192-193.

pg. 194: Chapter 7:
FROM LA BAMBA TO THE INTERNET/ BRINGING IT ALL HOME

pg. 194: On the Signpost Up Ahead:
Life Magazine article: *Life* magazine. 'Hidden sell' technique is almost here. March 31, 1958. pg. 102.

pg. 198: In and Out Burger:
To be perfectly clear, I am merely proposing a hypothesis as to how the name may be interpreted unconsciously. I do not know the management of In- N-Out Burgers® or any other party intended the name, or the company logo, to be interpreted. "In-N-Out" is a federally registered trademark.

Furthermore, I sincerely think In-N-Out Burgers® are delicious, and I eat them all the time. All the food is prepared from scratch after the customer orders it. None of it is ever frozen, and the french fries are cut in the individual stores. (See McNichol, Tom. The secret behind a burger cult. *New York Times.* August 14, 2002.)

pg. 200: Macy's Biggie:
I discovered the Macy's Biggie in the men's athletic department of Macys in San Jose, California in 2001. Several readers have commented that the tattoo may also refer to "Biggie Smalls" a.k.a. "Notorious Big," a rapper who was gunned down in Los Angeles.

pg. 202: Too Much Pleasure:
Thank God She's Late: The idea that men unconsciously fantasize about impregnating women was also proposed by Wilson Bryan Key in *Subliminal Seduction*, in relation to a Camel cigarette ad.

pg. 204: Beat Your Husband:
I discovered this ad on the Internet in 2001.

pg. 206: Dialing Down The Center:
This commercial was frequently shown on television in March, 2003. Readers have commented that Carrot Top's pointing finger also resembles a penis and testicles.

pg. 210: The Subliminal Sex™ Story:
The SEX design: Neslon is the one on the right. Sadly, he passed away in 1998. Please contact me at SubliminalSex.com if you wish to request permission to reproduce the Subliminal Sex™ design.

Black and white SEX: Remarkably, the design does "work" reduced in black and white, though not quite as well.

Newspaper article: I blurred part of the text of the article to avoid copyright hassles.

pg. 225: Appendix A:
PROJECTS AND EXPERIMENTS

1. A device that kills cockroaches: Wilkie, William L. (1994). *Consumer Behavior.* Third Edition. New York. John Wiley and Sons, Inc. First published 1996. pg. 130-131.
2. An antiseptic cream: Hepner, Harry W. (1964). *Advertising: Creative Communication with Consumers.* New York: Mc-Graw Hill 4th edition. pg. 147-153. Discussed in Britt, Steuart H. (Ed.) (1966). *Consumer Behavior and the Behavioral Sciences: Theories and Applications.* New York: John Wiley and Sons Inc. pg.105-107.
3. An antacid: Dichter, Earnest. (1964). *Handbook of Consumer Motivations.* New York: McGraw Hill. pg. 118, 217, 306, 324, 458. Reprinted in Britt, Steuart H. (Ed.) (1966). (Cited above.) Ref. at pg. 63.
4. A greeting card company: Dichter, E (1964) and Britt, S.H. (1966). (Same as "An antacid" above.)
5. A hair coloring targeted at both mothers and their daughters: Dichter, Earnest (1964) and Britt, S.H. (1966). (Same as "An antiseptic cream" above.)
6. A low-cost department store: Smith, G.H. (1954) Motivation research in advertising and marketing. New York: McGraw Hill, pg. 18-23. Reprinted in Britt, Steuart H. (Ed.) (1966). (Cited above.) Ref. at page 103.
7. Shortening: Hepner, H.W. (1964) and Britt, S.H. (1966). (Same as "An antiseptic cream" above.)
8. Candy: Hepner, H.W. (1964) and Britt, S.H. (1966). (Same as "An antiseptic cream" above.)
9. A laxative: Smith, G.H. (1954) and Britt, S.H. (1966). (Same as "A low cost department store" above.)

pg. 229: Appendix B:
SERIOUS RESEARCH

Kilbourne "Marlboro Lights penis/rock" experiment: Kilbourne, William E., Painton, Scott, and Ridley, Danny. (1985). The effect of sexual embedding on responses to magazine advertisements. *Journal of Advertising.* 14(2): pg.48-56.
Ruth and Mostache: Ruth, William J. and Mostache, Harriet S. (1985). A projective assessment of the effects of Freudian sexual symbolism in liquor advertisements. *Psychological Report.* (56): pg. 183-188.

INDEX